**DO NOT REMOVE
CARDS FROM POCKET**

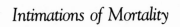

Intimations of Mortality

Intimations of Mortality

Time, Truth, and Finitude in Heidegger's Thinking of Being

David Farrell Krell

THE PENNSYLVANIA STATE UNIVERSITY PRESS
University Park and London

Library of Congress Cataloging in Publication Data

Krell, David Farrell.
    Intimations of mortality.

    Includes bibliography and index.
    1. Heidegger, Martin, 1889–1976—Contributions to ontology.
2. Ontology—History—20th century.
I. Title.
B3279.H49K74   1986   111'.092'4   85-28409
ISBN 0-271-00427-4

In memory of my father
Matthew J. Krell
1907–1978

The clouds that gather round the setting sun
Do take a sober colouring from an eye
That hath kept watch o'er man's mortality.
—Wordsworth, "Ode: Intimations of Immortality
from Recollections of Early Childhood"

Contents

Preface

The eleven chapters of the present book offer in-depth studies clustered about four themes in Heidegger's thought: (1) the project of fundamental ontology, designated by the rubric "Being and Time, Time and Being"; (2) the question of *Alētheia*, or the truth and clearing of Being, the matter that is usually said to have preoccupied Heidegger only after his "turning" or "reversal"; (3) the history of philosophy conceived as a destructuring or dismantling of the history of ontology and as the history of Being; and (4) a poetics of Being for which mortality remains the incessant preoccupation.

The book represents neither a general introduction to Heidegger's philosophy nor an exegesis of particular texts. It focuses on a restricted number of issues in Heidegger's thinking, issues which, if I am right, enable us to perceive the thrust of his thought as a whole. My thesis is that a single *Grunderfahrung* or "fundamental experience" underlies Heidegger's work from *Being and Time* through all the later writings. The issues I have selected for discussion arise as a unitary constellation out of that single experience. The title I have chosen for the book lends a name to the constellation.

Despite appearances, the title is not in the first place a reply to Wordsworth. I had been wavering between two working titles: (1) "To Become Mortal," recalling a phrase from Heidegger's essay "The Thing" ("The rational animals must first become mortals"); and (2) "Intimations of Being," *Anklänge des Seyns*, which is the refrain of Heidegger's *Contributions to Philosophy: "On Ereignis"* (1936–38). I was leaning toward the second title. I wanted to avoid any "anthropological" emphasis in my account, simply because it has dominated discussion of Heidegger in the English-speaking world, and to stress Heidegger's "ontological" intentions and import. At the same time I resisted the temptation to scorn existentialism and to deny Heidegger's essential role in it, however grudging his own commitment to it may have been. For me it was no insult that Heidegger was mentioned in the same breath with Kierkegaard, Jaspers, Camus, and Sartre; although his mastery of the history of metaphysics far exceeded theirs taken collectively, I feared the tendency to scholasticize Heidegger. The first of my two titles would transform him into an ardent existentialist, and that would be inaccurate; the second would dub him the Magus of Being, and that was boring. *The fact is that for Heidegger all intimations of Being are intimations of mortality.* When we are most accurate Heidegger is least boring.

In the retrospect that all prefaces provide it is clear to me that no single style pervades the following chapters. They are sometimes strictly historical in approach, sometimes phenomenological; occasionally they appear to be speculative, even fanciful. It is as though each style displaced the others for a time, decentering any apparently privileged point of reference or manner of referral. In *What Calls for Thinking?* Heidegger celebrates "multiplicity of meaning" as the very element of thought. However much my own response to Heidegger's thinking tries to capture its "fundamental experience," that experience proves to have endless ramifications. Its network of roots infiltrates and cracks every fundament. The subversion of foundations and dispersion of styles in my own work are expressed in that seemingly harmless word "intimations," which is all that mortal interpreters are heir to.

Acknowledgments

Much of the material in this book has appeared earlier elsewhere in somewhat different form. I am grateful to the editors of the following scholarly journals and anthologies, not only for permission to revise and reprint this material, but also for their generous reception of the original pieces. My thanks to:

John Sallis, for material in *Research in Phenomenology*, vols. V (1975), 77–94; VII (1977), 238–58; and X (1980), 208–34.

Wolfe Mays, for material in the *Journal of the British Society for Phenomenology*, vols. VI, no. 3 (October 1975), 147–56; and XIV, no. 3 (October 1983), 271–82.

Robert Lechner, for material in *Philosophy Today*, vol. XXVI, no. 2/4 (Summer 1982), 126–38.

Richard Rorty and Eugene Freeman, for material in *The Monist*, vol. LXIV, no. 4 (October 1981), 467–80.

David Wood and Robert Bernasconi, for material in *Time and Metaphysics* (Warwick, England: Parousia Press, 1982), 121–60.

Mazzino Montinari, Wolfgang Müller-Lauter, Heinz Wenzel, and Jörg Salaquarda, for material in *Nietzsche-Studien*, vol. V (1976), 255–62.

Nancy D. Simco, for material in *The Southern Journal of Philosophy*, vol. XIII, no. 2 (Summer 1975), 197–204.

Frederick Elliston, for material in *Heidegger's Existential Analytic* (The Hague: Mouton, 1978), 247–55.

My thanks to two readers for The Pennsylvania State University Press who offered acute criticisms; to John Sallis, who read the entire manuscript and offered many helpful suggestions; to Helm Breinig, for tidbits and repasts; to Nick Land, who helped with the proofs so generously; and to Dennis Goldford and Chris Kentera for taking the risk.

Abbreviations of Works Cited

I. Works by Martin Heidegger in German

EM   *Einführung in die Metaphysik.* Tübingen: Max Niemeyer, 1953.

EHD   *Erläuterungen zu Hölderlins Dichtung.* Vierte, erweiterte Auflage. Frankfurt am Main: Vittorio Klostermann, 1971.

FS   *Frühe Schriften.* Frankfurt am Main: Vittorio Klostermann, 1972.

G   *Gelassenheit.* Pfullingen: Günther Neske, 1959.

H   *Holzwege.* Frankfurt am Main: Vittorio Klostermann, 1950.

Hk   *Heraklit.* With Eugen Fink. Frankfurt am Main: Vittorio Klostermann, 1970.

ID   *Identität und Differenz.* Pfullingen: Günther Neske, 1957.

KPM   *Kant und das Problem der Metaphysik.* Vierte, erweiterte Auflage. Frankfurt am Main: Vittorio Klostermann, 1973.

LR   "Letter to Richardson." In William J. Richardson, S.J., *Heidegger: Through Phenomenology to Thought.* The Hague: Martinus Nijhoff, 1963.

NI, NII   *Nietzsche.* Two volumes. Pfullingen: Günther Neske, 1961.

SG   *Satz vom Grund.* Pfullingen: Günther Neske, 1957.

SZ   *Sein und Zeit.* Zwölfte, unveränderte Auflage. Tübingen: Max Niemeyer, 1972.

TK   *Die Technik und die Kehre.* Pfullingen: Günther Neske, 1962.

US   *Unterwegs zur Sprache.* Pfullingen: Günther Neske, 1959.

VA   *Vorträge und Aufsätze.* Pfullingen: Günther Neske, 1954.

W   *Wegmarken.* Frankfurt am Main: Vittorio Klostermann, 1967.

WhD?   *Was heisst Denken?* Tübingen: Max Niemeyer, 1954.

ZSdD   *Zur Sache des Denkens.* Tübingen: Max Niemeyer, 1969.

20   *Prologomena zur Geschichte des Zeitbegriffs.* Martin Heidegger Gesamtausgabe, Band 20, edited by Petra Jaeger. Frankfurt am Main: Vittorio Klostermann, 1979.

21   *Logik: Die Frage nach der Wahrheit.* Martin Heidegger Gesamtausgabe, Band 21, edited by Walter Biemel. Frankfurt am Main: Vittorio Klostermann, 1976.

24   *Die Grundprobleme der Phänomenologie.* Martin Heidegger Gesamtausgabe, Band 24, edited by Friedrich-Wilhelm von Herrmann. Frankfurt am Main: Vittorio Klostermann, 1975.

26   *Metaphysische Anfangsgründe der Logik im Ausgang von Leibniz.* Martin
          Heidegger Gesamtausgabe, Band 26, edited by Klaus Held. Frankfurt am
          Main: Vittorio Klostermann, 1978.

32   *Hegels Phänomenologie des Geistes.* Martin Heidegger Gesamtausgabe, Band
          32, edited by Ingtraud Görland. Frankfurt am Main: Vittorio Kloster-
          mann, 1980.

39   *Hölderlins Hymnen "Germanien" und "Der Rhein."* Martin Heidegger
          Gesamtausgabe, Band 39, edited by Suzanne Ziegler. Frankfurt am Main:
          Vittorio Klostermann, 1980.

II. Works by Heidegger in English Translation

BW   *Basic Writings.* New York: Harper & Row, 1977.

EGT   *Early Greek Thinking.* New York: Harper & Row, 1975.

Ni 1   *Nietzsche: The Will to Power as Art.* New York: Harper & Row, 1979.

Ni 2   *Nietzsche: The Eternal Recurrence of the Same.* New York: Harper & Row,
          1984.

Ni 4   *Nietzsche: Nihilism.* Translated by Frank A. Capuzzi. New York: Harper &
          Row, 1982.

PLT   *Poetry, Language, Thought.* Translated by Albert Hofstadter. New York:
          Harper & Row, 1971.

III. Works by Nietzsche are cited as *SI*, *SII*, and *SIII*, indicating the three-
volume edition by Karl Schlechta: Friedrich Nietzsche, *Werke in drei Bänden.*
Sechste, durchgesehene Auflage. München: Carl Hanser, 1969. With the
following exception:

WM   *Der Wille zur Macht: Versuch einer Umwertung aller Werte.* Ausgewählt und
          geordnet von Peter Gast unter Mitwirkung von Elisabeth Förster-Nietz-
          sche. Stuttgart: Alfred Kröner, 1964 [1906; 1930].

IV. Works by Hegel are cited by volume and page of the *Theorie Werkausgabe*,
e.g., *20, 197.* Frankfurt am Main: Suhrkamp, 1969–71. Two of Hegel's works
are cited in another edition:

PG   *Phänomenologie des Geistes.* Philosophische Bibliothek. Sechste Auflage.
          Hamburg: Felix Meiner, 1952.

Enz   *Enzyklopädie der philosophischen Wissenschaften, 1830.* Philosophische Bibli-
          othek. Siebente, durchgesehene Auflage. Hamburg: Felix Meiner, 1969.

Introduction

The theme of mortality—finite human existence—pervades Heidegger's thought before, during, and after his magnum opus, *Being and Time*, published in 1927. Mortality is surely not a thought unique to him. Perhaps Montaigne is all we ever needed: "I sense twinges of the death in me, continually, in my throat, in my kidneys. . . ."[1] And it is also true that Nietzsche and his predecessors in the School of Suspicion grounded us long before the Freiburg philosopher began to teach. Yet there is something particularly implacable about Heidegger's thinking of mortality, rooted in the experience he calls *oblivion of Being*.

The thought of mortality is not merely a logical exemplum or anthropological finding for Heidegger. Neither logic nor anthropology contains the secret of its power. Only when we realize that the concealment and darkness surrounding death have something to do with every minute of *anthropos'* life, with every one of its discoveries and adventures, every announcement of its speech, and every flash of its thought do we begin to descry the range and power of Heidegger's thought. Not as funereal melodramatics or as despair and destructive nihilism. But as a *thinking within anxiety* and on the descent, a *descensional reflection* determined to keep its feet on the earth.

It is telling that when in a recent article Otto Pöggeler seeks "new ways" to go with Heidegger he takes inspiration from Werner Marx's study, "The Mortals," finding in this oldest of Heideggerian themes "not this or that detail . . . but the matter of genuine need."[2] At the present juncture, that of "Introduction," it is a matter of anticipating what the theme of mortality—embedded in the larger question of Being's forgottenness—has to do with the four areas of inquiry staked out in the present volume. Those four areas have the following titles:

    I. Intimations of Time and Being;
    II. Intimations of Truth and Turning;
    III. Intimations of a History of Being;
    IV. Intimations of Mortality.

Let me now introduce each of the book's four parts by sketching briefly their contents and by suggesting something concerning the movement of the inquiry in them. In what manner they reflect Heidegger's "fundamental experience" is of course a question no introduction can make fully clear.

I

Heidegger's *Being and Time* continues to surprise us with the complexities of its provenance and its project. As is well known, this principal work of twentieth-century philosophy is but a fragment or torso: Heidegger never wrote its planned second half, and the third division of the first half, "Time and Being," never saw print. The possible reasons for Heidegger's failure to proceed with this "reversal" of *Being and Time* into "Time and Being" have dominated discussion of his work for decades. The first chapter of the present volume examines an early manuscript by Heidegger that is especially fruitful for insight into the provenance of *Being and Time*, namely, Heidegger's unpublished review (dated 1919–21) of a book by Karl Jaspers, *Psychology of Worldviews* (1919). Chapters two and three then inquire into the fate of *Being and Time* as "fundamental ontology" by examining the texts of lecture courses Heidegger taught at Marburg during the late 1920s. Part One of the volume thus covers the years 1920 to 1930 in Heidegger's career. Yet "Intimations of Time and Being" extend far beyond the bounds of that decade. Although the 1920s may well have been the richest decade of Heidegger's life, the question pursued there remained problematic up to the end.

Only a detailed study of Heidegger's Marburg period (1923–28) could broach adequately the question of the origins of *Being and Time* or of the "fundamental experience" underlying the work. Yet even a detailed study of this period would prove insufficient if it did not take into account Heidegger's development during the years 1909 to 1922 when he was a student and young *Dozent* in Freiburg. Heidegger's Jaspers review is the single most important document of that first Freiburg period. It clearly indicates the direction Heidegger was taking toward *Being and Time*, a route that took him from Husserl's *Logical Investigations* and transcendental phenomenology of consciousness, by way of Dilthey's philosophy of life and hermeneutics of history, to Jaspers' Kierkegaardian philosophy of existence—existence in its "factical life-in-process" and "limit situations." Yet soon quite beyond Jaspers. For the question of Being, or, rather, the peculiar *oblivion* of that question, obtrudes in the very methodological matters that Jaspers presupposes, neglects, takes for granted. Heidegger's challenge to Jaspers is a *fundamental* one, inasmuch as it is Jaspers' *access* to the "limit situations," the foundations of his hermeneutic, that remain altogether unexplained. What astonishes is how far Heidegger had already advanced along the path of the "question of Being" by 1921, that is, by the time of his lecture courses on the "hermeneutics of facticity" and "phenomenology of religion." My first chapter therefore traces the earliest stretches of Heidegger's journey toward *Being and Time* and articulates that astonishment.

Chapters two and three sustain the sense of surprise by observing how quickly Heidegger allows the intimations of Time and Being to resound beyond the limits of his own major work. In *Being and Time* Heidegger inquires into the question of the meaning of Being by investigating the particular being that poses questions and yearns for answers—the finite human being. The guideline for both his inquiry into Being and his investigation of existence is the phenomenon of *time*. Not only has the latter served to distinguish various "regions" of beings in traditional metaphysics; it also bears a special relationship to human beings and their history. The significance of historizing, temporalizing time becomes the principal quest of Heidegger's fundamental ontology. Yet we know that in later years Heidegger distances himself from the term *fundamental ontology* and from his own penetrating analyses of *ecstatic temporality*. What are the reasons for Heidegger's doubts? Are those reasons altogether compelling? Or is there a way to retrieve Heidegger's analyses of temporality and of finite human existence from their entanglement in fundamental ontology? Would such recovery reveal an unsuspected unity in Heidegger's career of thought, no matter what twists and turns it undergoes? These are some of the questions posed in the second and third chapters of this book. And they recur throughout the volume.

II

Heidegger's question of Being and Time, Time and Being, is above all else and from the outset a question concerning *truth*. The very meaning of Da-sein, our being in the world, is an openness, uncoveredness, or disclosedness of beings and of ourselves. Heidegger understands truth to be that free space in which all other kinds of truths—for example, those in which propositions are in accord with states of affairs—find their place. His preferred word for the uncoveredness of beings is the Greek expression *A-lētheia*, taking the alpha as privative and *Lēthē* as meaning concealment in general. Why Heidegger's projection of the meaning of Being upon *time* must advance to a "metaphysics of truth," and in what sense concealment as such is an intimation of mortality, are questions taken up in the three chapters of Part Two.

Chapter four pursues the development of Heidegger's inquiry into truth from the year 1907, when Heidegger first read Franz Brentano's dissertation, *The Manifold Meaning of Being according to Aristotle* (1862), through *Being and Time* and on into the later work. Brentano's interpretation of the "second" meaning of "being," "being in the sense of the true," however much it remained tied to the Scholastic-Aristotelian categories, brought together for Heidegger the notions of Being and Truth. He would never allow them to be put asunder. (The fact, incidentally, that in Part Two of this study we are cast back to a period that antedates the Marburg period indicates that no straightforwardly "developmentalist" approach to Heidegger's thought suffices: the final chapter of Part Two will thematize the insufficiency of all such approaches.)

The proper matrix for "being in the sense of the true" proves to be what Heidegger ultimately calls *physis*—not "nature" in any usual sense but the upsurgence of beings into unconcealment. Such upsurgence, and the decline, departure, and concealment it inevitably implies, occur in and as the "clearing" of Being, *die Lichtung des Seins*. This central concern of Heidegger's thought is the theme of chapter five. Here I analyze the transitions undergone by the notion. The principal difficulty with *Lichtung* and the need for transition lie in the word's reference to the tradition of natural and supernatural *illumination*. Heidegger contends with the glare of the luminous-numenal tradition by stressing a second sense of *Lichtung*, one captured in the homonymic English adjective "light," meaning "light-in-weight," buoyant. Only if there is a clearing or lightening of occlusion can luminosity penetrate. Yet the irremediable duplicity of clearing and concealing, lightening and oppressing, opening and closing, betrays the finitude—the intimations of mortality— within Being itself.

We find a great deal concerning *Lichtung* in Heidegger's later work; yet the notion is central to *Being and Time*. The course of chapter five thus involves both a departure from and a return to Heidegger's major work, where the idea of a lighting or clearing first appears. Given the necessity of such a return, what are we to say about Heidegger's notorious "reversal" or "turning" after *Being and Time?*

I will already have commented on the *Kehre* in chapter two. Yet the turn has become such an omnipresent theme in Heidegger scholarship (not a soul has heard of Heidegger that does not know he had a "reversal") that I will speak to it again, in greater detail, in chapter six. The ultimate difficulty will prove to be, not that Heidegger underwent no *Kehre*, but that he was always caught up in one.

The immediate task of my sixth chapter is to displace the customary interpretation of Heidegger's *Kehre* (as a successful turn from Man to Being, from existentialism to ontology, from anxiety to releasement, and so on) and to examine Heidegger's two discourses on the "turn." First, Heidegger descries an *impending* turn in and for our technological era, by which the oblivion of Being and the possibility of disclosure or *alētheia* as such are revealed. Second, Heidegger refers us to the *unsuccessful* effort of his own thought to turn from the question of Being and Time to that of Time and Being, to reverse the question of the essence of truth to the question of the "truth of essence." The unsuccessful reversal—the failure of the project of *grounding* Being on a projection of Time— proves to be an index of the impending turn in the history of Being itself: the unsuccessful reversal discloses *alētheia* as a possibility of revealing, a possibility that occurs in and as the eschatology of Being. The latter engenders a turn toward, and not away from, the intimations of Time and Being.

III

It is an error of the most ruinous sort to suppose that Heidegger's preoccupation with the history of Being had to wait upon some "turn" in his thinking. From the outset of his teaching activity in Freiburg the *history* of philosophy served Heidegger as the essential counterweight to phenomenology. Herein lies the source of his later break with Husserl.

Some years ago I was told how Heidegger once accompanied his master to the train station—Husserl was off to deliver a programmatic lecture on the role of phenomenology in all the sciences and disciplines. The assistant asked the mentor where *history* fit into his schema. Husserl stopped short.

"Good heavens! I forgot about history!"

Heidegger never forgot about it.

Whether the focus was on Aristotle or Plato, Schelling or Hegel, Aquinas, Descartes, Leibniz or Kant, the early Greek thinkers or Nietzsche, the history of philosophy remained Heidegger's unique *camera obscura*. Yet there was nothing eclectic or purely historicist about his approach. For it was always a matter of destructuring and dismantling the mechanisms of the transmission or tradition of historical knowledge as such. And it was always the same question that he posed to the great thinkers of the Western intellectual tradition—the question of Being and of the unhappy fate of disclosure. Even when the preserve of Being's truth closed its doors to him, when in the late 1950s and 1960s he was no longer confident enough to asseverate on "the truth of Being," the epochal granting of Time and Being remained for Heidegger a problem of history and destiny, *Geschichte* and *Geschick*. He did not try to counter the oblivion of Being by forgetting about the history of metaphysics and the thinking of metaphysicians; he did not flee the experience of finitude and mortality to some splendid Olympian isolation. Dialogue with prior thinkers was always the only way.

Yet dialogue with the dead did confront peculiar obstacles. Heidegger knew full well that in the thinking of history Hegel was his sole genuine predecessor. The need to confront *the* philosopher of history and culture became obvious to him at the time of his Habilitation dissertation in 1916. In the 1950s he was still lecturing on Hegel, in the 1960s insisting that students of Heraclitus study Hegel's *Logic*. On May 16, 1975 Heidegger emphasized to me the importance of his essay, "Hegel and the Greeks," which placed the grand historian of spirit in the context of a history of Being. Yet never for a moment did Heidegger conceive of the history of Being as a continuation of Hegel's history of spirit. A number of things made such continuation impossible. For example, Nietzsche.

Indeed, the figures of Hegel and Nietzsche loom omnipresent in Heidegger's inquiries into the history of Being, no matter which philosopher is being questioned. My next three chapters therefore forego all attempts at a comprehensive account of Heidegger and the history of philosophy; they revolve instead about a set of questions which at first appear to be mere suspicions but which then expand into a kind of reflection I call *descensional*. Descensional reflection responds to intimations of a history of Being.

Why should Heidegger's point of departure preclude anything like a history of spirit? What does Nietzsche's position at the outermost point or *eschaton* of the history of metaphysics signify for that point of departure? How does Heideggerian hermeneutics differ decisively from Hegelian ontotheology? Can such hermeneutics guarantee any "results" in and for the history of philosophy? Or would results of any kind be fatal to hermeneutics conceived of as descensional reflection? Does Heidegger's "step back" out of metaphysics and into its "essence" safely remove us from the snare of ontotheology? Or do we, after the Nietzschean-Heideggerian eschatology, require a shift of ground and an alter(n)ation of styles such as Jacques Derrida has attempted? Or, finally, are Derridean traces themselves intimations of mortality?

The three chapters of Part Three pose these questions with some persistence. Chapter seven seeks to outline the difference between Hegel's history of spirit and Heidegger's history of Being. The crucial interruption of spirit's trajectory proves to be the thought of Nietzsche. Heidegger's thinking of finitude, mortality, and the history of the oblivion of Being joins Nietzsche's descensional reflection. It proves to be what chapter two calls a thinking *within* anxiety. The problem of course is how such reflection can conduct its hermeneutics of history—whether and how it can allow the multiplicity of philosophers in our history to get a fair hearing.

Chapter eight proceeds to examine Heidegger's reading of Nietzsche more closely. As its title, "The Last Thinker of the West," suggests, these two thinkers may be seen as converging in the descending arc of the history of Being as eschatology. For contemporary interpretation Heidegger and Nietzsche remain conjoined: their impact on Continental Philosophy today is a shared impact. Chapter nine, "Results," therefore alters the thrust of the suspicion concerning Heidegger's history of Being—that it is merely inverted Hegelianism—by considering the history of Being as a history of *nihilism*. For Heidegger, the mere search for results in the history of the West, its philosophy and its civilization generally, is akin to what Nietzsche called passive, reactive, or incomplete nihilism—nihilism in its usual destructive sense. Yet Heidegger himself interprets *technology* as the result of Western thought about Being from Plato through Nietzsche. Do these two sets of results jibe? The ambivalence of all "results" for hermeneutical philosophy, whether it involves itself in the texts of earlier thinkers or tries to decipher the erratic text of contemporary technological civilization, is the result of "results." Descensional reflection shies from stating unequivocal results. Nevertheless, it insists on the following:

However problematic Heidegger's thinking of the eschatology of Being may be, however much it brings him into proximity to ontotheology, both his appreciation of past thinkers (for example, the early Greeks) and his dogged efforts to achieve another kind of thinking (a nonrepresentational, noncalculative thinking) merit the most serious study. Perhaps the most auspicious way to approach Heidegger's "other" thinking is to inquire into its relation to poetry—poetry not as an aesthetic object but as an eminent instance of intimations of mortality.

IV

Why does Heidegger's question concerning Being and Time, which naturally enough develops into an inquiry into truth and the history of Being, culminate in a poetics of Being? Why does it not produce a logic or proclaim an ethics? Or at least promulgate an aesthetics?

It is a long way from fundamental ontology and its descriptions of factical life-experience to a metaphorics of clearing and presence, and a longer way still to a poetics of *Ereignis*, the granting of Time and Being to thought. Indeed, that way never comes to a decisive end. The reversal of Being and Time into Time and Being is never over and done with in Heidegger's thought. True, the shift from "scientific" phenomenology, fundamental ontology, and metaphysics of truth to meditation on the work of art, especially the work of poetry, *poiēsis* itself, marks the most significant transition in Heidegger's long career. Yet it is *truth* that the artwork sets to work, and truth (as disclosure and unconcealment) is a matter of crucial importance in *Being and Time* and in the Marburg lecture courses that precede it. The importance of language in the question of truth as unconcealment is apparent to readers of sections 31–34 of *Being and Time*. There, especially in section 33, "Assertion as a derivative mode of interpretation," it becomes clear why Heidegger produces no tractatus and no logical investigations. The kind of language that is suited to meditation on disclosure is neither assertive nor prescriptive. Rather, it is evocative. While the language of fundamental ontology is often too busy with grounds, orders of implication, and possible horizons to trust pure evocation, it does pose questions that provoke perpetual recommencement of the analyses. And while the language of Heidegger's later thought becomes increasingly evocative—as the two chapters of Part Four show—such evocations are always in service to the provocations of *Being and Time*. Yet what can possibly conjoin intimation and provocation?

Chapter ten suggests that "the gift of the poetical life" (Ricoeur), even if Heidegger gives it the name *Gelassenheit*, "releasement," is by no means release from the situation of *anxiety*. In fact, I shall try to show that Heidegger's later reflections on poetry sustain a *thinking within anxiety*. Such reflections may be viewed as an essential continuation and enrichment of Heidegger's efforts in *Being and Time* to let death be.

Although the intimations of mortality in Heidegger's poetics of Being could just as easily have sent me to Hölderlin or Rilke or George, the poet interrogated most closely here will be Georg Trakl. Trakl is Heidegger's contemporary, much more so than the others. The reasons for my choosing Trakl for a discussion of Heidegger's poetics—in a way he is the most recalcitrant candidate—should become clear during the book's final chapter, which focuses on love and death. It is significant that in a number of his later lectures, including "Time and Being" and "What Calls for Thinking?", Heidegger appeals to Trakl's poetry for insight into language and the mortal condition. The language we find in Trakl scarcely lends itself to a metaphorics of Being or a meditation on the holy; and the kind of mortal man and woman we find in Trakl's lines has precious little to do with philosophical anthropology. With Trakl we find ourselves everywhere on the verge of things unthought and unsaid. Perhaps unsayable. It is not surprising that when in the early 1950s Heidegger began to speak publicly about this poet whom he had been reading for some thirty-five years very few of his students and colleagues were able to follow; it was more reassuring to tarry with Hölderlin's gods and Rilke's angels, as tenuous as they had become, or to hasten on to Stefan George's sturdy Nordic Norns. When Trakl—two years older than Heidegger but dead sixty-two years before him—evokes "The Nearness of Death" we can be certain that his poetry resounds with intimations of mortality. The stroke of love only serves to strengthen and confirm those intimations.

Trakl's ambiguous *Geschlecht* is the "generation" of men and women "struck" by love and death. That theme leads me back and down to my point of departure. Heidegger projects a fundamental ontology of finite Dasein. The fundament itself proves to be finite, the horizon of the project interminably open. Ontology confronts its own history as the oblivion of Being, a history in which Being comes to nothing. However Icarian the projects of a history and poetics of Being may appear to be, Heidegger's thinking remembers to be what it always was—the downward way, the way of response to intimations of mortality.

PART ONE
Intimations of Time and Being

1 From Existence to Fundamental Ontology

Remembering Hannah Arendt

While in the throes of a change in vocation from psychiatry to philosophy Karl Jaspers published a lengthy treatise entitled *The Psychology of Worldviews* (1919).[1] He had composed the book hurriedly, writing it down and sending it off to the printer without re-writes or extensive corrections. In the opening pages of this eminently personal work, which tried to communicate nothing less than its author's conception of human life and purpose, Jaspers remarked with a tinge of self-criticism that "it is senseless to want to say everything at once" (J, 7). Leaving form to benign neglect, Jaspers pursued in all directions the content for a "psychology of psychology" which would dare to occupy "the outermost boundaries" of existence, in order to learn "what man is" (J, 5). In his 1954 Foreword to the fourth (substantially unchanged) edition, reflecting on the work's sacrifice of formal outline and perspective to existential experience, Jaspers explained, ". . . I thought about nothing else than authentic human being" (J, x).

After Jaspers' death in 1969 friends found among his papers an unpublished study of *The Psychology of Worldviews* by Martin Heidegger. Heidegger had originally planned the study as a review of Jaspers' book. Jaspers himself received a copy of the typescript in June, 1921. More than five decades after Jaspers received his copy, Heidegger reluctantly consented to the essay's publication in a collection of critical articles on Jaspers' philosophy.[2] In September, 1975 he informed me of his intention to make the Jaspers review the very first of his *Wegmarken* in the new Collected Edition.

Heidegger had been working intermittently on the manuscript since the appearance of Jaspers' book, concurrent to his own return to Freiburg University after the war in 1919. At that time he was an "assistant" to Husserl, although he had received his *venia legendi* (the right to lecture as a *Privatdozent*) three years earlier. During the period of the essay's composition Heidegger taught courses on phenomenology and transcendental value-philosophy, on the philosophical foundations of medieval mysticism, on the phenomenology of intuition and expression, as of religion, and on Descartes' *Meditations*. Perhaps most interesting in the present context is a seminar held during the winter semester of 1919–20 on Paul Natorp's *General Psychology*. At the present time only one of the texts of these courses is available in print. Yet the Jaspers review is the most significant piece of work we have from Heidegger's hand stemming from the first Freiburg period (1909–23), before the move to Marburg and the publication of *Being and Time* (1927). As I shall try to show in my "Conclusions" below, of all the early writings it is especially valuable for insight into Heidegger's way toward *Being and Time*. For in it are unmistakable intimations of ideas basic to Heidegger's magnum opus, nascent structures and analyses which appear much earlier and in a more mature form than anyone might have imagined.[3]

Heidegger's typescript, some 12,000 words long, shows no articulated divisions except for a brief "Appendix" at the end. Nevertheless, the text proves to have certain natural joints, and may be considered as having five sections:

(a) an introductory appreciation and criticism of Jaspers' book (pp. 70–76, 1. 37);

(b) a section focusing on "the phenomenon of existence" (pp. 76–89, 1. 21);

(c) the preparation of a new starting-point for the analysis of the phenomenon of existence (pp. 89–94, 1. 32);

(d) a recapitulation of both appreciation and criticism (pp. 94–99);

(e) an "Appendix" (pp. 99–100) offering suggestions for revisions in a possible second edition.

Since Heidegger's suggested changes were never adopted,[4] I shall incorporate this "Appendix" into my account of the general criticism. Sections (a) and (d) belong together, while sections (b) and (c) contain the most original and constructive material. I shall offer a particularly detailed account of (c), where Heidegger's own projected starting-point emerges, consider the three references to Jaspers' book in *Being and Time* itself, and offer some concluding observations. Chapter one thus has five parts: Appreciation and Criticism; The Phenomenon of Existence; Toward a New Beginning; References to Jaspers in *Being and Time*; and Conclusions.

APPRECIATION AND CRITICISM

Heidegger lauds the "self-reliance and significance of achievement" in Jaspers' *The Psychology of Worldviews* (70). The work's aim is to explore the "substantial totality" of man's spiritual being by advancing to the very limits of his psychic life. Its purpose is not to promote any particular view of the world but to clarify in a philosophical way all such possible views. "Worldview" thus loses some of its historicist implications: Jaspers understands it as "the ultimate nature and totality of man, . . . his preoccupation with the whole" (J, 1).

Heidegger hones in on the "principal issue" of Jaspers' intended philosophical psychology. He asks whether "the choice and manner of application of the methodological means genuinely correspond" to the motifs Jaspers himself wishes to display; that is, whether "these motifs and tendencies themselves have been grasped radically enough" in terms of what Jaspers himself wishes to accomplish (71). For such critical purposes no "standard measure" of philosophical rigor can be applied. Heidegger's own critique must therefore go beyond the usual logical and historiological limits. In fact, the epistemological presuppositions behind all such "standards" live a "shadowy existence" in a philosophical tradition that is congested and in decline. At the very outset of his review of Jaspers' work, one of the central themes of Being and Time thus comes to the fore: the destructuring of the history of ontology (cf. Being and Time, section 6). Heidegger speaks of a "destructuring of what is transmitted in our intellectual history," relating that destructuring from the start to "the explication of the original motivating situations from which fundamental philosophical experiences spring" (72). In this way Heidegger expresses his "strong suspicion of all Lebensphilosophie that revels in indeterminability and assumes an apparent originality" (72). Only a factically rooted historical self-criticism can successfully dismantle all those presuppositions and preconceptions that occasion the discrepancy between who we are and who we think we are. Such self-criticism may seem to be a detour in Jaspers' (or anyone's) study of man, but according to Heidegger it is the only way (73). It is finally time to ask whether we have adequately comprehended "what we ourselves ostensibly 'have' and 'are'—in connection with the fundamental question of the meaning of the 'I am' " (73). It is this "preliminary work" (74) that is lacking in Jaspers' study.[5]

Jaspers' The Psychology of Worldviews hopes to establish the horizon of the totality of human psychic life by locating its "limit situations." Man stands out, according to Jaspers, "in certain decisive, essential situations that are bound up with human being as such and are inevitably given with finite existence [Dasein]" (J, 229). For Jaspers, the "primal phenomenon" of human life is the subject-object split and the resulting antinomial character of existence (J, 42; 232). In fact, the subject-object split determines the outline of Jaspers' own treatise, which first analyzes the subjective "engagements" (Einstellungen) possible for the psyche (J, 52–138), and then elaborates the objective "world images" (Weltbilder) corresponding to them (J, 139–216.)[6] Behind this central motif of the subject-object split hides a certain set of presuppositions which Jaspers uncritically adopts. Heidegger italicizes the following principal complaint: "In the very starting-point [Problemansatz] a preconception [Vorgriff] of the psychic, articulated in a definite way, is pre-given and works its effects" (74). He continues:

> If genuine psychology is to enable us to see "what man is" [J, 5], then preconceptions concerning the ontological meaning [Seinssinn] of this totality of psychic-spiritual life lie within the prerequisite and proper scope of the task. So do those preconceptions about the possible method of clarifying life as it is supposedly lived, and also those about the basic meaning of that from which something like "possibilities" can emerge at all. [75]

Here we sense something of Heidegger's later definition of Dasein as "possibility-being" and "ability to be" in which basic structures of the "I am" are brought to light without special appeal to "psychic life," as indeed already belonging to "our factical life-experience" (75). Hence the *method* for exposing the preconceptions of the subjectivist tradition is to trace their genesis in a concrete analysis of the basic possibilities of human existence. So long as the problem of method is not made thematic, however, the analysis cannot genuinely advance. In the fourth section of his review, which recapitulates his appreciation and criticism, Heidegger explains why this circle (cf. SZ, section 2) is unavoidable. If existence or *Dasein* is the "object" to be examined, no mere "observation" of it is adequate unless its own interpretive behavior becomes an issue for it; in other words, unless it becomes aware of its own *history* (95). Existential explication requires more than a typology or description of certain human behaviors; it must be more than a "looking around to see what is there," more than a regional depiction. For its *own tendency* is to search for the *whole*. Nor can it spare itself this task by appealing to the "infinitely flowing" character of life, which will not allow its particularity and individuality to be fixed in concepts.

> Instead of repeating again and again the oft-quoted *individuum est ineffabile*, it is high time we ask what sense the *fari* [speech] should have, and what kind of grasping should come to expression. We should also ask whether the above dictum doesn't presuppose a certain way of conceiving the individual that is ultimately rooted in an aesthetic, extrinsic observation of the "whole personality." Such extrinsic observation still remains in force even when the personality is "understood" in immanent-psychological fashion: the objective, image-like aspect is maintained (cf. for example Dilthey). [96][7]

Indeed, what has just been described is the image of the world that Jaspers' own observations propagate—although Jaspers' *verstehende Psychologie* wishes to refrain from all such propagation. "Mere observation does not give what it most wants to give, namely, the possibility of radical re-examination and decision, as well as a . . . rigorous consciousness of the necessity of methodical interrogation. . . . As one advances in reflection, one can make others aware only by going ahead a stretch of the path oneself" (98). It is not enough to reserve this methodological problem for a "general psychology." Failure to see the pervasive influence of unclarified preconceptions in all specific or derivative psychologies is "a mistaking and an underestimation of the genuine methodological problematic" (98). Jaspers cannot simply observe and describe helter-skelter what is "there"—he must broach "a radical interrogation [Befragen] which keeps itself in the question" (99). Yet the "primary Befragte" (cf. SZ, section 2) is the "there" of the questioner himself, Dasein or Existenz.

THE PHENOMENON OF EXISTENCE

The formal object of inquiry for both Jaspers and Heidegger is "existence." This is "the phenomenon of the 'I am,'" whose "ontological meaning" is to be interpreted (76). Heidegger remarks parenthetically that "the fundamental meaning of all philosophical concepts and conceptual matrices" rests in the problem of "existence" (76–77). The nucleus of Jaspers' understanding of existence, and the "strongest" part of his entire analysis, is the description of the "limit situations."

Jaspers discusses three "limit situations" that exhibit the pathos of existence—its striving, the opposing contradictions, and the resultant antinomies.[8] "For our experience, absolute accident, death, and guilt seem to stand everywhere at the limit" (J, 230). The last two come to play a central role in the analysis of Dasein (cf. SZ, sections 49–53; 58–60). But for Jaspers they are primarily evidence of the subject-object split and of the presumably essential human need for unity, totality, and infinity. These notions are common to the Lebensphilosophie of the day, which also leaves them unclarified (78–79).[9] Yet these philosophies of life express a tendency toward the phenomenon of existence, which Heidegger, in a free adaptation of Jaspers' use of the word (cf. J, 380), divides and italicizes as "Da sein" (79–80). He credits Jaspers with having led Lebensphilosophie to the central issue of the "phenomenology of existence," but faults him for being unable to explicate the latter according to the "applicable conceptual means" (80). Heidegger's aim in this critical appraisal is "to discuss the leading preconception [i.e., the phenomenon of existence] with regard to what it intends and how it intends it; that is to say, to delineate conceptually the phenomenon of existence with respect to its own suitability . . ." (83).

For Jaspers, the limit situations have meaning only by virtue of what in some unexplained way lies beyond the limit, namely, "the infinite totality of life," particularly "the endless life of the spirit" (80). Heidegger criticizes the covert manner in which biological infinitude is borrowed for "the spirit" without an attempt to clarify either of these phenomena (81). A hopelessly obscure appeal to several senses of "infinity"—this is what results from Jaspers' "mere observation." Even if Jaspers wishes to deflate the pretensions of metaphysics by invoking the "stream" of transient life, the metaphysical substructure of totality and infinity perdures (82). Such "specifically Bergsonian argumentation," in Heidegger's view, because it overlooks all problems concerning "significance, concepts, and language," cannot offer more than "a very rough and vague elaboration" of what "the fundamental meaning of life and of our whole life-experience" might be (82).

As I have already observed, Jaspers' leading preconception regarding the phenomenon of existence—the psychic *Urphänomen*—is the subject-object split (83). Effectively presupposed thereby is a "fundamental reality" of something "unsplit," as it were, toward which life strives. Heidegger insists that it makes little difference whether one overtly defines this Absolute in traditional metaphysical ways or makes covert appeals to it (84). Resisting Jaspers' starting-point, and anticipating his own later work, Heidegger suggests that life's striving must be more closely defined as the factical inclination toward one's own existence; in other words, as an a priori structure "of the disclosure [*Aufschliessen*] and holding open [*Offenhalten*] of a horizon of expectations with respect to concrete preoccupations" (84–85). Such a definition should produce the genuine structures for explicating the fundamental experience (*Grunderfahrung*) of existence.

Nevertheless, Heidegger appreciates Jaspers' individual analyses of the limit situations, especially that of death. Jaspers exhibits clearly the antinomial nature of death, "a universal situation" which at the same time is "a specific, individual" one. He makes much of man's "utterly unique relation to his own death, incomparable to any universal or particular experience of the death of the Other" (*J*, 261). The relevance of Jaspers' account of death for Heidegger's *Being and Time* (cf. section 47, "The possibility of experiencing the death of others and of grasping a whole Dasein") is unmistakable; but Jaspers' eclectic account, replete with extended quotations from Buddhist religious texts, Goethe, and Kierkegaard, differs sharply from Heidegger's programmatic analysis. Also lacking in Jaspers' account is a description of man's *access* to such limit situations (87), something Heidegger's analysis of anxiety will attempt to supply (cf. SZ, section 40). Heidegger's admiration of Jaspers' empassioned description is riddled by doubts concerning the role such accounts—and their recounting—play in existence as such. "Our critical observation therefore finds itself again and again thrown back to the problem of preconceptions" (87).

Jaspers' sources for the "antinomies" of existence and its striving for the "infinite" are, of course, Kant (cf. especially the first antinomy of *The Critique of*

Pure Reason) and Kierkegaard, who further "purifies" infinity of its theological trappings (88). Yet do these sources provide an adequate base for a full explication of existence? Or do they not by virtue of concepts transmitted in the metaphysical tradition—infinity, totality, contradiction—cover over the fundamental experience Jaspers himself wishes to expose? Heidegger suspects that the latter is the case, and that a new point of entry into the phenomenon of existence is needed.

TOWARD A NEW BEGINNING

Existence is . . . a definite manner of Being, a certain sense of the "is" which "is" essentially the sense of (I) "am." It is a sense that is not possessed genuinely in any sort of theoretical opinion, but rather in the process of the "am," which is an ontological mode of the Being of the "I." Formally designated, existence suggests the Being of the self understood in such fashion. . . . Decisive is the fact that I *have myself*—the fundamental experience in which I encounter myself as a self, so that, living in this experience, I can question *its* meaning in an appropriate way, corresponding to the sense of my "I am." [89]

These words appear, not in *Being and Time*, but in the central pages of Heidegger's review of Jaspers' *The Psychology of Worldviews*, completed before June, 1921. (Cf. *SZ*, sections 9 and 25.)

The fundamental experience of existence with which all explication must begin is one that "radically and purely involves me myself [*um mich selbst geht*]," not as a particular instance of some "universal," but as this (my) experience itself. Explication of such experience must guard against the perpetual danger of objectifying the "I" as some sort of "stream of consciousness" or "nexus of life-experiences" which would congeal the meaning of the "am." Such "objectifying preconceptions" must be subjected to "radical suspicion" and untiring scrutiny (90).

All theoretical explanations, seeking as they do the "what-it-is" of things, distort the way in which I have my self and trouble myself about it in the factical life I lead in my environment. The "I" must be taken not as "the concept of an empirical subject" but as "the full, concrete, historical, factical self" (90). Formally, of course, the "I am," as a meaning of Being, a "how" of Being,[10] can be transmuted into the form "he, she, it is," the form of statement that tells "what-it-is." Yet the last-named modes are appropriate to the Being of beings at hand, *vorhanden* (90), in a way that existence never is.[11] The fundamental experience of having my self cannot be reduced to any immanent-psychic act of consciousness, for which the "am" is reduced to an "I" that is present-at-hand.

The "am" is not so readily accessible to interpretation. For experience has an "authentically historical extension into the past," which is itself experienced within an always presupposed (*vorweggesetzt*[12]) horizon of expectations. Heidegger elaborates:

> The decisive task is the phenomenological explication of the "how" of this process of experience, within the whole complex of problems involving the phenomenon of existence, according to its fundamentally *historical* meaning. . . . We must achieve the meaning of the explication itself as an interpretive process that corresponds to this task. We must maintain access to the *explicata* themselves, in accord with their essential character as *hermeneutical* concepts, as essentially open to ever-renewed interpretation. . . . [91]

The phenomenological basis for the explication of existence must be the facticity of its own fundamental experience (cf. *SZ*, section 12, p. 56, and section 41). The latter is essentially "historical," in that it is experienced in process as a factical life-situation, *enacted, executed,* and *achieved* in the course of a life-history (*ein sich selbst so erfahrendes* VOLLZUGSGESCHICHTLICHES *Phänomen*) (91). This process yields the "how" of "the self's taking trouble concerning itself [or: preoccupation with itself, *Bekümmerung des Selbst um sich selbst*]" (91). Heidegger later calls such *Sichbekümmern* (in section 41 of *Being and Time*) *Sorge*, "care."[13]

Bekümmerung betrays a peculiar union of past, present, and future for the self. The phenomenon of existence, whose basic experience is a taking trouble concerning itself, is disclosed (*erschliesst sich*) as radically *historical* (92).[14]

On the basis of this process of *Sichbekümmern*, existence may be said to possess conscience (92), a concept central to the later existential-ontological analysis of Dasein (cf. *SZ*, sections 54–60). Conscience, in turn, provides the basis for an original understanding of historicality in a narrower "historiological" sense (cf. *SZ*, section 76). Furthermore, the essential relatedness of having-a-self to history in an original sense—from which the discipline of "history" derives—and to having-a-conscience is usually covered over and hidden. Existence has a tendency to "fall" into ready-made meanings and possibilities, so much so that a new exposition of the phenomenon of existence must be bound to a destructuring of the tradition.[15]

With that we arrive at the most striking of all the intimations of *Being and Time* in this early essay. It merits extended quotation.

> With respect to what it experiences, our concrete, factical experience of life has its own tendency to fall into the "objective" meanings of the

experienceable environment. From the prevailing ontological character of the objective meanings which this falling experiences we can understand that the self, with respect to the meaning of its Being, can be experienced in an objectified sense ("personality" or the "ideal of humanity"). Such a direction for experience comes to the theoretical grasp and to philosophical conception in ever stronger measures as the experienced and known past insinuates itself into the present situation as an objective tradition. As soon as this particular burden of factical life [i.e., the past] is seen in terms of tradition (which is to be understood in a manifold sense), a burden that fatefully exercises its effects most directly in the worldly experiences of one's having-a-self, the insight develops that the concrete possibility of bringing phenomena of existence into view and specifying them in genuine conception can manifest itself *only when* the concrete, relevant, and effectively experienced tradition is destructured, precisely with reference to the ways and means by which it specifies self-realizing experience; and *only when*, through the destructuring, the basic motivating experiences that have become effective are dismantled and discussed in terms of their originality. Such destructuring actually remains bound to one's own concrete and fully historical preoccupation with the self. [92–93]

The central question of a new beginning for the exposition of the phenomenon of existence closes with a discussion of the problem of method and an enumeration of several concrete tasks (94). The problem of method, of the initial steps of such exposition and of its access to the phenomenon, cannot remain extrinsic to the interpretation itself. The genuine problem—largely ignored in Jaspers' work—is "the method of the historically-in-process interpretive explication of the concrete, fundamental ways of experiencing one's factically preoccupied having-one's-self" (94). Without specifying the several tasks outlined at the end of this third section of the review, we can still attend to their general character and to Heidegger's own direction in search of a new beginning. The latter resists quite strongly any interpretation of the "self" in terms of current psychological notions, and hence tries to surpass from the outset the subjectivist understanding of the "I am" that supports such notions.

The point is not casually to introduce the personality and then to *apply* to it something gained from some philosophical tradition or other. The point is to take the concrete self as the starting-point of the problem and to bring it to the appropriate fundamental level of phenomenological interpretation, namely, that related to our factical experience of life, in this way bringing the concrete self to "givenness." From our necessarily restricted remarks one thing should have become clear: the authentic phenomenon of existence designates a manner of access appropriate to it; the phenomenon of existence is to be had only in a definite way of achieving the "how" of experience; precisely this *how* of the appropriation [*Aneignung*], and even of the *very beginning* of its appropriating, is decisive. *The factical, historically-in-process life in the factical "how" of this problematic of the self's preoccupation with and appropriation of itself belongs originally to the meaning of the factical "I am."* [93]

It is surely not out of place to recall that the questions of *existence, history*, and a "new beginning" in *method* had been brewing for some time in Heidegger.[16] Husserl's young assistant had been reading Dilthey at least since 1917. Dilthey fulfilled two vital functions for Heidegger. First, he elevated Bergsonian *Lebensphilosophie* beyond Bergson's own intuitionism to a sophisticated hermeneutics of history. Second, he fortified Heidegger's growing resistance to the bloodless transcendental consciousness of Husserl's *Ideas I* (1913) by considering the full thinking-willing-feeling life of historical human beings, hence proving himself to be, as Pöggeler puts it, "a better phenomenologist than Husserl." Even Heidegger's admiration for the *Logical Investigations* did not blind him to his own task, which required him to place practical, "lived" truth on the same level as theoretical, cognitive truth: the transcendental ego would have to be brought to confront its finitude as factical, historical, life-in-process. The word "process" (*Vollzug*) is particularly important—we confront it constantly in the Jaspers review. Heidegger always and everywhere prefers *Vollzugssinn* to the more Husserlian *Gehaltssinn:* the sense of historical process, enactment, and execution is more decisive than any eidetic content or cognitive import. "Religious" experience offers a number of striking examples of such factical, process-bound life-experience, although the fact that the word has to appear in quotation marks indicates that it has a special sense in Heidegger's case.

During the winter semester of 1916–17 Heidegger had taught a number of courses for the Catholic theology faculty in Freiburg, even though by that time Catholicism had become problematic for him. It is not—as Husserl believed—that his interest in Luther and Kierkegaard had "converted" him to protestantism. I imagine Heidegger's rejection of his Jesuit training and his faith to be similar to that of his fictional contemporary, Stephen Dedalus, though far less passionate and bitter. Whatever his own religious state of mind, Heidegger acceded gladly to Husserl's wish after the war that Heidegger devote his teaching to problems in the phenomenology of history and religion, in order to counterbalance Oskar Becker's work in the phenomenology of mathematics and the natural sciences. In the winter semester of 1920–21 he taught an "Introduction to the Phenomenology of Religion."[17] There he chose the model of belief in the

Second Coming of Christ in early Christian communities as one "factical experience of life" that would burst the constraints of eidetic phenomenology. He referred to Paul's epistles, especially I Thessalonians 4–5, where Paul invokes the Christian's hope in Christ's return. That return would follow not in chronological but kairological time, which is to say, at the fitting season. The critical period or fitting season was not a temporal object for prediction and control but, on the contrary, a matter of the risks of an open future. The *Parousia* of Christ's Second Coming was of neither present nor past nor future, but a moment or "flash of an eye" (*Augenblick*) encompassing and transcending the ordinary dimensions of time. The early Christian experience was not one of mere expectation; the Christian did not simply await the Christ; his or her vigilance or wakefulness, as a factical life-experience, required a new conception of both history and temporality.

In his course on "Augustine and Neo-Platonism," taught in the summer of 1921, Heidegger argued that while Augustine originally thought in terms of the factical experience of his own life he falsified that experience by subsuming it under neo-Platonic concepts. To Augustinian philosophy Heidegger opposed Luther's rejection of the Patristic-Scholastic adaptation of Greek metaphysics and science and his decision to commit the world and its works to the Cross. In all this Heidegger had been impressed by Franz Overbeck's interpretation of *eschatology* as the core experience of the early Christians, one that found its echoes in Augustine, medieval mysticism, Luther, and Kierkegaard. Yet Heidegger's interest was not primarily religious or theological. What intrigued him in the Christian experience was the way in which life-in-process was grasped as a whole, gripped in the "hour of salvation," an hour that was as much an instant as a lifetime. What captivated him was the factical, historical experience of life represented in such a grasp.

At least since his 1919–20 lecture course on "Fundamental Problems of Phenomenology" Heidegger had viewed such life-experiences as the proper theme of phenomenology, the "science of origins." According to Pöggeler, however, it was not until the years 1922–23 that Heidegger attained the decisive insight into the "hermeneutics of facticity" which he had been practicing for some time. His insight was that although life-in-process or factical existence was defined by *time* the traditional metaphysical sense of time (as "presence," based on the "presentness" of things) touched only the shallowest dimension of life. This crucial insight is not fully present in the Jaspers review of 1919–21 or in any of the courses contemporaneous with it; but that Heidegger is on the very verge of it is clear from his emphasis on the necessity of a "destructuring" of the tradition. Heidegger's state of mind—better, the state of the *question* in him—at the time of the Jaspers review emerges clearly from an interior monologue fashioned for him by Pöggeler and Hogemann (pp. 53–54).

Here the "new beginning" envisaged by Heidegger for philosophy of life, philosophy of existence, and hermeneutical phenomenology takes on well-defined contours.

> To have a self—which is what life is all about—is not to have an isolated subject, and certainly not an ego as object. It is rather the process by which life achieves or loses a certain familiarity with itself. . . . Life settles itself into its world. It is not an ego that must first build bridges to things. . . . The problems of logic and of language thus receive a new foundation. . . . "Meaning" is not a world on its own, to be grasped as static and inert; it is rather the primal own-ness of factical life and must be conceived in accord with its structure in terms of life. Life, in its factical character, is a nexus of meaningfulness. To be sure, a particular human proclivity may level such meaningfulness to sheer reification or "objectification." But such objectification has to be grasped as a "de-vitalizing" of life: as a result of it, living loses its "tendentious" structure; loses the meaningful relations to its world; loses its life. Because it exists in process, within its factical, meaningful contexts, life occurs in "situations." It draws on the fundamental sense of its self when it grasps itself in process [*Vollzug*]. This way it comprehends itself as "historical" life; this way it is on the way to its origins.

To this imagined monologue only one or two thoughts specifically aimed at Jaspers must be adduced:

> Life must be conceived of and described in terms of *existence*, and existence in terms of *how* I have my self. Such descriptions must dismantle the notions our tradition attaches to the self. Yet neither description nor destructuring can afford to be careless of *concepts*. Life-in-process is not a pot of freely flowing porridge. Enthusiasm is not enough. Though there be process, yet there is *method* in it.

REFERENCES TO JASPERS IN *BEING AND TIME*

Heidegger mentions Jaspers three times in *Being and Time*, at pp. 249n., 301–2n., and 338n. All three references are to Jaspers' *The Psychology of Worldviews*. Because the second reference is of central importance I shall consider it last.

First reference. At the end of section 49, "The delimitation of the existential analysis of death against other possible interpretations of the phenomenon," Heidegger invites a comparison between his existential analysis of death and those of Wilhelm Dilthey, Rudolf Unger, Georg Simmel, and "especially"

Jaspers' *The Psychology of Worldviews*—its general theory of the "limit situations" and "death" in particular. "Jaspers conceives of death along the guidelines of the phenomenon of the 'limit situation' which he explicates and whose fundamental significance surpasses all typology of 'engagements' and 'world images' [*Einstellungen und Weltbilder*]." (Jaspers' first two chapters, we recall, were entitled "Engagements" and "World Images.") Thus even six years later, in *Being and Time*, Heidegger finds Jaspers' particular analyses of the limit situations stimulating, but the structures in which they are confined tenuous and unenlightening.

Third reference. In section 68a, "The temporality of understanding," Heidegger refers to Kierkegaard's interpretation of "the moment" (*Augenblick*) and also to Jaspers' *The Psychology of Worldviews*, pp. 108ff. and 419–32. Heidegger's opposition to Jaspers' Kierkegaardian view of "the moment" in terms of "time and eternity," as the "cancellation of time, the present of the eternal" (*J*, 112), is vigorous. The "moment" Heidegger wishes to speak of in section 68 of *Being and Time* cannot be clarified by reference to the derivative conception of time as a series of "now" points (cf. *SZ*, section 81). Nor is it an escape from Dasein's past and future: Dasein's resolute openedness (*Entschlossenheit*) preserves its authentic present from complete dispersal precisely by holding onto its past and future. Jaspers' interpretation of the "moment" wanders toward that unclarified "eternity" or "infinity" Heidegger had criticized in his review and which he continues to resist in *Being and Time* (cf. *SZ*, pp. 330–31).

Central reference. Toward the close of section 60, "The existential structure of the proper ability to be that is evidenced in conscience," where Heidegger defines Dasein's "situation" in terms of openedness, authenticity, and the call of care, Jaspers' *The Psychology of Worldviews* is once more invoked. That work's problematic goes in the direction of "thematic existential anthropology," which should describe in more detailed fashion than a fundamental ontology of Dasein can various "factical existentiell possibilities" for such phenomena as conscience. With reference to Jaspers' book Heidegger continues:

> Here the question of "what man is" is posed and defined in terms of what he essentially can be (cf. the Foreword to the first edition). From this the principal existential-ontological significance of the "limit situation" comes to light. One misses the philosophical import of *Psychologie der Weltanschauungen* entirely if one "utilizes" it solely as a reference-work for "types of worldviews."

Several pages later (*SZ*, 308), Heidegger employs Jaspers' term *Grenzsituation* in a passage that clearly exhibits the word's "principal existential-ontological significance."

The indeterminacy of one's own ability to be, although it has become certain in our resolution [*Entschluss*], manifests itself *wholly* first of all in being toward death. Anticipation brings Dasein before a possibility that is constantly certain, yet which remains undetermined at every moment as to when possibility will become impossibility. Anticipation makes it manifest that this being has been thrown into the indeterminacy of its "limit situation"; opened to it [*zu der entschlossen*], Dasein achieves its proper ability to be a whole.

That the limit situation of Dasein's being toward death, revealed in anxiety and sustained in anticipatory openedness, is essential to the very idea of an existential analysis and fundamental ontology of Dasein, is revealed clearly in a reading of the methodologically pivotal sections of *Being and Time*.[18] All these sections testify to the importance of concrete phenomenal grounds, existentiell possibilities, and ontic testimony for phenomenological, existential-ontological investigation. The "limit situation" disclosed in anxiety—where the disclosure and what is disclosed are existentially selfsame (cf. section 40, p. 188)—and supported by conscience as the call of care, in other words, Dasein's being thrown into death, is the most abyssal phenomenal ground, the most proper existentiell possibility, and the most compelling ontic testimony.

CONCLUSIONS

Heidegger's praise of Jaspers' *The Psychology of Worldviews*, whose *content* offered much that Heidegger had been looking for, is tempered by his criticism of the work's jumbled *form* and lack of sustained *method*. In his Foreword to the fourth edition, Jaspers concedes that the language of his early work "achieved no kind of form at all" (*J*, viii). While still affirming the book's basic posture and tendency (*J*, xii), he admits that it is "somewhat unpreoccupied" with philosophical rigor (*J*, viii). Many of its concepts simply "swept over" him and were "not systematically thought through" (*J*, ix).[19]

I have dealt with Heidegger's criticism of Jaspers' preconceptions at some length, although in the preceding section we saw something of Jaspers' more positive contributions to Heidegger's analysis of Dasein. These may be reduced to two essential matters. First, Jaspers' very language—especially such terms as *Existenz, Existenzphänomen*, and *Dasein*—suggests how the starting-point of the prevailing "philosophy of life" may be surpassed. Second, the idea of a "limit situation" which would expose the essential character of existence, and the description of death as such a situation for each existence, foreshadow the methodological importance of the analysis of death in *Being and Time*.[20]

Before summarizing the ways in which Heidegger's review points toward his major work, we should note several essential aspects of *Being and Time* that are not yet present in the earlier piece. For it would be foolhardy to argue that the project of *Being and Time* assumes its definitive shape prior to the Marburg years, 1923–28. In this early piece the terms *Jemeinigkeit* and *Eigentlichkeit* do not appear, although the notions seem to be brewing. Dasein as "being in the world" is not explicitly invoked, nor, understandably enough, are the detailed structures of Dasein's being-in or the worldhood of the world presented. The existential structures of *Befindlichkeit*, *Verstehen* and *Rede* do not arise as such. Also missing is the crucial conception of temporality (*Zeitlichkeit*) as the very essence of Da-sein and the horizon of the question of the meaning of Being in general. While implied in such phrases as the "*Seinssinn* of the (I) am," the priority of the question of Being itself does not come to light. The distinctions between ontic and ontological, existentiell and existential, are lacking; the definitive formulation of the project of a phenomenological existential analysis, conceived as fundamental ontology, does not yet appear. Yet what is genuinely surprising is the extent to which the Jaspers review anticipates what Eugen Fink has called Heidegger's "breakthrough work."

We might now try to list the most striking of the foreshadowings of *Being and Time* in this early writing:

Awareness of the problem of method and a desire that the exposition of the "phenomenon of existence" thematize the problem of its own phenomenal access and process. Even at this early date the exposition is called a *hermeneutics*.

Attention to the *ontological foundations* of such hermeneutical exposition. Existence is a mode or "how" of Being, in the form (I) "am," disclosed as *historical* Being.

Insistence on a concrete, factical, and complete account of the historizing Being of the "am," based on genuine *experiences*, not theoretical constructs; in a manner appropriate to the basic experience of *having-my-self*, not to beings present at hand.

Resistance to the derived subjectivist interpretation of the (bracketed) "I," and the proposed *destructuring* or dismantling of the Cartesian tradition.

Finally, we might try to locate the proper place of this essay among the other of Heidegger's "early writings." His doctoral dissertation, *The Doctrine of Judgment in Psychologism* (1914), does seem the work of an *unhistorischer Mathematiker*, as Heidegger styled himself in its Foreword. For whatever reasons, the dissertation remains strictly within the confines of the neo-Kantian approach of his directors. Nevertheless, Heidegger's resistance to the psychologistic reduction of phenomena is present in both this work and in the later Jaspers piece. For the dissertation, the matter to be safeguarded is the ideal content of judgment, whereas in the Jaspers review it is the ontological sense of the "am"; but the opposition to psychologism is itself constant. The Habilitation dissertation, *The*

Doctrine of Categories and of Judgment in Duns Scotus (1916), shows the extent to which the problem of historical interpretation, primarily through the study of Wilhelm Dilthey's writings, had shaken the apparently secure formal-systematic approach of the young academic. In effect, this treatise exhibits Heidegger's incipient return to his original interest, metaphysics (rather than theory of knowledge), awakened by his early contact with Franz Brentano's dissertation on "being" in Aristotle—discussed in chapter four, below. The Jaspers review manifests a much stronger emphasis on the problem of history—in keeping with the *venia legendi* lecture of 1916, "The Concept of Time in the Discipline of History"—and a corresponding shift of interest away from the primarily episte-mological concerns of the Habilitation dissertation itself.

Heidegger's first published article, "The Problem of Reality in Modern Philos-ophy" (1912), spurns the neo-Kantian standpoint of these later dissertations in favor of a "critical realism" more attuned to the Aristotelian-ontological than to the modern-epistemological approach to philosophy. In a sense, this "opus one" of Heidegger embodies more of the Heidegger of *Being and Time* (cf. sections 13 and 43), and therefore also more of the Heidegger of the Jaspers review, than do his own later "school" writings. On the other hand, the discipline exercised in these dissertations in the neo-Kantian and Husserlian style doubtless contributes to Heidegger's awareness of the problems of approach, method, and structure— and to his later criticism of Jaspers in these respects.

However, none of these early writings indicates as clearly as the Jaspers review does the fundamental direction eventually taken by the author of *Being and Time*. Heidegger's review exhibits tendencies away from epistemology toward ontology, away from mathematical formalism toward hermeneutical exposition, away from timeless truths to the disclosures of history, away from problems of essence toward those of existence. At the same time, Heidegger's direction maintains the rigor, precision, and definition typical of each of the former. It culminates in a work no one may call "early," whose interlacing of content and form, matter and method, does not cease to astonish.

What we must now proceed to examine is the way in which Heidegger's criticisms of Jaspers "come home"; that is, how they recoil on his own project of fundamental ontology in *Being and Time*. For Heidegger's methodological rigor will soon crack the fundament of his own magnum opus.

2 Fundamental Ontology, Meta-Ontology, Frontal Ontology

For John Sallis

Heidegger opens the treatise *Being and Time* with a reference to the perplex of "being" in Plato's *Sophist*. Two questions follow:

> Do we today have an answer to the question of what we really mean by the word "being"? By no means. And so it is fitting that we raise anew *the question of the meaning of Being*. Yet are we today perplexed because we cannot understand the expression "Being"? By no means. And so we must first of all awaken an understanding of the meaning of this question. [SZ, 1]

May we presume that the question of Being has by now become a familiar part of our tradition, readily accessible to our deliberation and critical judgment, ultimately "in hand," *zuhanden?* Does some sort of technique lie at our disposal for the confident manipulation of Heidegger's question? Have we so soon become assiduous tinkers of "Being"? True, over half a century has elapsed since the publication of *Being and Time*. Yet I myself am so far from a critical reassessment of that work that apart from several brief references to it I will refrain from discussing what is in effect my protracted first reading of *Being and Time*.

Instead, this chapter will raise some questions involving three other texts, texts of lecture courses Heidegger taught at Marburg in 1925–26 (*Logik*), 1927 (*Grundprobleme der Phänomenologie*), and 1928 (again, *Logik*). Obviously, I will be able to invoke only a few motifs of these lecture courses, those most proximate to the themes of fundamental ontology and meta-ontology. But which motifs? How find the focus?

Before narrowing the focus to the three texts mentioned, I want to broach the general problem of the formulation *Fundamentalontologie*. Here I want to explore at medium range, as it were, one dead-end approach to the problem, to see whether a more fruitful way opens up. Two critical remarks by Heidegger on the fate of his own project in *Being and Time*—one concerning the question of temporality, the other on the language of metaphysics—will introduce the fundamental-ontological themes of the Marburg lectures, which I want to focus on quite closely. Finally, by returning to what I take to be the irreducible enigma of fundamental ontology, I want to widen the focus of the discussion, widen it excessively, in order to get into view the radical dispersion of contemporary European thought in its retreat from fundamental ontology and its collision with what I shall call "frontal" ontology.

The present chapter will therefore advance through three stages: first, the formulation "fundamental ontology" and the search for an opening; second, two themes from the Marburg lectures—(a) temporality of Dasein and the temporal quality of Being in general: the ecstatic unity of horizon for the understanding of Being, and (b) metaphysics of truth and ground, or "meta-ontology": the *logos* of hermeneutic vs. scientific phenomenology; third, the dispersion of contemporary European thought in transition from fundamental to frontal ontology, exemplified in the thought of Jacques Derrida.

FUNDAMENTAL ONTOLOGY

An ample literature demonstrates that mere reversals of titles—such as *Being and Time, Time and Being*—do very little to clarify obscure questions. Still, let me try to reverse the components of the term *Fundamentalontologie*. Presumably, *Fundamentalontologie* is the quest for "ontological founding" or an "ontological fundament." Concealed in this reversal, which seems cogent enough, is an error which, if unnoticed and left uncorrected, distorts Heidegger's fundamental ontology from top to bottom. For the fundament Heidegger seeks is by no means an *ontological* one. Throughout *Being and Time* and the Marburg lectures Heidegger stresses that the fundament is irremediably ontic. The kind of testimony and demonstration that the hermeneutical-existential analysis of *Being and Time* invariably requires is "ontic," "factical," "concrete," rooted in "original experiences of Dasein." And when introducing his students to *The Basic Problems of Phenomenology* Heidegger insists:

> Ontology cannot be grounded in a purely ontological fashion. Its very possibility reverts to a being, which is to say, to the ontic realm: to Dasein. Ontology has an ontic fundament. . . . Hence the *first task* for a clarification of the scientific character of ontology is the *demonstration of its ontic fundament* and the characterization of this founding. [24, 26–27]

Ontology, whether "hermeneutical" or "scientific," has its roots in ontic soil.

Yet are we clear in our minds about what a fundamental ontology can be which searches for a fundament that is expressly not ontological but ontic? As for the founding itself, can it be ontological if the foundation is ontic? Does it really help if we recall that the fundamental analysis of Dasein is preparatory and provisional? Is it "preparatory" in that a repetition of the analysis will advance from an ontic to an ontological fundament? Is it "provisional" in that the investigation into the temporal quality of Being in general will transcend the limitations implied in the word "ontic"? If the outcome of the preparatory fundamental analysis of Dasein be designated in the phrase "finite transcendence," what would "transcendence" of ontic limitations mean for the hermeneutic of Dasein?

These questions are merely evaded when we go the route prescribed by most theorists of the "turn." Most often the Kehre—discussed in greater detail in chapter six below—is defined with reference to a phrase employed in 1938 by Heidegger himself: the turn from Being and Time to the later works, from Heidegger-I to Heidegger-II, is a turn from "man's relation to Being" to "Being, and the Truth of Being, in relation to man" (LR, xxi). Phrased more crudely, Heidegger's is a turn from Man to Being. Such a turn ostensibly accomplishes the move from mere ontic investigation (into Man) to ontological inquiry (into Being). It is essential that we loosen the grip such developmentalist theories of the "turn" have had on us. For the sake of such a loosening, let me propose a thesis: If there were a dramatic "turn" of this sort in Heidegger's career of thought (and I underscore the "if" and embrace the subjunctive), then it would be a turn, not from man to Being, but from the neutral designation Da-sein to homo humanus, to der Mensch, die Sterblichen; in other words, a turn from Being to Man. [1] If the developmentalist theory of the "turn" is helpful at all, it is only because it speaks precisely contrary to the case.

However matters may stand with my thesis, theories of the turn offer no fruitful way to take up the question of Fundamentalontologie as Fundamentalontik, the search for an ontic foundation for the question of the meaning of Being. Are we then clear in our minds about the relationship between the question of the meaning of Being (die Fundamentalfrage) and the path Heidegger follows in fundamental ontology? For even though he lets the title "fundamental ontology" drop, Heidegger insists that the path taken is a "necessary" one for his fundamental question (SZ, v). Why "necessary"? Because if the fundamental question is raised at all it is raised by a particular being who at a particular moment of historical time is prodded by the question. To put it another way: If the meaning of Being is at issue, and if meaning is projected in an understanding, that is to say, if there is some understanding of what is being asked about in the question, and, finally, if "understanding" is one of the existential structures of Dasein, one of the structures that constitute its mode of Being, then an analysis of Dasein cannot be avoided. Not only can it not be avoided: once undertaken, it can be neither abandoned nor circumscribed. The circularity of Being and understanding-of-Being confronts the questioner full face, like a sculpture of the Egyptian Middle Kingdom: frontally.

Although Heidegger never turns away from the question, he does turn toward it, incessantly, and always critically. Two of his criticisms may help us to open a path into the labyrinth of fundamental ontology.

1. Heidegger had long been aware that the oldest responses to the question of the meaning of Being were intimately and mysteriously bound up with Time. He defined the "provisional goal" of *Being and Time* as "the interpretation of *Time* as the possible horizon for any and every understanding of Being in general" (SZ, 1). The "first part" of that treatise—the only part, and it but two-thirds complete—is entitled "The Interpretation of Dasein with a View to Temporality and the Explication of Time as the Transcendental Horizon of the Question of Being." Its two completed divisions offer a "preparatory fundamental analysis of Dasein" and a repetition of that analysis in terms of "Dasein and temporality."

Of that repetition Heidegger remarked in his letter to Richardson, a letter he also read to the participants in the Todtnauberg Seminar on "Time and Being" (LR, xiii; ZSdD, 55):

> Die in *Sein und Zeit* gekennzeichnete ekstatisch-horizontale Zeit ist keineswegs schon das der Seinsfrage entsprechende gesuchte Eigenste der Zeit.

> Ecstatic-horizontal Time, as characterized in *Being and Time*, is by no means what is most proper to Time as sought in accordance with the question of Being.

The protocol to the Todtnauberg Seminar defines "what is most proper to Time" when it asserts that Heidegger's major work sets out on the path of *Zeitlichkeit des Daseins*, within the context of an interpretation of Being as *Temporalität*, in order "to find a concept of Time—to find what is proper to 'Time'—on the basis of which 'Being' is granted as *Anwesen*: presencing" (ZSdD, 34).

Question: Why and how does ecstatic-horizonal Time fall short of the meaning of Being as presencing?

In pursuit of that question I shall examine the second part of the 1927 Marburg course, especially sections 20 and 21 (*"Zeitlichkeit und Temporalität,"*

"Temporalität und Sein"), along with sections 12 and 13 of the 1928 *Logic*. However, by mentioning the title "logic," which seems an anomaly in the context of a question concerning temporality, I introduce a second critical remark by Heidegger.

2. The title of the "first half" of *Being and Time*, to repeat, is "The Interpretation of Dasein with a view to Temporality and *the Explication of Time as the Transcendental Horizon of the Question of Being*" (my emphasis). The words following the "and" apply to the projected third division of Part One: "*Time* as the transcendental horizon of the question of *Being*," hence, "Time and Being."

Of that division Heidegger wrote in his "Letter on Humanism" (*W*, 159; *BW*, 207–8):

> Der fragliche Abschnitt wurde zurückgehalten, weil das Denken im zureichenden Sagen dieser Kehre versagte und mit Hilfe der Sprache der Metaphysik nicht durchkam.

> The division in question was held back because the thinking failed to say this turning and did not succeed with the help of the language of metaphysics.

Heidegger expands this critique of the language of the projected third division of *Being and Time* some pages later, noting that the "wholly different dimension" sought in his treatise "falsifies itself insofar as it is not yet able to retain the essential help of phenomenological seeing while dispensing with the inappropriate concern for 'science' and 'research'" (*W*, 187; *BW*, 235).

Question: Why and how does the attempt to "explicate" Time as the "transcendental horizon of the question concerning Being" founder in its very discourse?

In pursuit of that question I shall again take up the two lecture courses mentioned, focusing on the "Appendix" to the second major division of the 1928 logic course. The Appendix is entitled "Designation of the Idea and Function of a Fundamental Ontology," and it introduces the term *meta-ontology*. Of essential importance will be to discern how the two questions posed here intertwine. For that I will have to refer to Heidegger's *first* logic course, taught in 1925–26, while the treatise *Being and Time* was in preparation.

BEING, TIME, AND TRUTH: META-ONTOLOGY

Why and how does ecstatic-horizonal Time fall short of the meaning of Being as presencing? Why and how does the attempt to "explicate" Time as the "transcendental horizon of the question concerning Being" founder in its very discourse? Why and how do these two questions intertwine?

The second half of *Basic Problems of Phenomenology* is devoted to "the funda-mental-ontological question concerning the meaning of Being" (*24*, 321). Its point of departure and return is the phenomenon of the understanding of Being: to raise the question of the meaning of Being requires that a tacit understanding of "something like Being" be operative. But "to grasp understanding-of-Being means first of all to understand *that* being to whose ontological constitution understanding-of-Being belongs: Dasein" (322). Now, the existential analysis of Dasein culminates in the insight that "*The ontological constitution of Dasein is grounded in temporality* [Zeitlichkeit]" (323). Hence temporality must also be the condition of the possibility of ontology as such, the horizon upon which something like Being can be projected explicitly. The phenomenon of *Zeitlich-keit*, viewed as the condition of the possibility of both understanding of Being and an articulated ontology, receives the title *"Temporalität"* (324). Heidegger's question is "whether in fact Time is that upon which Being itself is projected—whether Time is that on the basis of which we understand something like Being" (397; 406).

In *Basic Problems* Heidegger duplicates the structural analyses of temporality found in *Being and Time*. But now the orientation is far more explicitly histor-ical, paying particular heed to Aristotle and Kant, that is, to two of the three figures who were to have appeared in Part Two of *Being and Time*, the "Destruc-turing." Especially striking is Heidegger's preoccupation with *metabolē* ("change" or "alteration") in Aristotle's *Physics IV*. He translates the word as *Umschlag* or *Übergang*, "turnabout" or "transition," words he will later apply to the transmutation of his own fundamental ontology.

Of Heidegger's detailed analysis of time in Aristotle I will report nothing here,[2] except to say that it culminates in an account of the existential structures of "original Time" or "temporality of Dasein": *Gewärtigen*, "awaiting," in rela-tion to the ecstasis of the future; *Behalten*, "maintaining," in relation to the ecstasis of having-been; and *Gegenwärtigen*, "presenting," in relation to the present (365). Associated with each mode of original Time is a particular possibility-of-Being for Dasein: *sich selbst vorweg*, being ahead of itself; *sich selbst behaltend, in dem was es schon gewesen ist*, maintaining itself in that which it already has been; and *sich selbst bei Vorhandenem aufhaltend*, tarrying alongside things that are at hand. The last-mentioned has always been preeminent in the history of ontology, with its interpretation of Being as "presence at hand," on the horizon of "presenting," such an interpretation itself "falling" into the "ordinary" understanding of time as an infinite series of now-points and into oblivion of the difference between beings and Being. In contrast to the tradi-tion, Heidegger grants primacy to the ecstasis of the *future*. For understanding-of-Being is projected in understanding, the existential pro-jection or fore-casting of Dasein as possibility-being; all significance and meaning are to be found in the network of purposeful relations in which Dasein, for its own sake, is always ahead of itself, future-bound to the end.

Heidegger emphasizes the preeminence of the future ecstasis in the 1928 *Logic* (section 13). Here the very unity of the temporal horizon as such is determined out of the future. The *Umwillen* ("for the sake of") which expresses the possibility-being of Dasein is primary; it founds all the other modes of Dasein's comportment to beings (26, 273). The fact that Dasein exists "for the sake of itself," the fact that its own being-in-the-world is an issue for it, constitutes what Heidegger calls "the primal phenomenon of ground in general" (276; 282). The *Umwillen*, itself grounded in the ecstasis of the future, may thus be identified with the *epekeina tēs ousias* of Plato's *Republic* (VI, 509b 6–10): it is beyond Being, serving as its horizon and condition of possibility (284; cf. 24, 402).

Yet precisely here a doubt arises. For Heidegger specifies one region of problems surrounding the issue of "ground" itself as "interpretation of the essential retrogression of grounds into one ground," and he identifies that one ground as "thrownness in itself" (26, 278 and 174; cf. SZ, 308). Furthermore, he relates this "retrogression of grounds, that is, this reversal of Dasein," to the "'circle' in understanding" that characterizes the fundamental ontology of *Being and Time* (278; cf. SZ, section 2, and elsewhere). Yet if "thrownness," *Geworf-enheit*, expresses the facticity of "always already having been," of *Gewesenheit*, and if all grounds lead back to it, then how can the ecstasis of the future be primary? Can the meaning of Being be projected without explicit reference back to the "always already there" of our understanding of Being?

Another difficulty emerges in the *Basic Problems*. Ahead of itself, Dasein tarries alongside beings: the only explicit reference beyond the self to *beings* occurs in the ecstasis of the *present*. Can the meaning of Being be projected without an opening onto beings? Would that not overshoot the ontological difference, as it were, and so miss the mark? To put it another way: Is the primacy of "presenting" in the tradition simply the result of a lapsus, of "ensnarement," *Verfallen*? If the analysis of Dasein embodies the truth of subjectivity from Thales to Hegel (cf. 24, 320, 444, and 453; 26, 19–21 and 189–90), is there a truth of *Vorhandenheit* that has not yet been absorbed?

That question becomes crucial when Heidegger takes up for the second time Kant's "thesis on Being," "Being is not a real predicate" (24, 445ff.; cf. 35–107). For Kant, Being is equivalent to absolute position or perception. But perception has its ground in the ecstasis of the present—neither of the future, nor of having-been—insofar as all "presenting" presupposes "a mode of uncoveredness and unveiledness, that is, of truth" (446), and since this mode, in turn, is projected upon the horizon of *Praesenz*. Kant's identification of Being and perception, phenomenologically interpreted, suggests the identity of *Sein* and *Anwesenheit* or *Praesenz* (448). It is for the sake of the truth of *Vorhanden-*

heit, that is, for the sake of the unconcealment of beings, and not merely as a convenient "example" (cf. 431), that Heidegger projects the problem of Temporality and Being (section 21) upon a recovery of *Zuhandenheit/Vorhandenheit*. The being on or at hand, the being handy or no longer in hand of beings, are themselves modes of a primal phenomenon, to wit, presence/absence, which Heidegger subsumes under the rubric *Praesenz*.

At this point Heidegger concedes something vital. *Praesenz* is not at all the moment of the present, it is not simply *Gegenwart* (433–34). "The very term *Praesenz* indicates that we are *not* referring to any ecstatic phenomenon, as we are with [the terms] *Gegenwart* and *Zukunft*, at least not to the ecstatic phenomenon of temporality with regard to its ecstatic structure" (435). The tension in Heidegger's *temporale Interpretation* among all three ecstases with regard to "primacy" and "ground," and the way in which the horizon of *Praesenz* points beyond the ecstatic phenomenon as such—these constitute a first reply to the question of why and how the ecstatic-horizonal analysis of Time falls short of the meaning of Being as presencing. That Being is always already projected on an understanding of Being, and that this projection has *something* to do with Time, so much is certain. "But the direction of the possible projection of Being as such . . . is questionable, undefined, and uncertain" (458). Heidegger is compelled to recognize the entanglement of his own analysis in "a fundamental untruth" (459). "Without our knowing where the error in our interpretation lies, we may rest assured that an error is also concealed in the *temporale* interpretation of Being as such—and not just any arbitrary error" (ibid.). The error has to do with the ontic-ontological oscillation of fundamental ontology as such. Being must be projected on the horizon of its understandability, but precisely this "founding act" of ontology is precarious since it remains enmeshed in the ontic realm: this has been the case throughout the history of ontology, and Heidegger cannot rescue his temporal interpretation from the implications of that history. He knows that already in the summer months of 1927.[3]

The problem of primacy, of grounds and grounding, of the a priori—for these designate but one project of thought—has been lodged at the center of ontology ever since Plato's and Aristotle's labors on origins and causes. In relation to the question of whether what comes first does so in the process of cognition (*proteron pros hēmas; ratio cognoscendi*) or in the nature of things themselves (*proteron physei; ratio essendi*), the problem of ground generates the further problem of ontological explication or thematization, that is, the problem of *Wissenschaft* in general. Essential to "science" is a lucid sense of purpose and of limits. Such limits may be considered the horizons of a discipline—for horizons do constitute boundaries and limits. In both *Basic Problems* and the 1928 *Logic*, where the horizon of Being as Time is under scrutiny, Heidegger remains sensitive to the issues of *Grund*, the a priori, explication or thematization, and limitations. Such issues interpenetrate in the very *discourse* of Heidegger's phenomenological ontology. Although I shall discuss them individually in what follows, they must be thought together in their interpenetration as replies to the second of my guiding questions.

Let me begin with the problem of the a priori. Heidegger's persistent question during the later Marburg lectures runs as follows:

> To what extent does temporality make the understanding of Being in general possible? To what extent is Time as temporality the horizon of the explicit understanding of Being as such, insofar as it is to become the theme of the science of ontology, which is to say, of scientific philosophy? [24, 388]

If temporality serves as the horizon for the explicit understanding of Being it must somehow be *prior to* that explicit understanding. How then can ontology lay claim to apriority? That Time is the a priori of our understanding of Being is evidenced by the fact that the term "a priori" is itself a determination of Time: it is "the earlier," *das Frühere* (461). Heidegger hopes in some way to transfer the apriority of our understanding of Being to the articulated ontology itself. He refers to the "primal fact" of the "*Temporalität* of the understanding of Being" (462) as evidence for the supposition that all explicitly ontological determinations of Being possess apriority, indeed in a radical sense. For Time is not merely a priori, "earlier," but "the earliest without qualification [*das Früheste schlechthin*]" (463). Thus the "transcendental science" of ontology becomes *temporale Wissenschaft*, and all its assertions become "a priori propositions" (460–61; 26, 184–89). Heidegger alludes to Platonic recollection as an early indication of the a priori character of ontology: ontological knowledge is remembrance, *Wiedererinnerung*, and requires a kind of backtracking, *Zurückkommen*, in the direction of Being (461–65; 26, 186; cf. KPM, 227). *Yet how can the propositions of Heidegger's ontology lay claim to being a priori if they are responses to a prior ontic understanding of Being?*

We ought to recall once again the outcome of Heidegger's recovery of "presenting" and the ecstasis of the present. The horizon of presence/absence, that is, of *Praesenz*, cannot be reduced to any of the temporal ecstases as such. Whether *Praesenz* is temporal at all is a question that no a priori proposition can settle. We may also wonder whether "the earliest" is still a *temporal* determination at all. Does it not tend to overlook the "already" rather than to return to it and recover it? In Augustine's ontotheology God is in some sense "the earliest," since he precedes all past times "in the sublimity of an ever-present eternity," *celsitudine semper praesentis aeternitatis* (*Conf.* XI, 36, 16). However much Heidegger may reproach the ontotheological interpretation of an atemporal a priori as being a *lucus a non lucendo* (462), is not the claim that temporality constitutes the source of all possible understanding of Being as the earliest, the first and the last, quite reminiscent of Augustine's eternity? If Being is always projected upon a prior understanding of Being, is not the traditional distinction between *ratio cognoscendi* and *ratio essendi* thoroughly undermined? Must not a *hermeneutical* ontology hold out in the comparative degree, never insinuating itself in the superlative? Must it not strive always to recover its ground, never dreaming of absolute possession? Must it not grow excruciatingly aware of the hazards of its own discourse?

The *logos* of ontology is "to project *explicitly* [ausdrücklich]" that which is "*already* projected in prescientific experience or understanding" (399). It is to grasp (*begreifen*) explicitly the difference between Being and beings which is always already active preontologically, *impliciter*, in Dasein (454). It is to realize the possibility that what is prescientifically revealed can become an *object* of scientific research (456). Heidegger even employs the prejudicial phrase "objectification," *Vergegenständlichung*, to describe the "primal act" of thematization in ontology (398). Yet he is under no illusions concerning the pitfalls that await such realization or objectification:

> We are confronted by the task, not only to go forward and backward from beings to their Being, but also—if we are inquiring into the condition of the possibility of our understanding of Being as such—*to inquire out beyond Being into that upon which Being itself, as Being, is projected.* That seems a risky undertaking—to inquire beyond Being. It has perhaps resulted from the fatal embarrassment of philosophy, that it has run out of problems. It is apparently nothing more than the desperate attempt by philosophy to assert itself in the face of the so-called facts. [399]

Heidegger's own "desperate attempt" to inquire beyond Being reverts to the problem of truth as unconcealment, *alētheia*. All ontological investigation requires a prior understanding of what is being asked about. Such understanding rests on an "unveiling," ultimately on the "uncoveredness" of beings. Yet "all unveiling requires a prior illumination" (401), "a *light-granting, luminous horizon*" (402; cf. 447). These are distinct foreshadowings of the themes of *Lichtung* and *Ereignis* (the granting of Time *and* Being), which will emerge once again in Part Two of these *Intimations*. Yet the difficulty of an adequate discourse for "scientific" ontology persists. For the problems of explicitation, thematization, and a priori proposition cry for a hermeneutically circumspect phenomenological analysis, one that responds to the problem of truth as unconcealment. Astonishingly, we find such an analysis in the *first* logic course, taught at Marburg in 1925–26.

In his *Logic* of 1925–26 Heidegger demonstrates that the *Zurückkommen* or "backtracking" inherent in ontology has implications less propitious for its discourse than those suggested by the reference to Platonic recollection. He shows that the apparently straightforward conceptualization of something as the "subject" of a succinct and streamlined "proposition" presupposes "a perpetual backtracking." For the Being of Dasein, as "concernful having-something-to-do-in-the-world, is . . . always-already-farther-on with that something" (*21*, 147). Proposition and definition constitute a drastic reduction from the "hermeneutic" to the "apophantic" *as*. Heidegger's analysis of the existentiality, thrownness, and ensnarement of Dasein, as *Immer-schon-vorweg-sein-bei-etwas*, therefore has baneful implications for the language of science, including the science of ontology: the kind of unveiling or uncovering performed by predication and definition, by propositional discourse as such, rests on a *Wiederverbergen*, a covering up again of what is revealed, indeed an obfuscation of the Being of beings. In propositional discourse the being collapses into an anonymous, artificial, isolated being at hand; properties are allotted to it or stripped from it; and at length the statement or proposition itself becomes something at hand that is handed on as traditional doctrine. At that juncture the "covering up again" is itself covered over and forgotten. *The result is oblivion of Being and a deficient mode of discourse for all of Western philosophy.* Heidegger concludes:

> Definition by proposition is therefore never a primary uncovering of and original relation to beings; and therefore such *logos* can never be made the guideline for the question of what the being is. . . . [But this implies] that the phenomenon of definition cannot be made the point of departure for an inquiry into Being, inasmuch as that inquiry is to grasp the phenomenon of Being at its roots. [159–60]

Yet what could be more assertive than a *logos* that "grounds" one phenomenon in another as its "condition of possibility" and which claims to have located the "primal fact," the superlative a priori, in temporality? Is not the will and intention to ground, the very project of founding, already cast in the traditional mold of *definitio,* demarcation and delimitation? Is not the omnipresent horizon of such discourse inevitably proposition and definition (*horismos*)? These suspicions can be neither quelled nor corroborated, since, as Heidegger says, "the mode of Being possessed by that phenomenon we call *language* is up to our own day fundamentally obscure, . . . ontologically altogether enigmatic" (151). Yet the suspicion remains intact, and flourishes.

Heidegger's first logic course adds a further dimension to my discussion above of his later vacillation on the question of primacy with regard to the three temporal ecstases. In section 15, "The Idea of a Phenomenological Chronology," he discusses "the temporality of thematization" (207). Here he stresses the rootedness of all thematization or explicitation in the ecstases of having-been and the present. Every possibility-of-Being for Dasein, including the project of thematic discourse, "has as its fundament being-already within a world" (212). Such having-been expresses in fact the a priori character of *facticity* for speech. At the conclusion of the course Heidegger asserts the primacy of the present, of *Gegenwärtigen*, although here too the "already" is cited as an "indication of the a priori of facticity" (414). As for the *future* ecstasis, Heidegger insists that "every awaiting [*Gewärtigen*] understands that to which it is related as such as something that is possibly present [*als mögliches Anwesendes*]; it understands itself as awaiting a presenting" (412). The very last page of the transcript contains the following passage:

> Uncoveredness, or truth of assertion which is bound to the world, suggests presentness [*Gegenwart*]. But Being suggests presence [*Anwesenheit*]. This means that the meaning of Being is grasped in terms of presentness, in which alone something like presence is possible. Being in general cannot be conceived otherwise. [415]

We have seen how the later courses put into question the relationship of *Anwesenheit* and *Gegenwart*. But that the truth of assertion, thematization as such, risks a "covering over again" of what is uncovered, that *Wiederverbergen* is the very facticity of philosophical discourse, Heidegger is never able to forget. Such facticity is the most recalcitrant of the limitations ontology must confront. Yet there are others as well.[4]

In *Basic Problems* and the 1928 *Logic*, the growing sense of limitations manifests itself principally in the following issues: the finitude of Time (*Endlichkeit der Zeit*, to be discussed in the following chapter), the experience of the "ground" of Dasein as an "abyss," and renewed confrontation with anxiety and "the nothing," *das Nichts*. It is fitting that my own discussion of the finitude of Time be deferred (if only for a dozen pages), since such deferral reenacts Heidegger's own hesitation with regard to this central difficulty. After considering the modes of *Abhandenheit* (the "missing" of what is normally on hand) and *Absenz* (the shadow of *Praesenz*, always implied in the latter though seldom expressed in these lectures as such), Heidegger confronts the problem of negativity or nullity (*das Nichts*) in terms of temporality. "To what extent is Time itself the condition of possibility for nullity in general?" (443). After alluding to Hegel's formulation of the identity of Being and Nothing, Heidegger confesses that he—and perhaps his students also—"are not prepared to penetrate into this obscure matter" (ibid.). The problem of the finitude of Time is indeed a labyrinthine one. We recall Heidegger's treatment of the finitude of *Dasein* and of *Sein* in "What Is Metaphysics?", "On the Essence of Ground," and *Kant and the Problem of Metaphysics,* all published in 1929. But what about the finitude of *Time?* How can phenomenology, conceived as the science of ontology, recover in a radical way the claim of the a priori unless it pursue the questions of the finitude of Dasein and the finitude of Being to the point where they converge in the finitude of Time—if converge they do? Or must Heidegger's understanding of the project of "Time and Being" undergo a fundamental transition?[5]

To the second major division of his 1928 logic course ("Metaphysics of the Principle of Sufficient Reason as the Fundamental Problem of Logic") Heidegger appends several pages devoted to a "Characterization of the Idea and Function of a Fundamental Ontology" (26, 196–202). These pages are absolutely essential to the problem of the finitude of interpretation and the inevitability of *transition.*

The term *Fundamentalontologie* suggests preparation of the foundations for ontology in general. The "founding" is to advance through three phases:

> First, the demonstrative grounding of the intrinsic possibility of the question of Being as the fundamental problem of metaphysics—the interpretation of Dasein as temporality; second, explication of the fundamental problems contained in the question of Being—the *temporale* exposition of the problem of Being; third, the development of the self-understanding of this problematic, its task and its limits—*der Umschlag* [the turnabout, transition, recoil, envelopment]. [196]

The third phase, in which understanding of Being and the question of Being are to be confronted by a new effort at self-understanding, requires careful consideration. For development of the self-understanding of the project constitutes a reassessment and critique of fundamental ontology conducted at a level of supreme complexity and sophistication. Particularly difficult to interpret is the *Umschlag*—Heidegger's topological depiction of the evolving self-understanding of the project undertaken in *Being and Time. Umschlag* is the word he uses to translate Aristotle's notion of *metabolē,* alteration or transition in the most general sense. It is as though Heidegger's choice of that word now aims to exhibit something of the temporal unfolding or maturation of his own question, as though a peculiar *recoil* typifies fundamental ontology, such that it must *turn about,* back to the problem of its *envelopment* in the history of metaphysics, such a turnabout being its only way to advance.

The phase of *metabolē* receives the name *Metontologie.* Although there is little choice but to translate it as "meta-ontology," we should not imagine it as having been constructed on the pattern of "meta-language," "meta-ethics," or the like. The *meta-* refers to the tradition of metaphysics as such, which Heidegger still hopes to rejoin in a positive and fruitful way. For the third phase wants to broaden the scope of the existential analysis of *Being and Time* beyond mere "historiology of metaphysics" and beyond all efforts to define and describe *"humanitas."* This it hopes to do by appealing to the "full concept of metaphysics" and by recognizing the "radicality and universality" of the ontological problem. For, as Heidegger now concedes, "Fundamental ontology does not exhaust the concept of metaphysics."

Within fundamental ontology itself a latent tendency toward "an originary metaphysical transformation" evolves; it is actualized when the full problem of Being discloses itself. As we know, ontology recoils incessantly upon its point of departure—"the primal phenomenon of human existence," which understands something like Being. Yet factical existence is already confronted by the presence of nature, indeed by "a possible totality of beings," a totality that is "already there." Thus the third phase of Heidegger's "founding" is to introduce the theme of *das Seiende-im-Ganzen,* "being as a whole," a theme that will become dominant in *Kant and the Problem of Metaphysics,* "On the Essence of Ground," and "What Is Metaphysics?" For *das Seiende-im-Ganzen* is that toward which fundamental ontology itself must *turn.* In such a turn ontology affirms itself as a repetition or recovery (*Wiederholung*) of the ancient preoccupation with the Being of beings. Since the preoccupation is *enveloped* within "the historicity of our understanding of Being," that historicity must be dismantled and meticulously examined. In this Appendix and throughout the Marburg lectures the theme of the *Destruktion* (that is, *Being and Time,* Part Two) resounds again and again. In an article published several years ago[6] I suggested that the *Destruktion* propels its way forward in Heidegger's project to the point where it postpones indefinitely the third division of Part One, "Time and Being." Perhaps we can grasp the necessity of that postponement by recalling that when Heidegger poses the question of the temporal quality of Being (cf. *24,* section 21) he does so by repeating his analyses of being handy and at hand, which is to say, the modes of Being that are applicable to beings in general, to *Seiendem,* and—to a certain extent—to *Seiendem-im-Ganzen.* (Only to a certain extent, however, since the "slipping away" of beings as a whole in the experience of anxiety, as described in "What Is Metaphysics?", is not an inversion of *Zuhandenheit* or *Vorhandenheit* but a wholly different relation to beings.) At all events, the outcome of the repetition is the emergence of a peculiar vacillation on the question of primacy with regard to the temporal ecstases and a tentative uncovering of a horizon (*Praesenz*) not explicitly temporal in character. It is noteworthy that when Heidegger speaks in the Appendix of the *metabolē* of his own project he says that it suffers "the dissolution of horizons." Not only does each ecstatic horizon dissolve upon that of openness as such, but the horizon of openness puts into question the very formulation of the problem of "Time and Being." Heidegger's project was to proceed from an analysis of *Zeitlichkeit des Daseins* to an inquiry into *Temporalität des Seins überhaupt. . . .*

But this *temporale* analysis is at the same time the *turn* [*die Kehre*] in which ontology itself turns back and enters into the ontic metaphysical realm in which it tacitly already stands. Ontology must be brought to the transition that is latent in it by means of the impetus of radicalization and universalization. Then the turn occurs, and the result is a transition into meta-ontology. [201]

The question of course is whether the language of metaphysics ("radicalization" suggesting the search for a ground, "universalization" suggesting an induction or deduction in the direction of beings as a whole) will be adequate to this turning of the self-understanding of the project. But the resurgent *Destruktion* already hints at the answer to the question. In the Appendix Heidegger emphasizes that his recovery dare not attempt to absolutize the problem of "origins" as its "eternal task." The task is rather to discern "new origins" in the ceaseless dissolution of once secure horizons. "On the basis of the finitude of Dasein," proclaims Heidegger, "always and everywhere labor on factical possibilities." Yet "because philosophizing is essentially a matter of finitude, every concretion of factical philosophy must fall prey to its factical aspect."[7]

The insurmountable finitude of all interpretation, which remains ensconced in its ontic-metaphysical matrix, requires of an interpreter "the capacity for transformation." Not that the inquirer is to dash off, breathless for something novel: the central problematic remains simple, but it contains a surfeit of problems that demand "renewed vigilance."[8] The capacity for transformation empowers a perpetual turning about origins and horizons. To describe this kind of turning Heidegger couples the word "meta-ontological" with what would seem to be a "pre-ontological" signification: he speaks of *eines metontologisch-existenziellen Fragens*. The implication is that the transition from fundamental ontology to meta-ontology by no means abandons the ontic-existentiell situation of inquiry as such. That situation is frontal, in the sense that there is no eluding it. Inquiry is not an academic discipline, a learned knack, but an *Existierkunst*, an "art of existence."[9] *Existierkunst* grants to the inquirer an ability to be totally devoted to the inquiry in progress, to be gripped by it, and yet to be utterly clear about the inexpungeable finitude of one's own devotion. Yet inquiry is not arbitrary—at least not when it seeks a transformation of the fundamental problem of philosophy as such, that is to say, the problem of Being. Inquiry into Being constitutes nothing less than "the given concretion of the ontological difference," differentiating itself within and as the history of the question of Being. Only in that way can philosophy make a difference.

It remains for us now to draw out the essential implication of meta-ontology—the self-understanding of the project of fundamental ontology—as the radical finitude of interpretation, interpretation as response to the most remote intimations of Time and Being. Elsewhere in the 1928 logic course Heidegger invokes the themes of "freedom in its finitude" (253) and "finite reason" (256); he stresses the need for a more concrete analysis of transcendence based on reconsideration of "care," especially its "facticity" and "individuation" (270). He speaks too—in a way that adumbrates what he will discuss at length in his *Introduction to Metaphysics* of 1935—of the *resistance* of beings, such that they are experienced as a whole "as that in the face of which transcendent Dasein is impotent" (279). These discussions betray Heidegger's waxing confrontation with the *Nichts*, as the *nihil originarium* of world, the negativity of what has "gone missing" and of radical absence, the closure of horizon implied in "the finitude of Time," and finally, or first of all, the nullity announced in the "finitude of Dasein."

That announcement is twofold, referring to the being-toward-death of Dasein and to the hermeneutic encirclement or envelopment inherent in all recovery. One way of understanding the move from fundamental to meta-ontology, and indeed the incipient move beyond both of these to what I am calling *frontal* ontology, is to ask about the convergence of these two voices of finitude, one the whelming resonance of Being, the other the daimonic no-saying of interpretation in transition. Heidegger refers to this complex of finitude in a long marginal note (26, 211n.) that discusses finite transcendence in terms of Being as the overpowering and the holy. A parenthetical remark at the close of the first paragraph of this note reads:

> (Zu bedenken bleiben: Sein und *daimonion*. Seinsverständnis und *daimonion*. Sein qua Grund! Sein und Nichts—Angst.)

> (It remains for us to consider Being and the daimon, or perhaps understanding of Being and the daimon. Being as ground! Being and nothingness—anxiety.)

The exclamation point of "Being as ground!" points perhaps in the direction of "On the Essence of Ground," which at its conclusion insists on the "thrown" character of all world-projection, on the absorption of Dasein in the midst of beings, on the situation of possibility-being "within its destiny," on the irremediable impotence of Dasein before the fact "*that* transcendence temporalizes," on the essence of ground (freedom) as *the radical absence of grounds* (the abyss: *Abgrund*), and on the remoteness to which Dasein in its proximity to Being is inevitably exposed (*W*, 70–71). Accordingly, the daimonic "no" holds all interpretation in suspense. *Die Angst verschlägt uns das Wort.* "Anxiety robs us of speech" (*W*, 9; *BW*, 103). Such deprivation does not reduce interpretation to utter silence but, as we shall see (for example, in chapter ten, below), lets silence infiltrate the speech of intimative interpretation: anxiety is the source of whatever rigor hermeneutics possesses. Thinking proceeds—if it is to proceed at all—*within* anxiety.

In *Being and Time* Heidegger italicizes a passage on the exceptional mode and mood of anxiety, exceptional in that it exposes *"the existential selfsameness of disclosure with what is disclosed"* (SZ, 188). In anxiety an uncanny convergence—a frontal collision—of what is to be interpreted and interpretation itself occurs. To be interpreted is being-in-the-world *"as individualized, pure, [and] thrown possibility-of-Being."* The most proper possibility-of-Being is of course death, which *Being and Time* (section 52) calls the *unüberholbare,* "insurmountable," possibility. Somehow the *Unüberholbarkeit* of what is to be interpreted collides frontally with *Wiederholbarkeit,* the recovery, repetition, and reprise of interpretation. In section 68b Heidegger italicizes the following cryptic statement:

> *Vor die Wiederholbarkeit bringen ist der spezifische ekstatische Modus der die Befindlichkeit der Angst konstituierenden Gewesenheit* (SZ, 343).
>
> *The specific ecstatic mode of having-been, which constitutes the disposition of anxiety, brings us to confront recoverability.*

What tension sustains the relationship between the *Wiederholbaren* and the *Unüberholbaren,* the eminently recoverable and the ultimately insurmountable? The transition from fundamental ontology to meta-ontology and beyond it to frontal ontology turns not away from but toward the hermeneutic of Dasein. Recovery and repetition of the analysis of Dasein in its entirety might take its clue from the meta-ontological turn to *Seiendem-im-Ganzen,* focusing on the problem of the "whole": inasmuch as the "whole" of beings is disclosed in an exceptional way in their slipping away (*Wegrücken:* see W, 9; BW, 103), the disclosure of beings as a whole relates to the problem of the "whole Being" of Dasein. The latter issue opens onto the problem of the "end," *das Ende,* of Dasein, which is the crucial problem for the hermeneutic of Dasein as such (cf. SZ, 230–35). But the "whole" in both cases would refer to withdrawal and absence, and ultimately to the finitude of both time and interpretation. For the "whole," as withdrawn, becomes a "hole," an enigma.[10]

Posed in terms of the central enigma of the recoverable yet insurmountable, the metabolism of Heidegger's project may receive a new name, one that Heidegger himself did not devise. The name would suggest that contemporary thought has neither confronted nor circumvented the central enigma of fundamental ontology but is in dispersion before it, haunted by it on all sides: *Frontalontologie,* "frontal" ontology.

FRONTAL ONTOLOGY

Fundamental ontology remains unattainable. Frontal ontology cannot be circumvented.

A young Spanish philosopher, Eugenio Trias, at the close of his book *Filosofía y carnaval*, writes: "It would be worthwhile to write the *Being and Time* of the final decades of the twentieth century, an analysis that would revise fundamentally all the concepts implied in the idea of man. . . ."[11] We can only smile ruefully at the "worthwhile" proposal: "Fine, Eugenio! Be our guest!"

That it will not be written is due, not to scarcity of talent or lack of commitment, but to what Heidegger would have called a transformation of Dasein. In 1929, before an assembly of representatives from various faculties at the University of Freiburg, Heidegger could speak of a Dasein rapt to the passion of science. Fifty years later we can speak only of impassioned dispersion. Rather than laboring to enter the circle of Being and understanding-of-Being "in the right way," we struggle to escape its frontality and succeed only by scattering. The question of that circle, the question of the convergence of finite transcendence and finite interpretation, the question of the daimonic difference, has by no means been satisfactorily formulated. But we possess no means to speak to it. We haven't the language, or rather, all we have is the unraveling of language. With us it is not merely a matter of "almost" having "lost our speech in foreign lands": we have lost it definitively, at home, at the writing table.

I had planned to comment, if only by way of intimation, on the dispersion of contemporary European thought in various figures: in Ricoeur's "longer way," in Foucault's dazzling archeologies of the remnants of man, and in Lacan's purloined letters of the unconscious; but let me rein in my wanton steed and close with one brief reference to the thought of Jacques Derrida, a reference in the interrogative mood, since especially here I have neither competence nor insight.

Whence this dispersion in and of *the text?* I do not mean to hound Derrida with such a question, which comes easy, nor to scorn his work as sheer virtuoso performance, but only to ask about his *question.* At the end of his remarkable lecture, "The Ends of Man,"[12] which among other things puts into question the *exemplary proximity* of inquirer and inquiry in Heidegger's thought, Derrida speaks of two vigils or sorts of wakefulness, one guarding the meaning of Being and its domicile, the other celebrating a Nietzschean "active forgetfulness" of Being. The last lines of the lecture read: "We are perhaps between these two vigils or awakenings (*veilles*) which are also two ends of man. But who, we?"

Who, indeed? In his essay on "Différance,"[13] Derrida insists that the question "who?" addressed to *différance* founders in its very utterance, and so it does, as long as the "who" is thought as the undisturbed or the ultimately reconciled self-presence of the Subject. Yet while inscription of signs delays or defers by means of a simulacrum of presence a "need" or "desire," such needs and desires are never without a "who."[14] With Derrida's inscriptions, whether in dance, or as strategic-systematic tracing, or as "cries out of need" (NI, 310), the question of the "who" is deferred for reasons that merit respect—or at least deference. Therefore it is not a matter of browbeating Derrida until he inscribe his Ecce Homo. He does the work he has to do. No, the work "we" have to do. Etc.

In the Preface to the second edition of Daybreak Nietzsche encourages such deference:

> . . . Do not ask him what he wants to do down there; he will tell you himself soon enough, this seeming Trophonios, this subterranean one, as soon as he has "become man" again. For one forgets silence altogether when one has been, like him, such a long time a mole, such a long time alone. . . .[15]

When once again he becomes Mensch. . . . "Everyone knows what man is" (W, 82). With Derrida it may all seem to be a question of style, but style is the question of man in remoteness and proximity to woman, dispersed in sexuality/ textuality, passionate not over science but over traces. At the end of his footnote to a footnote in Being and Time Derrida fantasizes a mode of écriture "without history, cause, archē or telos"—Heidegger would say, without Woher, Worüber, Wohin, or Wozu—a mode of inscription that would "overturn all dialectic, theology, teleology, and ontology."[16] Heidegger awoke from that dream long ago. Can differance, as exercised in tracings, be incessant deferment? Does it not for the nonce trace itself? Or does it leave no trace of its own? Emerging from texts, plunging into texts, producing texts: that is its whence and whither. Wherefore? That question too must be deferred, again for reasons of deference. For deferral and differancing in texts is thoughtful response to the convergence of the eminently recoverable and the ultimately insurmountable, des Wiederholbaren und des Unüberholbaren, which "we" experience frontally.

But who, we?

The frontal ontological question of inquirer/inquiry persists, though not, as Derrida suggests, in a realm of proximity. It persists in the irreconcilable alienation of an anxious hermeneutics, in the frontality of a question we would always prefer to have left behind. It remains Martin Heidegger's achievement, without his having turned once and for all, to have confronted in the coils and recoils of his thought the unattained and unattainable, to have made the transition from fundamental, through meta-, to frontal ontology in such a way that contemporary thought cannot avoid or evade it even in diaspora. Fundamental ontology remains unattainable. Frontal ontology cannot be circumvented.

Yet what (is) this "frontality"? It is (not) the façade of an imposing theoretical edifice. It may be confronted perhaps in a *brow* or *forehead* (*le front, la fronte*), though neither of God nor Man nor any intermediary *Logos*.

Moby-Dick, chapter LXXIX:

> . . . But in the great Sperm Whale, this high and mighty god-like dignity inherent in the brow is so immensely amplified, that gazing on it, in that full front view, you feel the Deity and the dread powers more forcibly than in beholding any other object in living nature. For you can see no one point precisely; not one distinct feature is revealed; no nose, eyes, ears, or mouth; no face; he has none, proper; nothing but that one broad firmament of a forehead, pleated with riddles; dumbly lowering with the doom of boats, and ships, and men. . . .
>
> Champollion deciphered the wrinkled granite hieroglyphics. . . . How may unlettered Ishmael hope to read the awful Chaldee of the Sperm Whale's brow? I put that brow before you. Read it if you can.

3 The Raptures of Ontology and the Finitude of Time

For Robert Bernasconi and David Wood

In the ignorance that implies impression that knits knowledge that finds the nameform that whets the wits that convey contacts that sweeten sensation that drives desire that adheres to attachment that dogs death that bitches birth that entails the ensuance of existentiality.
James Joyce, Finnegans Wake

These intimations of Time and Being have traced Heidegger's advance from the limit situations of the philosophy of existence to the limits of fundamental ontology as such. Fundamental ontology metabolizes, confronts ever more profoundly the history of metaphysics in which it is ensconced. Frontal ontology experiences the closure of its horizons, or the interminable opening of ever new horizons, as the finitude of Time. To which we must now turn. For reasons that I hope will become clear I must begin this chapter with two epilogues, marked "A" and "B," and then work my way forward through the body of the chapter to its prologue.

A. In the previous chapter, and even in the present one, I have attempted and am attempting to reproduce the movement that Heidegger seems to have made from the "temporality of Dasein" to the "temporal quality of Being in general," from Zeitlichkeit des Daseins to Temporalität des Seins überhaupt. I have done so, and am now doing so, because Heidegger himself suggests that the project of "Being and Time, Time and Being" foundered in the course of that movement and that the "later" Heidegger was forced to abandon the analysis of ecstatic temporality in his search for "what is most proper to Time."

Yet after reading the text of Heidegger's 1925 lecture course, "History of the Concept of Time" (20), I wonder whether these attempts of mine are not misconceived. For in that lecture course much of what in Being and Time becomes the "preparatory fundamental analysis of Dasein" appears in fully developed form, while *nothing at all* of the analysis of ecstatic temporality appears there, not even the word *Ekstase*. Nevertheless, the temporal quality of Being in general *is already known*, at least insofar as Time can be proclaimed the "guideline" for the very question of Being: "The concept of Time . . . becomes . . . the guideline of inquiry into the Being of beings" (*20*, 8). The crucial problem is therefore not the movement from *Zeitlichkeit* to *Temporalität* but precisely the reverse; the crucial problem is the *original advance* in Heidegger's thought *from* the temporal quality of Being in general *to* the temporality of Dasein as revealed in *ecstatic analysis*.

When, where, and how does that analysis first arise? To repeat: the fact that it does not come to bear in the time lectures of 1925 is astonishing, because those lectures (at least in the retrospect that *Being and Time* provides) so beautifully pave the way for it. Ecstatic temporality appears as the sole "concrete" avenue of "research into Being" (422–23). When Heidegger defines the Being of Dasein as care, and care as "the being-ahead-of-itself of Dasein in its being always already alongside something" (408, in italics), we are prepared to espy in the *sich-vorweg* the ecstasis of the future, in the *immer schon* the ecstasis of having-been, and in the *bei* the ecstasis of the present. Indeed, Heidegger pledges that the "basic structure of care" will "later" be seen as deriving from that "constitution of Being" which "we will learn to understand as *Time*" (409). Yet the time lectures themselves postpone that learning experience indefinitely. The "second division" of the course[1] does not advance to an ecstatic analysis. In section 33, which poses the question of the "whole being" of Dasein, Heidegger is quoted as saying (424–25):

> On the basis of what has gone before, I could now make a leap and begin to say all sorts of things about *Time*. But in any case an understanding of what Time means would be missing; it would merely be a matter of uttering some statements about it. For that reason I shall choose the only possible path within the context of the present study, displaying by a series of individual steps the basis on which Time becomes visible in a particular way.

Those "individual steps" are themselves remarkable. They show how attention to the phenomenon of *death* dispels the dream of a totalizing grasp on Dasein. It is impossible to envisage a Dasein that is wholly present, that does not slip toward "that which it not yet is." The futural being of Dasein as possibility-being toward which Dasein relates; the possibility of death casting Dasein back onto itself, and thus onto its own past; the temporal Being of Dasein as such— all this culminates in the brief final section (section 36), "Time as the Being in which Dasein can be its totality." The "will be" or "becoming Being" (*Sein-werden*) of Dasein is here discussed with tantalizing brevity in terms of *Vorlaufen* ("running ahead"), *Gewesensein* ("having been"), future and past, understood as *Zeitigung*, "temporalization." "Not: Being is; rather, Dasein, as Time, temporalizes its Being" (442). The only thing that is missing is a detailed account of such temporalization, a description of the unity of the temporal structures that constitute Dasein *as* a whole and *as* being-unto-death. What is missing, as we shall see, are the *raptures of finite temporality*, the *raptures of ontology*.

We will still want to know when and where the ecstatic analysis first emerges. There is no hint of it in the second half of the 1925–26 logic course (*21*), which is actually a continuation of the time lectures. Does it appear in the summer semester of 1926, during the lectures on ancient philosophy, or in the winter semester of 1926–27, during lectures on the history of philosophy from Aquinas to Kant? Does it appear at all before *Being and Time* bursts on the scene? Whatever the case, the Marburg lectures show us that the ecstatic temporality of Dasein is not some "given" from which we might easily extrapolate "the temporal quality of Being." What came hard (and late) to Heidegger will not come easy (or soon) to us.

B. Even if we were able to track down the first stirrings of "ecstatic temporality" in Heidegger's Marburg period, we would want to know where he gets the idea of applying *ekstasis* to time. Not from Husserl, surely. In some nook and cranny of Bergson's writings, perhaps? Doubtful. I want to speculate that Heidegger *must have* taken the idea from Aristotle's treatise on time in *Physics IV*, 10–14. The words "must have" betray the fact that there are difficulties with my speculation.

The root-meaning of *existēmi* is "to cause to be displaced, changed, radically altered"; *ekstasis* is a departure from what used to be and a kind of dispersion. Euripides expresses an early sense of such displacement or radical alteration in *The Bacchai* at line 850: "Drive this man mad, distract his wits!" Aristotle refers to those lunatics who confuse their fantasies with actual memories as *existamena* (*On Memory*, 451a 10). And we recall his more general use of *ekstasis* in the sense of displacement in *On the Soul* (406b 13): "All movement is displacement of that which is moved." However, the crucial text for Heidegger would have to be *Physics IV*, 13, 222b 14–22 (although see also 221b 1–3). Aristotle is discussing *metabolē*, "change" in the most general sense (the sense Heidegger will apply to both Time and ontological interpretation in general), and *to exaiphnēs*, "the instantaneous" or "sudden" (Schleiermacher translates it at *Parmenides* 156d as *der Augenblick, das Augenblickliche*, "the moment" or "flash of an eye"), which was traditionally held to be neither motion nor rest, hence outside the time-series as such. In the following few lines Aristotle uses words based on *ekstasis, existēmi* three times:

The term "suddenly" [or: "instantaneous"] refers to what-has-departed-from-its-former-state [*ekstai*] in an imperceptible time . . . ; but all change [*metabolē*] is by nature a departing [or: "dispersion": *ekstatikos*]. In time all things come into being and pass away, for which reason some called it the wisest, whereas the Pythagorean Parōn called it the most stupid, since in it we also forget; and his was the truer view. It is clear, then, that in itself time must be . . . the cause of corruption [*phthora*] rather than of generation. For change in itself is a departure [*ekstatikon gar hē metabolē*], whereas it is only accidentally the cause of Becoming and of Being.

I make two claims concerning the passage. First, these lines *must have been* the source of Heidegger's notion of ecstatic temporality, *even though Heidegger himself in his detailed treatment of Aristotle's treatise on time completely ignores the passage.*[2] Almost as bewildering as Heidegger's omission is Jacques Derrida's total disregard of the passage in "*Ousia* et *Grammé*," an essay that often succeeds in recollecting what Heidegger seems to neglect in the Aristotelian and Hegelian accounts of time. Second, this passage is pivotal for any discussion of the metaphysical significance of time. In it time is declared to be merely incidental to Being *and* to Becoming; cited as the cause of dispersion and corruption; defined as the inanity of a contemptibly oblivious existence. The passage would have to be inserted into the second of the six phases of Nietzsche's "History of an Error: How the 'True World' Finally Became a Fable," the insidious phase in which the idea of a true world becomes Christian, becomes *female*.

It seems as though the view of time expressed in these lines hardly squares with what Aristotle says in *On the Heavens* concerning the revolutions of the translunary spheres as "the measure of all motions" (287a 23). After all, time in Aristotle's view is as much a Timaean "moving image of eternity" (*Timaeus* 37d 5) as a Paronian monument to stupidity. But such *imagery* in motion proves to be more *phantastikē* than *eikastikē*, more dissembling than resemblance; and such imagery in *motion* inevitably implies slippage, entropy, dispersal and decline. In and for the history of metaphysics, time is adversity.

Thus ends the second epilogue. We may now begin at the beginning.

"The Raptures of Ontology and the Finitude of Time." The emphasis here must fall on the word "time," because we are familiar with other applications of the term "finitude" in Heidegger's thought, to "Dasein" (in *Being and Time* and *Kant and the Problem of Metaphysics*), "Sein" (in "What is Metaphysics?") and even to "Ereignis" (in the final lines of the "Protocol" to the Todtnauberg Seminar on "Time and Being"). Yet what about finitude and *time?* Section 65 of *Being and Time* refers (once!) to *Zeit* as finite, while all other references are to *Zeitlichkeit*, human temporality. And the crucial determination of the Being of Time itself—

the projected third division of Part One, "Time and Being"—is, as we know, missing.

Let me attempt a preliminary posing of the problem of the finitude of time. The analysis of *Dasein* is to uncover the transcendental horizon for the question of the meaning of Being in general, and is to do so through an interpretation of human being as temporality. Now, if *Dasein* and even *Sein* itself may be said to be finite, then the *horizon* of the question of Being should somehow bear the traces of finitude. Yet how can a *transcendental* horizon, conceived ontologically as an a priori condition-of-possibility, be finite? Dasein may well be finite transcendence, but precisely if it is so, what can we determine about its "horizons"? What can we say of Time and Being *as such*?

To pose the problem another way: If Being "needs" Dasein for its manifestation and is thus permeated by the nothing, so that Heidegger can speak of it as finite, can one say the same of Time? Does Time "need" Dasein, precisely in the way Aristotle suggests in his treatise? Yet what sort of horizon can time and temporality be if they themselves are permeated by the nothing, by finitude, and if finitude and the nothing are associated with darkness, closure, withdrawal, and absence? How are we to conceive of an opening or manifesting of something that is inherently occlusive and concealing? How are we to conceive of the finitude of time?

We know that at the close of the 1920s Heidegger grew taciturn about the problem of temporality and of time in general. The 1930s were, as we shall see, years dedicated to the thought of *A-lētheia*, that is, the truth (as "preserve") or the history (as "destiny") of Being. That history was no longer investigated primarily with a view to Time, and certainly not in the context of ecstatic temporality. The meaning of Being as presence (*parousia, Gegenwart, Anwesenheit*) was somehow taken for granted from the 1930s on, but not further analyzed.[3] It is as though the analysis of ecstatic temporality in *Being and Time* fell short of the meaning of Being as presence, a meaning already descried in the *Destruktion* planned as Part Two of that work, and hence was dropped. Announcement of the public lecture "Time and Being" in 1961 thus caused quite a stir in Freiburg. Its later publication too aroused "Great Expectations." Everyone believed that the long silence was now to be broken, and that the "missing part" of *Being and Time* was now to be tacked on. Such hopes were—or ought to have been—frustrated.[4]

The most superficial posing of the problem of Heidegger's silence—in "developmental" terms—would be as follows: One might wish to search for clues as to the sort of impasse Heidegger confronted while elaborating the problem of the finitude of time, to search for clues to the thirty-five-year gap in Heidegger's reflections on time. Yet one would also have to recognize the essential continuity of the themes of finitude and temporality in Heidegger's thought. At the very beginning, in the *venia legendi* lecture of 1915, "The Concept of Time in the Discipline of History" (*FS*, 366), Heidegger's discussion contraposes time as quantitative measurement in physics to "time proper" (*die eigentliche Zeit*). Time proper is not yet spoken of as "finite," but is designated as "qualitative," hence as essentially heterogeneous and resistant to measurement. And at the end, in the Todtnauberg Seminar (September 1962), we witness still the search for "time proper." The *eigen* ("own") that is common to *Eigentlichkeit* ("ownness") and *Ereignis* ("propriation") itself expresses finitude: *Eigentum* is neither property nor possession, but boundary and limit. Thus, to counter the thirty-five-year gap, a fifty-year continuity! But so much for developmentalist caprices.

My plan is to begin (again) with a brief reference to "Time and Being" (1962), where the finitude of time plays a covert role in the interplay of time's three dimensions and an overt role in the theme of "withdrawal." I shall then turn to section 65 of *Being and Time* (1927), where the finitude of time is seen as bound up with the ecstasis of the *future* and with the priority of that ecstasis for existential ontology. Finally, I shall proceed as I did in chapter two, turning to those two lecture courses at Marburg subsequent to the publication of *Being and Time:* "The Basic Problems of Phenomenology" (summer semester 1927) and "Logic" (summer semester 1928). These texts, although they follow hard upon *Being and Time,* serve as a kind of bridge to Heidegger's later thought. "The finitude of time" is the unfinished span of that bridge. The lectures suggest that the "end" of finite Dasein is intimately bound up with the question of disclosure and the clearing of Being, the *horizon* as such; and they show that an analysis of ecstatic temporality fails to descry this horizon of disclosure or *Praesenz*. Nevertheless, I shall argue that a recovery of the ecstatic analysis may yet uncover in the *raptures of time* a way of spanning "finitude of Dasein" and "finitude of *Ereignis,*" the being-toward-an-end of Dasein and the epochal withdrawal of Being as such.

"TIME AND BEING" (1962)

That this lecture—one of Heidegger's last—is one of his most demanding is generally known. But let me try to summarize its basic structure and movement in a few sentences. The lecture gathers together the themes of Being, Time, and human being into a discussion of *Ereignis*, the granting of Time and Being to man. Being is defined as presencing and as a letting-come-to-presence (*An-wesenlassen; Anwesenlassen*); it is thus defined in terms of time, and especially the present. Yet beings are present *to man*. Beings approach us and linger in presence before us. Heidegger describes the granting of time as a "reaching toward," an "extending" or "handing to," *ein Reichen*, and this in two senses: first, time reaches humanity, is extended to it; second, time's three dimensions extend to one another their essential proximity (*Nähe*), so that proximity thereby becomes its fourth dimension.

In both cases time as *Reichen* accounts for the peculiar openness of man to beings. Yet the second case constitutes the source of genuine problems. Heidegger's question in "Time and Being" about time and its three—or four—dimensions is: "But whence the unity of the three dimensions of time proper?" (*ZSdD*, 15). That is precisely the question posed in the Marburg lecture courses of 1927 and 1928, except that in the later lecture Heidegger avoids the word "ecstasis," speaking of "dimension." The unity of the three dimensions cannot derive from one particular dimension—for example, the present. Rather, it must be the manner in which each dimension plays off of and passes on to the other two, the "*Zuspiel* of each to each," that defines the dynamic proximity of the dimensions.

Two details of this play of time's dimensions, details that involve some sort of negativity, merit our attention:

First, if the present cannot unify the three dimensions, then neither can future or past, since future and past manifest an element of negativity vis-à-vis the present: having-been (*das Gewesen*) is a denial or refusal (*Verweigerung*) of the present, while the future is in some way a withholding (*Vorenthalt*) of it.

Second, there is an element of negativity implied in *Reichen* itself, inasmuch as it is called "revealing/concealing." What is the relation of such negativity or closure to finitude as discussed in *Being and Time* and the works immediately subsequent to it? The granting of openness, of Time and Being, itself withdraws in closure; *Sichentziehen* ("withdrawal") and *Enteignis* ("expropriation") express the central enigma of Heidegger's later thought. But in what way are these words expressions of the existence of Dasein in time, perpetually displaced and expropriated by future and past, perpetually incited by an imperfect present up to the end?

BEING AND TIME (1927), SECTION 65:
"TEMPORALITY AS THE ONTOLOGICAL MEANING OF CARE"

At the close of section 65, by way of summary, Heidegger produces four theses on time and temporality:

A. "Time is originally the temporalization of temporality, which makes possible the constitution of the structure of care."
B. "Temporality is essentially ecstatic."
C. "Temporality temporalizes originally out of the future."
D. "Original Time is finite."

Perhaps a few brief, schematic comments on each thesis are called for, in order to remind us of the argument of section 65.

A. On temporalization (*Zeitigung*): "Temporality 'is' no sort of *being* at all. It is not; rather, it *temporalizes* itself" (*SZ*, 328; cf. 20, 442). On the structure of care: Care is "being-ahead-of-itself-already-in (a world) as being-alongside (beings encountered in the world)" (*SZ*, 327). Care may be sketched diagrammatically as follows:

Being ahead of itself	future
Being already in	having-been
Being alongside	present

B. On ecstatic temporality: The three ecstases of time correspond to Dasein's coming *toward* itself (*Zu-kunft*) as possibility, and thus *back onto* its having been (*Gewesenheit*), while always *by* beings (*Gegenwart*). With regard to this basic structure of ecstatic temporality Heidegger writes (*SZ*, 329):

> The phenomena of the *toward* . . . , *back onto* . . . , and *by* [or: *along-side*] . . . , reveal temporality as the *estatikon* as such. *Temporality is the original "outside itself" in and for itself*. We therefore call the designated phenomena of future, having-been, and present the *ecstases* of temporality. They are not prior to that a being which merely steps out of *itself*; rather, their essence is temporalization in the unity of the *ecstases*.

Heidegger describes such ecstatic temporalization in one remarkable sentence: "Having-been springs from the future in such a way that the future which has been (better, *is having* been) releases from itself the present" (*SZ*, 326).

Whence the terms *Ekstase, ekstatikon*, derived from the verb *existanai, existēmi*, "to displace," in Heidegger's analysis of temporality? His own etymology, the reference to *Existenz* and *ex(s)istere*, "to stand out," is hardly the place to terminate the discussion. True, the words "existence" and "ecstasy" share the same root: *sto, stare* derives from the Greek *sta-, histēmi* ("to set," "to place"), the Sanskrit *sthâ, sthalam* meaning "locus" or "place."[5] The Latin *ex(s)isto* or *ex(s)to* has an extensive history: in Livy, Cicero, and Augustine it means "to step out," "come forth," "emerge," "appear"; in Lucretius, Caesar, and Cicero "to spring," "proceed," "arise," "become." In Cicero's *De officiis* (*I*, 30, 107, and elsewhere) it means "to be visible or manifest in any manner," "to exist," "to be." In contrast, the Latin word *ecstasis* has a far more limited history. Lewis and Short cite Tertullian as a source for what one might call the Plotinian sense of *ekstasis*, that is to say, union of the soul with God by grace of a removal (literally, a displacement) from the s(a)ecular, by virtue of transport *beyond* Time. When in sections 68–69 of *Being and Time* (cf. *SZ*, 338–39 and 350) Heidegger translates the word *Ekstase* as *Entrückung*, "rapture," he *seems* to be thinking of *ekstasis* along these lines. What irony! *Heidegger says that time itself, "original" Time, and not some sort of transport beyond it, is ecstatic, while the derived "time"* of *"eternity"* is not. His famous polemic at the conclusion of section 65 announces a reversal of that iconization of time mentioned earlier, in epilogue "B," the time of Plato's *Timaeus,* time as a "moving image" of paradigmatic eternity (330–31):

> The problem cannot be: how does "derived," infinite time, "in which" what is at hand comes to be and passes away, become original, finite temporality; rather, the problem is: how does *in*appropriate temporality spring from finite temporality proper, and how does inappropriate tem-porality, *as in*appropriate, temporalize a *non*-finite time from finite time?

I will return to this essential matter—which is much more than a polemic—in the prologue that concludes the chapter.

C. On the primacy of the future: The priority, and even apriority, of the future ecstasis, the *Zu-kunft* of Dasein, is suggested by the fact that Dasein somehow confronts its own being possible, its being for its own sake, and moves toward its being as one whose Being is at issue for it. As the identity of the very term implies, the futural essence of *existence* is defined by futural *existentiality.* Yet, as we have seen, this priority of the future is what becomes increasingly questionable to Heidegger during the Marburg lectures of 1927 and 1928.

D. On the finitude of original time: At *SZ,* 329–30, Heidegger writes: "The future proper, which temporality primarily temporalizes insofar as it makes out the meaning of anticipatory resolve, thus reveals itself *to be finite.*" *Zu-kunft* is Dasein's coming toward itself as possibility-being, "existing as the insurmount-able possibility of nullity." The *finitude* of original time derives from the *futural* character of anticipatory resolve.

The problem may now be formulated as follows: If thesis C should prove untenable, then what can close the gap between B and D? That is to say, if the apriority of the future ecstasis cannot be maintained, what will conjoin ecstatic temporality and finitude? In other words, what is the relation of Time as such to finitude, the negative, and the nothing? The tension involved in the assertion of the apriority of the future emerges already in sections 68–69 of *Being and Time.* Heidegger italicizes the following sentences there (*SZ,* 350):

> Temporality temporalizes completely in each ecstasis. That is to say, the totality of the structural whole of existence, facticity, and falling, that is, the unity of the structure of care, is grounded in the ecstatic unity of any given complete temporalizing of temporality.

Such ecstatic unity "illuminates the Da originally" and constitutes disclosure, openedness, clearing, A-*lētheia.* But, to repeat, how is the finitude of Time itself, and not merely of the *Zukunft* of temporality, related to the clearing? What is the temporality, not of *Entschlossenheit*, but of *Er-schlossenheit*, of unified disclosedness as such? How does finitude prevail there? What is rapture?

THE MARBURG LECTURE COURSES OF 1927 AND 1928

At the outset—for it is finally time to begin—I want to cite the pages in these Marburg texts that are essential for this topic (may the citation be an invitation to the reader!): *Grundprobleme der Phänomenologie* (24), sections 19–21, especially pages 377–78, and 428–45; and *Metaphysische Anfangsgründe der Logik im Ausgang von Leibniz* (26), sections 12–13, especially pages 264–73.[6]

In the preceding chapter I tried to show that Heidegger's fundamental ontology founders after *Being and Time* at least partly because it seeks to locate a "fundamental" temporal ecstasis. Heidegger insists on the apriority of the future ecstasis, in reaction against the tradition that dwells on "the present" (*Gegenwart*) and takes Being for granted as something at hand (*Vorhandenheit*). Yet at the same time he realizes that there must be a "truth" to that tradition, that the omnipresence of "presence" may in fact not be the result of a mere lapse—of *Verfallen* ("ensnarement").

It is noteworthy that Heidegger's preoccupation with the horizon of *Praesenz* in 1927 and 1928 is not new. That concept plays a vital role in the 1925 lectures on the concept of time (discussed in epilogue "A," above), which comprise a "first draft" of *Being and Time* Part One, first division. In section 23 of the time lectures Heidegger refers to the "peculiar *Praesenz* of the environing world" (20, 252), the "specific *Praesenz* of the world as an established and familiar totality of references" (255). Such presence—Heidegger also uses the words *Anwesenheit, Gegenwart,* and even *Appraesentation*—is of two principal types: the presence of what is most readily at our disposal in the workaday world, the handiness of tools and utensils; and the presence of what is always already at hand, if only by way of a general mise-en-scène, in our encounters with things in the world. The former is called a "founded presence" (262), founded not on being at hand, however, but in the structure of care (*Sorge*) as a whole. For being at hand too is founded on the presence to us of our concerns, while all our concerns or dealings are grounded in care. Care is "the primary worldly *Praesenz*" (270–71). An "alternation of presence" characterizes our activities in the environing world, an alternation which, Heidegger says, can be clarified only in terms of the phenomenon of time. The way we encounter beings in the world can be explained solely by the "presence-already of the world" (267). That pervasive familiarity of the world in which I am—and here Heidegger relates the *ich bin* to *Sein-bei*, that is, to in-dwelling (*Innan, Wohnen*) in presence (213)—is a function of time itself. *"Dasein itself,"* Heidegger emphasizes, *"is Time"* (267).

The workings of "alternation of presence" and the dimensions and dynamism of the "Time" which Dasein is—none of these things are explained in 1925. Nevertheless, even though the ecstatic analysis is still outstanding in 1925, and even though the term *Praesenz* does not figure in the analyses of sections 14–24 of *Being and Time*, a peculiar tension prevails in both the treatise and the earlier lecture course between (1) an ecstatic analysis of care, examining the possibility-being of finite, anxious Dasein and hence emphasizing the originary ecstasis of the *future*, and (2) the "preparatory" analysis of the presence of Dasein to its everyday world of circumspection. The quotidian world of familiar affairs and concerns arises from the *Gegenwärtig-werden-lassen* (letting-become-present; cf. *Seinlassen* and *Freigabe* in *SZ*, 84–85) of beings, the coming to presence not only of tools but also of signs, symbols, words, and language itself—in short, the presencing of significance as such. Can the apparently "solid" and dependable backdrop for the world of meaning be said to rest on the alternating current of fleeting raptures? The fact that *Praesenz* plays no role in the analyses of the "worldliness of the world" in *Being and Time* may indicate that something in the analysis of ecstatic temporality militates against it. We might then understand the principal task of these later lecture courses in 1927 and 1928 as one of reintroducing the notion of *Praesenz* by means of a recovery of the analyses of environment and of being handy or at hand, the task of trying to synthesize the presence of beings with a properly futural Dasein.

When in the 1927 *Basic Problems* Heidegger comes to acknowledge Kant's understanding of perception and of Being itself as requiring the backdrop of *Praesenz/Absenz*, his suspicions concerning the imputed apriority of the future become truly subversive of his own fundamental ontology. In fact, as we saw in the foregoing chapter, not merely the future ecstasis but the *entire ecstatic analysis* is threatened. For *Praesenz* is not merely the moment of the present; indeed, it cannot be identified with *Gegenwart* at all (24, 433–34). Heidegger's insight here sends shockwaves through his entire project: "The very term *Praesenz* indicates that we are *not* referring to any ecstatic phenomenon, as we are with [the terms] present and future, at least not to the ecstatic phenomenon of temporality with regard to its ecstatic structure" (435). These shockwaves are in fact themselves fundamental experiences of finitude, intimations of mortality, the traces of which Heidegger now tries to pursue. He advances (439ff.) in search of the temporality of negative modes of *Praesenz*, for example, the temporality of "missing something," the problem of my access to what has gone missing, and he even dares to speak of the "horizonal schema" of absence. If there is such a schema, then time itself is—if not the condition of possibility—the proper *site* of finitude and the nothing, not only for the anxious Dasein that is on its way to death but also for the bemused Dasein that cannot find its hammer.

Yet *why* is *Praesenz* judged to be nonecstatic? It is not as though ecstatic temporality has simply been dropped from the analyses of 1927 and 1928. Even during the winter semester of 1929–30, in his analyses of the fundamental attunement of "boredom," Heidegger is still on the lookout for the unity of the temporal ecstases. The question is whether *Praesenz* can be the unifier. What constitutes the unity and coherence of time? Do the ecstases converge in a single and singular ecstasy? Onto what sort of horizon—if any—would such *ekstasis* open?

"Time in itself, as future, having-been, and present, is *enraptured* [entrückt]" (377). *Entrückung*, rapture, becomes the key word for the unity of the three moments of temporalization. For it expresses something of the *Praesenz*, better, the presencing, *das Anwesen* (verbal), of beings. *Entrückung*, which Heidegger himself translates as *raptus* (26, 265), means sudden removal or transport, hence enchantment, entrancement, ecstasy: being outside oneself. But the "original outside-itself, the *ekstatikon*," Heidegger now repeats, is "ecstatic temporality" (24, 377). What does "outside" mean here? It suggests that "every *Entrückung* is in itself open" (378). Open to what? To the "horizon" of *ekstasis* as such. But what *is* this horizon? Heidegger replies, or concedes (438):

> The concept "horizon" in the vulgar sense presupposes precisely what we are designating as the ecstatic horizon. There would not be something like a horizon for us if there were not an ecstatic being-open-for . . . , and a schematic determination of the same, somewhat in the sense of *Praesenz*.

"Horizon" is thus not so much what the Greek word *horismos* suggests, namely, *Umschluss*, a boundary or containment (26, 269); rather, it is the original *Aufschluss*, the opening up of places and sites and possibilities in a world. "Horizon is the open breadth" (24, 378). The rapture of temporalizing temporality *"opens this horizon and keeps it open."* Thus what Heidegger earlier has called the *Öffentlichkeit* of original Time (373) must be understood literally: that temporality is "outside itself" actually means that it is "in itself already disclosed and open for itself in the directions of its three ecstases" (384; cf. 436). The term *Entrückung* or *raptus* specifically suggests the following: "Dasein does not merely gradually become an awaiting [*ein gewärtigendes*] by passing through a sequence of beings that come to it factually as futural; rather, such passing through advances step by step along the open path that the *raptus* of temporality itself has taken [*die offene Gasse, die der raptus der Zeitlichkeit selbst geschlagen hat*]" (26, 265). In the second logic course Heidegger offers a diagram of the open path along which futural Dasein comes toward itself and is cast back upon itself, an enigmatic diagram, to be sure:

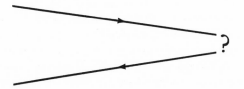

The interrogation mark signifies the inscrutability of the "horizon that remains open" (266). Perhaps the most radical formulation of the finite temporality of enraptured Dasein soon follows:

> The totality of the *Entrückungen* is not, as it were, centered in something that itself would be raptureless, nonecstatically at hand as a collective center for the instauration of and point of departure for the ecstases. Rather, the unity of the ecstases is itself ecstatic (268).

To the self-generating ecstatic unity of temporality Heidegger gives the names "animation" and "vibrancy" (*Schwung, Schwingung*), relating these words to Bergsonian *élan* and to the *Wurf* of *Geworfenheit* and *Entwurf* (268–69).[7] The animation and vibrancy of temporalization, the dynamism of Dasein and of Time, is the "ecstematic" ground of transcendence as such, constituting "world entry" (*Welteingang*) or the "worlding of the world" (*das Welten der Welt*). World is the source of the ontological difference, the "not" of "things." World is, in a sense, the *nihil originarium*; world entry is the "primal propriation," *Urereignis* (274). "Finitude of Time" hence becomes an expression of the essentially fecund no-thing of the difference. For the true *origo* remains "temporality itself" (272). "That there is something like temporality at all *is* the primal fact [*Urfaktum*] in the metaphysical sense" (270).

Heidegger's efforts during the 1930s to explicate the sense of *Entrückung* (for he *retains* this word during those years when so many words are disappearing from his vocabulary) and to explore its peculiar nature as both openness and closure cannot detain us now. But let me at least provide a number of references. In the third and final section of "The Origin of the Work of Art" (*UK*, 75, 85, 89) Heidegger refers to *Entrückung* as the "thrust" of the work of art into the open region, a thrust that "removes" us from the realm of the customary and introduces us to the truth of beings. Such thrust and removal are essentially historical (if not ecstatically temporal), inasmuch as they "transport" a people or nation to its historical task (see also 39, sections 6a–b and 9d, especially p. 109). In his first lecture course on Nietzsche, "The Will to Power as Art" (*NI*, 227–29; *Nil*, 195–97), Heidegger translates Plato's definition of beauty (in the *Phaedrus*) as *erasmiōtaton* with the word *das Entrückendste*, the superlatively rapturous. The superlatively rapturous is what removes mortals from their absorption in (non)beings and thrusts them toward the view upon Being. And in his discussion of "Wie wenn am Feiertage . . ." (EHD, 53–54), Heidegger describes the unity of what Hölderlin calls the "omnipresence" of nature as an effect of "the enrapturing," das Entrückende, taking the word as synonymous with Anwesen, presencing. Finally, there is evidence that the word Entrückung plays a decisive role in the sixth division of Heidegger's principal unpublished text of the 1930s, his Contributions to Philosophy: "On Ereignis."[8] There time-space is experienced as simultaneity of the temporal ecstases and proximity of space, both together occasioning the thrust (Entrückung) into the truth or clearing of self-concealing Being.

The upshot of these four references is that by the end of the 1930s Entrückung, while still associated with Gegenwart and Anwesen, has quietly been removed from the ecstatic-horizonal analysis of time and pressed into the service of history, the history of particular peoples, especially the Germans, and the history of the abyssal truth of Being.

Yet must ecstatic temporality be surrendered? To be sure, the project of grounding the temporal ecstases in some order of implication is to be given up. But cannot the question of the finitude of time be pursued, not only in the context of history, but also within the raptures of ecstasis? Is not the interminable opening of that open horizon—designated by an interrogation mark—an opening onto finitude, withdrawal, and closure? Does not Heidegger himself, in the very pages of Being and Time to which I referred earlier, insist that ecstasis implies a closing as much as an opening? He writes (SZ, 330): "The ecstatic character of the original future consists precisely in the fact that it closes [schliesst] the ability to be; that is to say, that the future is itself closed [geschlossen], and that as such it makes possible the un-closed [entschlossene] existentiell understanding of nullity." Even if we deny priority and apriority to the future, does that mean that ecstasis loses the character of closure? No, not if we focus on the dimension of having-been, since Gewesenheit too remains dark. Yet what sort of closure characterizes the rapture of the present (Gegenwart) in which beings are at hand (vorhanden) and stand in presence (Anwesenheit)? That is the question.

In the course of a discussion of the prevalent interpretation of Being as presence at hand and of the "lapsus" or "ensnarement" responsible for that interpretation, Heidegger cryptically refers to "the proper, essential finitude" of Time (24, 386). Inauthentic time is infinite, derived from an interpretation of the "now" in the "ordinary" experience of time. But "original Time" is finite and is the proper source of the derivative, "inauthentic" interpretation.[9] Be that as it may, Heidegger declines to discuss the finitude of time further "because it is bound up with the difficult problem of death" (387). Now, precisely this "difficult problem" serves as the culmination of the 1925 lectures and the center of *Being and Time* itself. Why do the 1927 and 1928 lecture courses fail to recover and recapitulate that problem? Any repetition of the analysis of Dasein would surely have to retrieve the analysis of death, or initiate a new one, inasmuch as this analysis constitutes the very heart of the interpretation of care, itself central to the interpretation of ecstatic-horizonal Time. How does the finitude of Dasein, its whole being as being unto death, yield an interpretation of the finitude of Time as such? Or must the latter yield the former? Is it not in the rapture of Time that we catch a glimpse of the dark side of world entry— since *Welteingang* is also the Stoic *ekpyrōsis* or conflagration—and the shadow of presence?

At the very juncture where Heidegger takes up the phenomenon of *Entrückung* or "rapture" (*Basic Problems*, section 21, "Temporalität und Sein"), discovering in the horizon of *Praesenz* a "primal phenomenon" of transcendence, the question of the finitude of Time recurs. However, we do not find here the synthesis of finitude and openness to beings that we are seeking. The *End-* of *Endlichkeit* at least appears to mean something else than *das Ende* in *Zum-Ende-sein*. Heidegger writes (437):

> The sequence of projections referred to earlier, projections that constitute a kind of regressus [*einander gleichsam vorgeschalteten Entwürfe*], namely, understanding of beings, projection upon Being, understanding of Being, projection upon Time, has its end in the horizon of the ecstatic unity of temporality. Here we cannot ground this more originally—we would have to enter into the problem of the finitude of Time. On this horizon every ecstasis of Time, which is to say, temporality itself, has its end. Yet this end is nothing other than the outset and point of departure for the possibility of all projection.

What *is* the outset and point of departure of all projection? "Ecstatic being-open-for . . ." (438). Yet is ecstatic openness an "end" simply in the sense of *telos*? Is it an "end" because it is a priori? If so, what would be the source of the finitude of Dasein in the sense of its being toward the end? Is there a common source for both the openness and the closure of horizons, one that would somehow embrace the uttermost closure? Would it not be possible, perhaps even necessary, once the notion of "horizon" as a transcendental foundation has been abandoned, to expand the analysis of ecstatic temporality in such a way that openness and closure, world and earth, clearing and concealing—the topics of Heidegger's later thought—would appear in their properly timely character?

What specifically should this reprise of ecstatic temporality seek to elaborate? How can finitude, the nothing, and death be joined to the preparatory analysis of the everydayness of Dasein *and* to the poetics of the clearing, the granting of Time and Being? My conclusion will take a few initial steps in the direction of such a reprise. As initial steps, they will serve as a somewhat overdue prologue.

"In itself time must be . . . the cause of corruption [*phthora*] rather than of generation. For change [*metabolē*] is in itself a departure [*ekstatikon*]." Perhaps a recovery of ecstatic temporality should stubbornly elaborate on the *metabolism* of Time. In his Marburg lecture courses Heidegger goes to great pains to interpret Aristotle's sense of the *nun*, the "now" of time, in terms of *metabolē*, which he translates first as *Umschlag*, "turnover," then as *Übergang*, "transition." *Übergang, metabolē*, becomes an important word for Heidegger. In his interpretation of Zarathustra's *Untergang* and of the "eternity of the Moment" in the thought of eternal recurrence of the same, Heidegger equates downgoing with going-over or transition, *Übergang*, that is, with the realization—tragic, Dionysian—that every moment is a moment of displacement and imminent collapse, that the "flash of an eye" is metabolic.[10] And in his 1928 logic lectures, searching for the word to characterize the fate of his own project of fundamental ontology in *Being and Time*, Heidegger can find no word more fitting than *metabolē, Übergang*, tragic transition.

Perhaps the unity of ecstatic temporality consists in tragic transition, an *Übergang* that is also *Untergang*, a metabolism that remains within time and is of time, a metabolism that confronts the certitude of its catabolism. (Such confrontation, and the frontality of finitude, are what I mean to indicate by contraposing *"Frontal"ontologie* to *Fundamentalontologie.*) "All change [*metabolē*] is by nature a dispersion [*ekstatikos*]." To be in time is to confront passing-away, transience, "corruption," *phthora*. "For ecstatic displacement is what transition as such is": *ekstatikon gar hē metabolē. Time itself*—whether written with big *T* or little *t*—*is ecstatic displacement to the mark of interrogation at the juncture of future and having-been, con-fronting the open horizon of the present world, a displacement that bears traces of its original darkness and eventual termination.*

As they stand in that curious passage from Aristotle's treatise on time, *ekstasis* and *metabolē* contribute to the establishment of metaphysics, that is, to the interpretation of Being as a being *beyond* Time. The passage appears to forget the horizon of that "beyond," appears to conjure in its stead a nonfinite realm, a "time" beyond all times, something Merleau-Ponty calls "the hypocritical sentiment of eternity."[11] Yet what intrigues Heidegger in Aristotle's detailed treatment of time is the way in which the *nun* itself is metabolic, ecstatic; a qualitative alteration that is not simply transience or corruption. The *ek-* of time's *ekstasis* is balanced by an *eis*, an "into," an advance (*Vorlaufen*): the "now" itself is *ek tinos eis ti*, "out of something, into something."[12] That is as straightforward a definition of Heidegger's *Innerzeitigkeit*—and of temporalization as such—as one could wish. It also suggests something of the *Zuspiel* of each dimension of time to the others, the passing-on-to-one-another mentioned in "Time and Being" (1962) which is nonetheless also a withholding or even refusal of the present. And it surely makes Time essential (not merely incidental) to the genesis of beings and the upsurgence of Being.

Nevertheless, if the ecstatic *nun* is not sheer corruption, neither does it leap beyond *phthora*, which would become another name for tragic transition. *Phthora* would no longer be a region of incorrigibly corrupt beings, of slippages and botched icons. It would no longer require the celestial repair shop that practices the metaphysico-moral technique. Nor would it simply be what "The Anaximander Fragment" calls it, to wit, the "departure" of beings from unconcealment into concealment (*H*, 315; *EGT*, 30). *Phthora* would be a name for the ephemeral rapture that is every bit as much a rupture, both in the lives of men and women and in what Heidegger calls the "history of Being." *Phthora* would name both the withdrawal or withholding of the granting—the granting of Time and Being in the epoch of metaphysics—and the raptures of anxious, bemused Dasein.

PART TWO
Intimations of Truth and Turning

4 The Manifold Meaning of Alētheia

For Walter Brogan

Do the intimations of mortality in Heidegger's thought evanesce once he has abandoned the project of fundamental ontology? Or does the object of his fundamental ontology—finite existence as the site of all understanding of Being—perdure even after the meta-ontological and frontal ontological turns? Does not the site of such understanding of Being, broaching as it does the questions of the *truth* and the *clearing* of Being, persist in bearing traces of finitude? That truth is always accompanied by untruth, and clearing by concealing and withdrawal—are these not also intimations of mortality in Heidegger's work?

The following three chapters will try to trace these intimations in Heidegger's interpretation of truth as *alētheia* and of the clearing of Being as revealing/concealing. They will do so by focusing on three quite specific themes: first, Heidegger's early "discovery" of the question of truth and being in Brentano's Aristotle; second, the burgeoning notion of "the clearing" in *Being and Time* and in the later work; and third, the question of the imputed "turning" from Man to Being in Heidegger's career of thought.

Let me now address the first of these themes. One of the four senses attributed to "being" in Franz Brentano's dissertation on Aristotle is *on hōs alēthes,* "being in the sense of the true." Does Brentano's account of "being in the sense of the true" have significant bearing on Heidegger's response to *alētheia* as the uncon-cealment of beings in presence? This chapter tries to answer that question by offering (1) a general account of Brentano's thesis, (2) a detailed résumé of its third chapter, concerning *on hōs alēthes,* (3) a condensed treatment of what John C. Caputo has called Heidegger's "alethiological" notion of Being, and (4) a summary of results.

"BEING IN THE SENSE OF THE TRUE"

Of the four leading Aristotle scholars in nineteenth-century Germany three were intimately involved in the early history of phenomenology. In his *Lectures* on the *History of Philosophy* Hegel celebrated Aristotle as "more comprehensive and speculative than anyone" (*19*, 132–33). Hegel's contemporary, the Prague philosopher Bernhard Bolzano (1781–1848), promoted serious study of Aristotle while developing the first rigorous critique of psychologism. While Friedrich Adolf Trendelenburg (1802–72) bitterly criticized the Hegelians and in general had little to do with the origins of phenomenology, one of his most gifted students of Aristotle ably compensated. Franz Brentano (1838–1917) dedicated his doctoral dissertation *On the Manifold Meaning of Being according to Aristotle* (1862) to Trendelenburg before becoming the single most important influence on Carl Stumpf (1848–1936), Alexius Meinong (1853–1920), and Edmund Husserl (1859–1938). If we therefore find Husserl's young assistant at the University of Freiburg teaching courses from 1919 to 1923 that seem a curious compound of phenomenology and Aristotle, the historical precedents—Hegel, Bolzano, and Brentano—make the mélange perhaps a bit less exotic.

Heidegger lectured during the winter semester of 1919–20 on "Selected Problems of Recent Phenomenology" and that summer conducted a seminar for beginning students on Aristotle's *De anima*. His seminar for the following winter semester consisted of "phenomenological exercises" while for the advanced students he read "phenomenological interpretations" of Aristotle's *Physics*. In the summer semester of 1922 he lectured on "Phenomenological Interpretations of Selected Aristotelian Treatises on Ontology and Logic," leading a seminar for younger students on the *Nicomachean Ethics*. For the winter and summer semesters preceding his departure for Marburg Heidegger conducted phenomenological exercises based on two texts: Husserl's *Ideas I* and Aristotle's *Physics IV* and V. Although a number of topics involved Augustine, Descartes, Kant, and others, the interlacing of the titles "Aristotle" and "phenomenology" remains striking.[1]

During his last year of gymnasial studies at Constance in 1907 Heidegger had received from his rector and fellow Messkirchner, Conrad Gröber, a copy of Brentano's dissertation on "being" in Aristotle. It seems a strange gift for a rector to have presented to a young man who was on his way to the Jesuit seminary in Freiburg. Brentano had renounced the priesthood in 1873 as a result of struggles surrounding papal infallibility and the anti-Modernist attitude of the Roman hierarchy, left the Church altogether in 1879, gained a wife and simultaneously lost a Vienna professorship in 1880. A strange gift also because of its abstruse subject-matter, although the young Heidegger had shown a penchant for taking long walks in the company of difficult books. The *peripatos* with Brentano and Aristotle proved to be one of the longest for Heidegger. In 1963 he called Brentano's book "the chief help and guide of my first awkward attempts to penetrate into philosophy." He continued (*ZSdD*, 81):

The following question concerned me in quite a vague manner: If being is predicated with manifold significance, then what is its leading, fundamental signification? What does Being mean?

Such were the beginnings of the "question of Being."

Beginnings are more consequential than they at first seem, Brentano warns at the outset of his own inquiry, for they determine all that follows.[2] "And so it happens that whoever in the beginning brushes aside even a bit of the truth is led farther and farther along a path through errors a thousand times as large." Thus Brentano paraphrases Aristotle (*De coelo* I, 5, 271b 8), taking as the starting-point of his own researches the various meanings of "being," *das Seiende, to on,* in first philosophy. Yet the sundry meanings of being are not solely Brentano's starting-point but Aristotle's as well. Brentano argues that "first philosophy must take its departure precisely from this establishment of the meaning of the name 'being'," inasmuch as it constitutes "the threshold of Aristotelian metaphysics."

The motto of Brentano's dissertation, *to on legetai pollachōs,* appears at *Metaphysics* Zeta 1, 1028a 10, but may also be found in slightly altered form at Epsilon 2, 1026a 33 and Gamma 2, 1003a 33. "There are many senses in which a thing may be said to 'be,' " Ross translates. Aristotle offers a list of such senses at each designated place, each list differing somewhat from the others. In Gamma 2 he elaborates the following meanings of "being": (a) substances, *ousiai;* (b) affections of substance; (c) way toward substance; (d) destructions or privations or qualities of substance; (e) that which is productive or generative of substance; (f) things related to substance, and (g) negation of such things and of substance as well. Here Aristotle adds the thought-provoking remark that according to the last sense we can say—in spite of Parmenides' stricture but in support of Plato's Eleatic Stranger—that nonbeing *is* nonbeing. Brentano does not pause to comment on this last remark before reducing all these meanings to four: (1) being that has no existence outside the intellect—the being of privations and negations of substance; (2) being of movement, generation and corruption—"For these are indeed outside the mind but have no finished and complete existence," Brentano adds, referring to *Physics III,* 1, 201a 9 on the various senses of "movement" (which prove to be as manifold as the senses of "being"!); (3) being that has a finished but dependent existence—such as affections and qualities of substance; and (4) the being of substances.

We notice that Brentano's reduction of the Gamma 2 list proceeds on the basis of the Leibnizo-Wolffian categories, themselves rooted in medieval Christian ontology, of dependent and independent existences inside or outside the mind. Such a reduction seems quite natural on the basis of a systematic

Thomistic-Aristotelian philosophy that is so tightly constructed that no opening for genuine inquiry can appear. Brentano assures us that all the other lists can be reduced in the same fashion, so that it is ultimately a matter of indifference which enumeration of the meanings of being he selects.[3]

As the basis for the structure of his book Brentano chooses the list at Epsilon 2, 1026a 33ff.[4] The meanings of being there cited are: (a) being in the inessential sense, *on kata symbebēkos, ens per accidens;* (b) being in the sense of the true, *on hōs alēthes, ens tanquam verum,* as opposed to nonbeing as the false, *mē on hōs pseudos;* (c) being in various senses deriving from the schema of categories, such as the "what," quality, quantity, place, time, etc.; and (d) being in potentiality and actuality, *to dynamei kai energeiai on.* Because Brentano wishes to stress the third of these meanings and because its treatment requires the most detailed elaboration, he reverses the places of (c) and (d), treating the problem of the categories last. Before taking up the meaning that most concerns us here, "being in the sense of the true," I must add a word about Brentano's treatment of the *Kategorienlehre,* which stands at the center of his own work.

Brentano elaborates the main thesis of his dissertation in its fifth chapter, on "being according to the schema of categories." He calls this the most difficult and important of all the meanings. This one chapter alone constitutes two-thirds of the book; here the secondary sources (Zeller, Prantl, Bonitz, Brandis) are brought into play. Especially important is the *Geschichte der Kategorienlehre* (1846) by his "most honored teacher," Adolf Trendelenburg. Brentano's immediate purpose is to modify Trendelenburg's view that the categories evolve from elements of grammar or parts of speech, by insisting that they are primarily significations of "real being." As analogous significations of being the categories have their *terminus* in the first of their number, *ousia* or primary substance. "Being," in the senses derived from the schema of the categories, is therefore not merely an "accidental" homonym; for all the other categories are directed "toward one and the same *physis,*" the *one* Being of *ousia.* And *ousia* is what is most real.

THE MANIFOLD MEANING OF ALĒTHEIA

Brentano's third chapter treats the question of "being in the sense of the true." It begins by asserting that for Aristotle truth and falsity are found only in judgments, which may be affirmative or negative. Brentano cites among other sources *De anima* III, 8, 432a 11, "Truth or falsity is a binding of concepts in the intellect." He adduces a passage from *Metaphysics* Gamma 8, 1012b 8, "Truth or falsity is nothing other than affirmation or negation."

But, Brentano now observes, "however much Aristotle in these and other places makes judgment the sole bearer of truth and falsity, however much he denies things outside the intellect and concepts outside of combination all participation in truth and falsity, he still seems in other places to assert precisely the opposite" (23). In the "lexicon" of his *Metaphysics*, Delta 29, 1024b 17ff., Aristotle notes that *pragmata* or things "that do have being" can be called "false" when they appear otherwise than as they (truly) are, for example, in sketches or dreams. Brentano affirms that this passage, "at least as it is formulated," contradicts those first cited. The issue is further complicated by Aristotle's attribution of truth and falsity also to the senses and the imagination in *De anima* II, 3, 428a 11 and 428b 18ff. Later (430b 26) Aristotle ascribes *alētheia* to both the *thought* that thinks the "what" of a thing in accord with what that thing essentially is and to the *vision* that perceives what is proper to it (for example, colors). Finally, in *Metaphysics* Delta 29, 1024b 26, Aristotle ascribes truth and falsity to *logoi* in the sense of definitions, or as Brentano translates, *Begriffe*, "concepts."

Brentano hopes to resolve the apparent contradiction—that truth and falsity reside *only* in judgment or predication *but also* in things, in imagination and the senses, in the mind (*nous*) and in definitions (*logoi*)—by distinguishing several senses of "true" and "false." *Not only "being" but also "truth" has manifold meaning.* The second of the meanings of "being" hence reenacts the drama of the whole: it does not so much say what being means as show how being *is*, which is to say, as manifesting various senses.

One may speak of "true" and "false" with regard to the judging intellect, simple representations and definitions, things imagined, or the things themselves. This does not involve one and the same predication of truth but implies a kind of relation. It does not name in the same way but *analogously*. Truth and falsity are predicated "not *kath' hen*, but perhaps *pros hen kai mian physin* (*Met.* Gamma 2, 1003a 33), not *kata mian idean*, but rather *kat' analogian* (*Nic. Eth.* I, 4, 1096b 25)." At this point (25 n. 11) Brentano refers his readers to the problem of analogy in his fifth chapter, section 3, the very section where we find the thesis of Brentano's work most clearly expressed. Brentano argues that "being" in the various senses derived from the schema of categories is a homonym, not of an accidental type, but unified by analogy—and not merely by the analogy of proportionality but by analogy with respect to the same *terminus*.[5] Like the Good and the One, Being is something other than a genus that disperses into species upon the addition of a difference.[6] The unity of analogy extends farther than that of genus, for it embraces even homonyms. Brentano argues that the unity of being with respect to the categories is *stronger* than that of proportionality. He reviews again at length the famous opening words of *Metaphysics* Gamma 2, 1003a 33ff.

We speak of being in many senses but always with a view to one [*pros hen*] and to one nature [*mian physin*]. Not simply in the way we use identical expressions [*homonymōs*] but in the way everything healthy is related to health, inasmuch as it preserves or restores health, or is a sign of health. . . . In precisely this way we speak of being in many senses, but always with a view to one source [*pros mian archēn*]. . . . And just as there is *one* science of the healthy, so it is in all such cases. For not only that which is expressed univocally [*kath' hen legomenōn*] is to be studied by *one* science but also that which is expressed in relation to one nature [*tōn pros mian legomenōn physin*]. For the last-named too in a certain sense is expressed univocally.

    . . . Obviously therefore it is proper for *one* science to study being insofar as it is being.

"Being" is not merely a homonym—a word whose sound accidentally suggests various things, like the "bear" who "bears" her cubs. Because it is not a synonym either it must be some curious third thing, to be pursued toward the *terminus* of primary substance.

However, what does all that have to do with "the true"? What is the *terminus* of truth? If it is spoken neither univocally nor simply homonymously, what is that *archē* and *physis* toward which it tends? Brentano's third chapter (26ff.) takes up these questions.

Aristotle says[7] that the true affirms where there is combination and negates where there is separation—in the things. "For him truth is accordance of knowledge with states of affairs." Brentano therefore considers the kind of truth or knowledge to depend upon the kinds of substance (for example, simple noncomposite substance) and asserts the priority of the known in the relation between knowing and the known (referring to *Metaphysics* Iota 6, 1057a 9). Contrary to the fundamental direction of Idealism, so vigorously opposed by his teacher Trendelenburg,[8] Brentano affirms that "our thought is dependent upon things" and that in order to be true it "must direct itself toward them" (29). He cites *Categories* 5, 4b 8: "It is because the matter [*to pragma*] is or is not that it may be said of speech [*die Rede, ho logos*] that it is true or false." Nevertheless, Brentano concedes that while the goal of desire remains "outside" the goal of knowledge "is found in the mind [*im Geiste, en dianoia*] itself." "But the mind knows the truth only when it *judges*" (30). Hence judgment or predication remains for Brentano that *terminus* to which all the analogous senses of "the true"—in *aisthēsis, phantasia,* or the *pragmata* themselves—tend. Just as health is predicated first of the body, and only by extension of diet and exercise, so is truth first ascribed to true judgments, and only by extension to those faculties or things judgment involves. There is a sense in which we may properly speak of false money or a false man, or of true coin and a true friend; but "the fundamental concept of truth remains always that of accordance of the cognizing mind with the thing cognized" (33).

Now, if the primary sense of "being" is *ousia* or substance, while that of "truth" is accordance of knowledge and thing, what does Aristotle mean by *on hōs alēthes?* Again citing *Metaphysics* Epsilon 4, 1027b 18, a passage whose clarity "leaves nothing to be desired," Brentano argues that truth and falsity are found only in *dianoia* or "judgment." Yet this answers only the "where?" question, not the "what?" question Brentano is asking. He now makes a somewhat daring attempt based on *Metaphysics* Theta 10, 1052a 5ff. He makes judgment—the affirmation or negation of a combination or separation in things—the subject (grammatical) of which being (*das Seiende*) is predicated. Of course, this cannot be merely the copulative "is" of normal predication; the kind of Being (*das Sein*) Brentano now means expresses the truth of the judgment as a whole. He offers an example.

Suppose someone wishes to prove to a friend that the sum of the angles of a triangle equals that of two right angles, and elicits from him agreement that the exterior angles of the intersecting line segments equal the opposite interior angles. The proof proceeds until a certain point in the demonstration is reached. The question then arises, "*Is* this, or is this *not?*" That means, "Is it true or is it false?"—"It *is!*" That is to say, it is *true*. This kind of Being is clearly of the highest importance—yet how can its "truth" be judged? The basic principles of all the sciences *cannot* be demonstrated. At the outset of the *Posterior Analytics*, 71a 11, Aristotle says that their "that they are" must be known beforehand.

Thus the meaning of "being in the sense of the true" appears to be decided. *Truth of predication is grounded in the ultimately nondemonstrable Being of beings.* Yet this decision soon falters.

Brentano now (36–37) introduces the curious cases where the being true of a judgment has no ontological (*reele*) implications, for example, in self-contradiction ("Every statement is false") and in affirmations involving things purely imaginary ("Centaurs are fabulous creatures"). Another such curious case is the affirmation that nonbeing *is*. In order to account for these cases Brentano must concede that the copulative "is," even when the subject of the sentence is a "real" concept, does not assure us of "the existent nature of being outside the mind" (38). Being in the sense of the true "has its ground in the operations of the human intellect, which combines and separates, affirms and negates, and not in the highest *Realprincipien* in terms of which metaphysics strives to know its *on hē on*" (39). It therefore has to do solely with logic, which has nothing to say about Being outside the mind. For logic "there is nothing left but the *on hōs alēthes;* and for this reason too, logic, as a merely formal science, is separated from the other parts of philosophy, which are devoted to the real."[9]

At this point Brentano's observations on "being in the sense of the true" come to an end. Yet something astonishing has happened here. As though in conformity to his reputation for being a dogged realist—a reputation based largely on his late work, however, much of it posthumously published—Brentano has been trying to demonstrate the analogical unity of both "being" and "the true." His major effort has been to show how "the true" expresses the accordance of judgment and thing (*dianoia* and *pragma*) and how the mind has to direct itself toward things and to conform to them in order to judge truly. True judgment must rest in the manifest Being of the *Sache*: "It is true" can be abbreviated to the expression, "It *is*." Such abbreviation actually directs judgment toward its ground. Thus *on hōs alēthes* would mean the *substantiality* of what is combined or separated in judgment. In other words, *alētheia* promises to reveal "being" in its supreme categorial determination. Yet in the end, because of arguments raised in traditional ontology and theory of knowledge (Epimenidean contradiction, dependent existence of things merely imagined in the mind, the problem of nonbeing), the meaning of being as truth collapses into something very much like solipsism.

Hegel had written: "Aristotle thinks objects, and since they are as thoughts, they are in their truth; that is their *ousia*" (19, 164). In the effort to aid his mentor Trendelenburg in depriving Hegel of his metaphysico-material logic, Brentano deprives metaphysics of speech and leaves logic nothing to say.

TRUTH AND BEING

Before achieving his own decisive response to the question of the meaning of Being in *Being and Time*, Heidegger had occasion to get involved once again with Franz Brentano's work. The brief third division of Heidegger's doctoral dissertation, *The Doctrine of Judgment in Psychologism* (1913),[10] offers a critical reply to Brentano's *Psychology from the Empirical Standpoint* (1874). Yet in this reply Heidegger himself remains absorbed in the problems of neo-Kantian and phenomenological epistemology—and that means in the tradition that caused Brentano to stress the importance of judgment and predication for the meaning of "the true." Heidegger's criticism of Brentano here has nothing to do with his later understanding of truth as disclosure, and I take note of it only in order to show how far Heidegger's own path was to take him.

Brentano allows the distinction between existential and categorial predication to collapse: the "is" of the existential statement "A sick man is" corresponds to the copula of the categorial assertion "Some man is sick." "Whether I say that an affirmative judgment is true or that its object is existing, whether I say that a negative judgment is true or that its object is not existing, in both cases I say one and the same thing."[11] We recognize this argument as the one that appeared at the climax of Brentano's consideration of "being in the sense of the true" in Aristotle, for which "it is true" means simply "it is."

Unlike Brentano, Husserl in the sixth of his *Logical Investigations* had preserved the distinction between the Being of the copular "is" of categorial assertion and the "is" that expresses *totale Deckung*, "total coverage" between meaning-intention and meaning-fulfillment or objective givenness.[12] In his doctoral dissertation Heidegger follows Husserl by criticizing briefly the meaning of the existential "is" in Brentano's psychology. When I assert that A is, where A first means "tree" and then the mathematical relation "a > b," the "is" has an equivocal sense. The mathematical relation especially must be seen "in its peculiar mode of actuality" as radically free from any psychic act that affirms or denies it. Heidegger thus raises the question "of the meaning of 'Being'" in judgment (*FS*, 35, 120, and 128). However, he adopts the solution suggested in the *Logic* of Rudolf Hermann Lotze—itself based on an understanding of the Platonic Ideas—that the peculiar mode of actuality for judgment is validity, *das Gelten*.

From the perspective of Heidegger's later work it is not difficult to criticize Brentano for emphasizing the meaning of being according to the schema of the categories.[13] Yet Heidegger too in his youth, pursuing the problem of being in terms of judgment and validity, does obeisance to the *Kategorienlehre*. His Habilitation dissertation treats—as we saw in chapter one—the problem of the categories in Scotist philosophy. But in his introduction and conclusion to that work (*FS*, 135–48; 341–53) Heidegger expresses growing dissatisfaction with any purely formal approach to the problem of the categories—that is to say, any approach that fails to take into account the general culture of the epoch in which the categories are discussed. Neither objectivistic Realism nor subjectivistic Idealism solves the problem of the *kind* of validity the categories may have. The answer seems to lie "*in a group of problems that lies deeper, disclosed in the concept of the living Spirit . . .*" (347). The latter has its metaphysically most important sense, not in the Subject of knowledge theory, but in an essentially historical, cultural development. In order to understand the categories in the Middle Ages, for example, study of medieval mysticism, moral theology, and ascetic tracts is indispensable (*FS*, 147 and 351).

Yet historical understanding cannot result from the mere collation of traditional views—a fault one may find in Brentano's dissertation and in Heidegger's own doctoral thesis as well. As I also noted in chapter one, however, by 1921 Heidegger's nascent philosophical project is bound to a "destructuring of the history of ontology." We may surmise from Heidegger's teaching activity of this period that his approach to Aristotle is essential to the destructuring. His novel approach to that philosopher induced Paul Natorp to secure Heidegger's appointment as a professor at Marburg in 1922. The contents of the manuscript on Aristotle that so impressed Natorp are unknown to us; but we do know that two years later Heidegger introduced a course on Plato's *Sophist*—where the problem of "being" is central—by discussing the meaning of *alētheuein* in *Nicomachean Ethics* VI, 3. Whatever Heidegger's approach to the question of Being may have been there, we may be sure that it had little to do with "clever games with categories and modalities" and much to do with *alētheia*.[14]

In *Being and Time* Heidegger attempts to recover the question of the meaning of Being and to seek an answer that goes beyond manipulation of the traditional categories. That the notion of Being is the most "universal" concept, characterized by the unity of analogy, undefinable by reference to beings and yet "obvious" in its meaning and import (*SZ*, 3–4), Heidegger learned from many sources—Brentano not the least among these. But his essential insight of 1922–23, that the meaning of Being was determined in advance for Greek ontology by a certain conception of Time, that *ousia* was not primarily the category of substance but the phenomenon of presence, is radically his own (*SZ*, 26). It is also important to note how quickly and decisively the question of the meaning of Being in *Being and Time* involves the question of truth. Section 7, "The phenomenological method of the investigation," defines *phainomenon* as "what shows itself from itself" and identifies this with "being"; it defines *logos* as *apophainesthai*, letting what is talked about be seen in its own terms. At this point the problem of true and false *logos* arises—and Heidegger rejects the primacy of the notion of correspondence between knowledge and state of affairs that dominated Brentano's account of truth. "The 'being true' of *logos* as *alētheuein*, in *legein* as *apophainesthai*, suggests taking the being that is being talked about out of its concealment and letting it be seen as unconcealed (*alēthes*), uncovering it" (*SZ*, 33). Here as well as in section 44 Heidegger reverses the traditional priorities that dominate Brentano's understanding of "the true." *Aisthēsis* and *noēsis*, as Aristotle cites them in *De anima* III, 3, 428b 26, are more original senses of the true, that is to say, of *uncovering*, than correctness of judgment (*SZ*, 33, 219, and especially 226). Predication or assertion is a derivative mode of interpretation, itself founded in the understanding of Being that Dasein always already possesses (*SZ*, sections 32 and 33). Such understanding of Being is in turn rooted in the disclosedness of world, Dasein, and Being; disclosedness founds all discovery and thus constitutes the original sense of truth.

In section 44 Heidegger reproduces a whole series of quotations from Aristotle's *Metaphysics*, culminating in the definition of philosophy as the science of truth (*epistēmē tis tēs alētheias*) and the science that studies being as being (*to on hē on*). For Heidegger's analysis of Dasein, the confluence of Being and Truth is fundamental: *on hōs alēthes* is not one among the many meanings of being but the very phenomenon of Being, a phenomenon that requires—as Heidegger had already insisted to Jaspers—*einen neuen Ansatz*, "a new starting-point" (*SZ*, 214).[15]

Heidegger himself was by now dubious as to whether a fundamental ontology of Dasein, conducted along the guideline of temporality, could provide that new departure. In addition to the problems adumbrated in Part One of these *Intimations*, one confronts the fact that no explicit "recovery" of section 44 takes place in the second division of *Being and Time* Part One. It is as though the failure of the ecstatic analysis of temporality to locate the unified horizon of Time, such failure devolving upon the interminably open horizon of presence/absence, requires a radicalization of the very themes of disclosedness, unconcealment, and the "lighted" or "cleared" *Da* of Dasein. Nevertheless, the decisive transition from the notion of truth as accordance or correspondence to that of uncovering is achieved in Part One of that work. Already in *Being and Time*, and not merely after some sort of *Kehre* conceived of as a "conversion" to Being, the double leitmotif of Heidegger's thought is the question of Being and the question of Truth.[16]

Earlier in this account of Brentano's treatment of "being in the sense of the true" I asked what *terminus* could serve as the focal point of the meanings of truth—in the manner that *ousia* served as the *terminus* for being. If we say "truth" always with a view to one, *pros hen*, whether it be one "source," *archē*, or one "nature," *physis*, what *is* that fundamental meaning of truth? We say "source," but as Heidegger notes at the outset of "On the Essence of Grounds" (*W*, 21) the word *archē* also has "manifold meanings." We say "nature," but the quotation marks suggest that this is not the sole possible translation of *physis*. Indeed, Heidegger's way of advancing the question of truth after *Being and Time* is to ask: What is the *physis* of *alētheia*?

In his essay "On The Essence of Truth" (*W*, 85; *BW*, 129) Heidegger briefly refers to *physis*, which for early Greek thinking is not so much a delimited region of beings as the upsurgence of *presence*. Presence is the meaning of *ousia*; upsurgence the meaning of *physis*; unconcealment the meaning of *alētheia*; and the gathering of these three into one is *logos*. Upsurgence into unconcealment is the primal phenomenon, by which the Being of beings, however much it loves to hide, does show itself. The one, whether it be conceived as the one *physis* or the one *archē*, is Being as movement (*kinēsis*) into unconcealment and return to concealment. Such is the transformed sense of the *on hōs alēthes*, which in Heidegger's view designates the fundamental task of all ontology from Aristotle onward.[17]

CONCLUSION

If I truncate the chapter at this point it is because the double leitmotif of Being and Truth dominates literally all of Heidegger's later work. To give an adequate account of it would take these *Intimations* quite beyond their bounds. Let me now summarize the chapter's findings and come to a conclusion.

Brentano offers an account of the manifold significance of being; Heidegger formulates the question of the meaning of Being. Brentano follows the tradition by emphasizing the importance of the categories, especially substance, in determining the primary sense of being; Heidegger puts these categories in question by reinterpreting the first of them as presence and by thematizing the problem of Time. Brentano again follows the tradition by designating assertion or judgment the primary locus of truth, although he tries (unsuccessfully as it turns out) to prevent the gap between judgment and thing from expanding into the subject-object split and the solipsistic chasm; Heidegger's interpretation of truth as unconcealment rather than correctness of judgment offers Brentano's interpretation what it needs in order to prevent the collapse into a solipsism that Brentano wishes to escape but cannot.

Heidegger's attempt to ponder *ousia* and *alētheia* as a unity concentric with *physis/logos* goes far beyond anything Brentano might have conceived under the title *on hōs alēthes.* (Yet when Heidegger insists that Aristotle's categories cannot be reduced to elements of grammar [*EGT*, 38] we recall Brentano's resistance to Trendelenburg's main thesis.) Perhaps Brentano's most positive achievement, viewed from the perspective of Heidegger's project, is best expressed in the following way.[18] For traditional metaphysics "being" is fundamentally "one." It is what perdures and subsists, embracing all in unity and identity. It is at the same time so broad in scope that it defies explanation and so obvious in meaning that it requires none. It is totality, Hegel says, and is therefore absolute indifference; and there is a sense in which it deserves to be met with absolute indifference. Pure Being is pure abstraction, destitution, really Nothing. It is the beginning, but, as the metaphysical definition of God, it is a beginning that can see to itself. For metaphysics Being is ultimately not a problem. For Brentano it becomes one. Brentano's problem is that the meaning of "being" is unclear in its historic beginnings in Aristotle. *By exposing the manifold meaning of being according to Aristotle, Brentano paves the way for putting an entire tradition into question.* That is not his express intention. His intentions are (1) to reach the threshold of Aristotelian ontology and (2) not to allow even a bit of the truth in the beginning to be brushed aside. Although it seems clear in retrospect—and it may only be the dazzling clarity of what Sartre and Merleau-Ponty call *l'illusion rétrospective*—that Brentano leaves a large part of "the true" unconsidered, it is nonetheless the case that the question of the "manifold significance of being" prompts the question of the "meaning of Being" and does so principally by drawing attention to the essential correlation expressed by *on hōs alēthes.*

Does Brentano's account of "being in the sense of the true" have significant bearing on Heidegger's response to *alētheia* as the unconcealment of beings in presence? On the occasion of his nomination to the Heidelberg Academy of Sciences in 1957 Heidegger replied (*FS*, x): "The question concerning the simple 'onefold' of what is manifold in Being—at that time [1907–8] churning helplessly, obscure and unstable—*remained the single,* unrelenting impulse, through many upsets, false turns, and perplexities, for the treatise *Being and Time,* which appeared two decades later."

Being as presence, and truth as *Lichtung* or the clearing of unconcealment, do remain unthought in Brentano's treatment of "being in the sense of the true." Yet Brentano names being and truth together and tries to think them together. His attempt therefore makes all the difference. It is the gift of a question given by one young thinker to another.

5 The Transitions of *Lichtung*

Remembering J. Glenn Gray

At the end of his essay, "The End of Philosophy and the Task of Thinking" (1964), Heidegger poses a series of intriguing questions. The most enigmatic asks: "Does then the title of the task of thinking run, not 'Being and Time,' but clearing and presence [*Lichtung und Anwesenheit*]?" (*ZSdD*, 80). The words "Being and Time" appear in quotation marks, used among other things to indicate titles of books. Yet I shall resist the temptation to raise the hollow question as to whether Heidegger intends some sort of abjuration of *Being and Time* here. Heidegger's appreciation and critique of his own magnum opus is a matter of public record. Nevertheless, the change in title does indicate a metabolism of thought, a transition. In what direction?

The change is not a mere substitution of terms, *Lichtung* for *Sein, Anwesenheit* for *Zeit.* In any case the substitution would presumably have to be reversed. For the earliest and most persistent "name" for Being is *Anwesenheit*, "presence." If it were a matter of sheer substitution the change in title would have to be *Anwesenheit und. . . .* And what? Is "clearing" a name for Time? We might be inclined to think so in light of Heidegger's use of the word in his lecture "Time and Being" (1962). In his discussion there of the "there is/it gives Time" we hear such phrases as "Time as the realm where the clearing extends a manifold presencing" (*ZSdD*, 17). Yet *Lichtung* is surely a name for the coming to *presence*, that is, the Being, of beings. In the "Letter on Humanism" clearing and Being are equated (*W*, 163; *BW*, 211). Our confusion increases when we remember that *Anwesenheit*, suggesting *Praesenz* and *Gegenwart*, is originally the word that impressed upon Heidegger the significance of the conjunction of Being *and* Time. In the phrase from "Time and Being" just cited, "manifold presencing" is of course a reference to Time. In short, by the time the title of the task of thinking has become *Lichtung und Anwesenheit* we are far beyond "reversals" of any kind. Being and Time, Time and Being—these pervade both clearing and presence. These name the selfsame, as Heidegger says, although they are not identical, each referring to the propriation, the "There is/it gives" Being and Time.

The final questions of Heidegger's "The End of Philosophy and the Task of Thinking" run: "But whence and in what way is there [*gibt es*] the clearing? What speaks in the *Es gibt?*" (*ZSdD*, 80). These final questions manifest something like a priority of the *clearing* over *presence* for the task of thought. That is doubtless because *Anwesenheit* has always worked its effects throughout the course of metaphysics as *ousia* and *parousia*, albeit unthought; whereas *Lichtung* is not as such a name granted by the tradition. Its root, *Licht*, "light," *lumen*, is of course omnipresent in Christian ontotheology. Yet Heidegger's *Lichtung* presumably struggles to say and to think something else. That struggle is what is meant by the chapter title, "The Transitions of *Lichtung*." My reason for taking up the transitions of *Lichtung* is that commentators, in their discussions of *Ereignis*, "propriation," have often forgotten that Heidegger's own way of giving *Ereignis* concrete meaning is through thought on *Lichtung*, the clearing of Being.

Heidegger supplies a great deal of information about the word *Lichtung* in the essay I have been discussing. He supplies it in conclusion to his remarks on Hegel and Husserl and by way of introducing the matter of *alētheia*. That introduction may be summarized in four steps.

1. For both speculative dialectic and transcendental phenomenology the matter of philosophy comes to shine forth, becomes present.

2. Such shining forth occurs within a certain luminosity or brightness, *Helle*.

3. Brightness itself requires an open or free space in which the strife of luminosity and obscurity can occur.

4. The name of such openness, the free region, is *die Lichtung*.

Heidegger now explains that the word *Lichtung* tries to translate the French *clairière*, the word itself being modeled morphologically on the forms—no longer current even in dialect—*Waldung* and *Feldung*. He adds:

> The forest clearing is experienced in contrast to dense forest, called *Dickung* in our older language. The substantive *Lichtung* goes back to the verb *lichten*. The adjective *licht* is the same word as "light" [i.e., not heavy]. To lighten something means to make it light, free and open; for example, to make the forest free of trees at one place. The free space thus originating is the clearing. What is light in the sense of being free and open has nothing in common with the adjective "light" which means "bright," neither linguistically nor in terms of the matter. This is to be observed regarding the difference between clearing and light. Nevertheless, it is possible that a factual relation between the two exists. Light can stream into the clearing, into its openness, and let brightness play with darkness in it. But light never first creates the clearing. Rather, light presupposes the clearing.

The passage tries to prevent *Lichtung* and *lichten* from collapsing into the meaning ensconced in the substantive *das Licht*, "the light." It makes special demands on both language and thought. Perhaps we should take a moment to consider the demands made on language—parallel though not identical—in German and English.

Lichten is in fact two verbs. The first is related to the adjective *licht* (Old High German *lioht*, Middle High German *lieht*) meaning "bright," "luminous." It stems from the Indo-Germanic root *leuk-*, "shining white," as in the words *leukos, lux, lumen*. In this sense *lichten*, used transitively, means "to make bright, to illuminate." In the passive voice, for example in Schiller's phrase, *taghell ist die Nacht gelichtet*, the word is only quasi-transitive, quite close to the (poetic) intransitive, *der Tag lichtet*. Goethe uses the intransitive to describe lightning: *nun wittert und lichtet es gut.*

However, *lichten* is also a form of *leichten*, related to the adjective *leicht* (Middle High German *lihte*), meaning "of little weight, not heavy." Its Indo-Germanic root appears in the Sanskrit *laghu* and the Greek *elaphros, elachys*, "small, lightweight." (Heidegger is therefore quite right to note that although their morphological history is one of increasing convergence the words have distinct origins.) *Lichten* in the sense of *leichten*, always transitive, means to make less heavy or to heave up and carry. One sets sail by "weighing anchor," *die Anker lichten*. In seaport towns small harbor vessels called *Leichter* or "lighters" are employed to disburden ships of their cargo. Recall Walt Whitman espying "the belated lighter" while "Crossing Brooklyn Ferry" (ll. 46 and 117). Elsewhere, on the parade ground or battlefield, one can thin the ranks, *die Reihen der Kämpfer lichten*. In a portion of the forest, as Heidegger relates, one can thin or clear the forest of trees, *den Wald lichten.*

The adjective *leicht*, in addition to its central meaning, also possesses a number of fascinating derivative senses. In architecture *leicht* suggests the opposite of squat or bulky—hence airy, soaring; *leicht* in general may also mean *nicht schwierig*, not difficult, easy; in terms of injury *leicht* means *gering*, slight or insignificant. Finally, *leicht* is related to the words *gelingen*, "to be successful," *Lunge*, "the lungs," and *lungern*, "to crave."

Everyone interested in the English-language parallels should read the twelve gripping pages of the *Oxford English Dictionary* that treat the cognates of "light." Here is but one sidelight, hardly a highlight, on the adjective "light" in the sense of "not heavy." As we have just seen, *elaphros* and *elachys* are related to the "lung," that airy, sponge-like organ that preserves us in the light of day, or the light of day in us. The connection of "light" and "lung" seems farfetched until we recall the rather skeptical account offered by Leopold Bloom (the "distinguished phenomenologist") of the resurrection of the dead in Christian dogma:

The resurrection and the life. Once you are dead you are dead. That last day idea. Knocking them all up out of their graves. Come forth, Lazarus! And he came fifth and lost the job. Get up! Last day! Then every fellow mousing around for his liver and his lights and the rest of his traps. . . . [Joyce, *Ulysses*, "Hades"]

The lights are the lungs. Perhaps, as *lungern* suggests, and the ancient Greeks attest, they are the seat of all *enthysiasmos*, here meaning the attunement of all disclosure.

So much for sidelights. What about the demands of *lichten* and *Lichtung* on Heidegger's *thought?* I will trace those demands in four texts: *Being and Time,* "The Origin of the Work of Art," "The Letter on Humanism," and "On the Essence of Truth," the first in some detail, the remainder more fleetingly.

Although the word *Lichtung* and its cognates do not appear often in *Being and Time,* the matter is omnipresent.[1] What in that treatise are called "existence," "openness to the world," "transcendence," "understanding of Being," "disclosedness of Being," and *Da-sein* revolve about the theme of clearing. Of the five direct references in *Being and Time* to *Lichtung* or to its terminologically employed cognates four are of central importance. The remaining one can be absorbed into consideration of the four key references, which are located in the following places: first, in section 28, on the thematic analysis of Being-in, especially p. 133 ll. 1–10; second, in section 31, on *Da-sein* as *Verstehen,* p. 147 ll. 1–3; third, in section 36, on curiosity, pp. 170–171 complete; fourth, in section 69, on the temporality of being-in-the-world and the problem of the world's transcendence, preliminary remark, p. 350 ll. 27–37 and p. 351 ll. 1–8. (The reference in section 79, p. 408 l. 7, fits easily into the thematic of the prior reference in section 69.)

The first reference. The thematic analysis of Being-in as such in chapter five imposes itself as a task because of the need to synthesize the concrete analyses of "world" (chapter 3) and "the who" (chapter 4) and in order to prepare the way for the designation of the structural whole of the Being of Dasein as care (chapter 6). Is such a synthesis really necessary? Not if we have been careful to prevent "world" from collapsing into the *res extensa* of categorial interpretation and the "who" of Dasein into the *res cogitans* of metaphysical subjectivity. Yet Heidegger is well aware of the burden of tradition, which as Karl Marx says of history in general, oppresses the brain of the living like a nightmare. And it is almost as though Heidegger could hear the utterances of future commentators who would find nothing more natural than to identify Dasein with the subject and world with the object. The thematic analysis of "being-in" is to awaken the reader from such a nightmare, in which the entire project of *Being and Time* would founder. Heidegger has no illusions about the difficulty of his task. For his earlier attempts to define Dasein as "the Being of the 'between'," and yet as the global phenomenon, may very well have roused the ghost it wished to lay to rest. It is at this point (chapter 5) that the word "Dasein" begins to appear as *Da-sein*, the separation paradoxically indicating the inseparability of world and self, and even of *Sein* and *Da-sein*, in disclosedness.[2] Heidegger now writes—and here it will be necessary to read the German text:

> Die ontisch bildliche Rede vom lumen naturale im Menschen meint nichts anderes als die existenzial-ontologische Struktur dieses Seienden, dass es *ist* in der Weise, sein Da zu sein. Es ist "erleuchtet," besagt: an ihm selbst *als* In-der-Welt-sein gelichtet, nicht durch ein anderes Seiendes, sondern so, dass es selbst die Lichtung *ist*. Nur einem existenzial so gelichteten Seienden wird Vorhandenes im Licht zugänglich, im Dunkel verborgen. Das Dasein bringt sein Da von Hause aus mit, seiner entbehrend ist es nicht nur faktisch nicht, sondern überhaupt nicht das Seiende dieses Wesens. *Das Dasein ist seine Erschlossenheit.* [SZ, 133]

> The ontically figurative turn of speech that refers to the *lumen naturale* in man means nothing else than the existential-ontological structure of this being; it means that this being *is* by way of being its *Da*. To say that it is "illuminated" means that it is lighted in itself *as* being-in-the-world, not by means of another being, but in such a way that this being itself *is* the clearing. Only for a being that is lighted existentially in such a way are things that are at hand accessible in the light, concealed in the dark. The *Da* accompanies Dasein from beginning to end. To lack it is not merely factually, but quite generally, not its way to be. *Dasein is its disclosedness.*

A few brief observations on this passage may be in order.

Lumen naturale is called an ontic image of man's Being. While it may serve as evidence for the analysis of Being-in it may not be taken as ontologically grounded and clarified. For it is not a being which, as ontic attestation, can serve to ground the analysis; it is rather one of the burdens of our tradition— "burden" meant here in both its musical and more oppressive senses.

Heidegger nonetheless tries now to make this image (*lumen naturale*) an icon of the existential-ontological structure of *Da-sein*. The attempt fails, for reasons that will become clear when we arrive at section 36, "Curiosity," the third reference to *Lichtung*.

That Heidegger is aware of the problematic nature of this particular burden or image is suggested by several peculiarities in the German text: (a) *meint nichts anderes:* the word "means" suggests perhaps that, in traditional doctrine at least, *lumen naturale* actually "says" something quite different; (b) *"erleuchtet"* appears in quotation marks, the "goose-feet" (*Gänsefüsschen*) in this case indicating that the illumination in question is not the work of the Paraclete; (c) *nicht durch ein anderes Seiendes:* written in defense, meaning "not illuminated by another being which would be characterized as *lumen supranaturale,* beyond the raptures of Time"; (d) *ist* and *als* are emphasized in order to preclude ontic-apophantic interpretation and to make room for an ontological-hermeneutical analysis (see the distinction between the apophantic and hermeneutic "as," *SZ,* section 33).

Note, finally, that although "light" and "dark" are introduced here they are restricted to the context of the disclosure of things at hand; there is a being that is *gelichtet* in such a way that things are accessible to it in the light—but *concealed from it* in the dark. *Lichtung* makes light and dark possible, but, at the same time, unlike a transcendental condition-of-possibility, does not flood the darkness and expunge all concealment. *Lichtung* seems to be something more—and yet less—than light. To it, at the end of the passage, Heidegger gives the name *Erschlossenheit,* one of the oddest words in the German language, containing the multivalent prefix *Er-.* It is one of those fundamental words of which Freud, following Karl Abel, postulated that they contain their opposite within them and thus are pregnant with opposition.[3]

The second reference. Section 31 of *Being and Time* discusses *Da-sein* as "understanding," one of the existential structures of the *Da.* As projection upon possibilities, Dasein possesses a kind of circumspection and vision that allow it to see what is at stake in its existence. What sort of vision is that? Heidegger calls it "vision of Being as such," *Sicht auf das Sein als solches,* "for the sake of which Dasein in each case is the way it is," *umwillen dessen das Dasein je ist, wie es ist* (*SZ,* 146). He also calls it perspicuity, *Durchsichtigkeit.* However, Heidegger immediately senses the proximity of a tradition that will distort his meaning. Perspicuity does not mean some knowledge or insight resulting from examination of self. It is not a matter of egocentricity or of the Puritan "inward journey." Heidegger continues (in a passage that needs no commentary):

> The expression "vision" must of course be preserved from a misunderstanding. It corresponds to the clearedness [*Gelichtetheit*] which we characterized as the disclosedness of the *Da.* Vision does not mean perception with the bodily eyes, nor pure nonsensuous apprehension of something at hand in its being at hand. Only *one* peculiarity of sight is taken up for the existential significance of sight: that it lets us encounter beings that are accessible to us as uncovered in themselves [*dass es das ihm zugänglich Seiende an ihm selbst unverdeckt begegnen lässt*]. Of course, that is what each of the "senses" achieves within its genuine domain of discovery. But the philosophical tradition from its inception is oriented primarily toward

"sight" as the mode of access to beings *and to Being*. Preserving the connection with the tradition, we may formalize vision and sight to such an extent that we achieve a universal term for characterizing every access, to beings and to Being, as access in general [*Zugang überhaupt*] (SZ, 147).

Just how dangerous it is to preserve the connection with the visualist tradition Heidegger exhibits in section 36, "Curiosity," with—

The third reference. Heidegger's analysis of curiosity begins with a retrospective summary of the existential structure of understanding and the primary, global phenomenon of disclosure.

> In the analysis of understanding and of the disclosedness of the *Da* in general we referred to the *lumen naturale* and designated the disclosedness of being-in as the clearing [*Lichtung*] of Dasein, in which a thing like sight first becomes possible. Vision was grasped with a view to the basic mode of all disclosure appropriate to Dasein, that is, understanding, in the sense of the genuine appropriation [*Zueignung*] of beings, beings toward which Dasein, along the lines of its essential possibilities of Being, can relate itself.

Yet Heidegger's reference to vision is now compelled to become part of the *destructuring of the ontological tradition*, insofar as the tradition is enslaved by "the desire to see." Heidegger cites the opening words of Aristotle's *Metaphysics*: *Pantes anthropoi tou eidenai oregontai physei*, which he paraphrases as follows: human being is shaped by the "care" of sight—the *orexis*, the prevailing *will* (in Nietzsche's sense) or passion, to see. Heidegger also identifies it with *noein*, the purely intuitive apprehending that constitutes "the fundament of Occidental philosophy" from Parmenides through Hegel.

As further testimony concerning the passion to see, which binds the most exalted *theōria* to the meanest oggling of curiosity mongers, and which Sartre so enticingly analyzes as the Actaeon Complex (*Being and Nothingness*, IV, 2, ii), Heidegger introduces Augustine's account of *concupiscentia oculorum* (*Confessiones* X, 35; SZ, 171). *Augenlust*, the passion of the eyes, becomes a word for sense-knowledge and cognition in general. That passion, "perilous in many ways," will haunt the Occident for centuries to come. Augustine writes:

> In addition to that concupiscence of the flesh present in delight in all the senses and in every pleasure—and its slaves put themselves far from You and perish utterly—by reason of those same bodily senses, there is present in the soul a certain vain and curious desire, cloaked over with the title of knowledge and science [*vana et curiosa cupiditas, nomine*

cognitionis et scientiae palliata], not to take pleasure in the flesh but to acquire new experiences through the flesh [*sed experiendi per carnem*]. Since this is rooted in the appetite for knowledge, and since the eyes are the princely sense, it is called in God's Scriptures concupiscence of the eyes.

Seeing belongs properly to the eyes. However, we also apply this word to other senses when we set them to the acquisition of knowledge. We do not say, "Listen how it sparkles," or "Smell how red it glows," or "Taste how it shines," or "Feel how it gleams." We say that all these are seen. Yet we say not only "See how it shines," which the eyes alone can see, but also "See how it sounds," "See how it smells," "See how it tastes," "See how hard it is." Hence, as has been noted, sense experience in general is called concupiscence of the eyes. . . .

That the passion to see is common to both *curiosity* and *theory* expresses two important theses in *Being and Time*: first, knowing is a *founded* mode of disclosure, by no means primary, hence not the keystone for an ontological analysis of Dasein; second, all theory—including phenomenological theory—presupposes a nonthematized lapse from handiness to presence at hand and must therefore be traced back to the world of everydayness—here in the phenomenon of curiosity. Yet both theses have repercussions on Heidegger's effort to preserve contact with the visualist tradition in his account of disclosure and clearing. Heidegger does not wish to reduce man's relation to beings to the status of a pure, presuppositionless, eidetic or intuitive apprehending. Far from it. He wants to restore the layers of complexity and richness that theory has always already stripped away. *Lichtung* ought to be a name for those layers of complexity, not an attempt

> To have squeezed the universe into a ball
> To roll it toward some overwhelming question.

To say that the visualist tradition tears away layers of complexity means that it claims to have located the *source* of light in a particular being. Heidegger does not say it in *Being and Time*, but he senses it and will later say it: the visualist tradition is inextricably onto-theo-logical.

The fourth reference. How does theory presuppose the lapse from what is handy to what is at hand? We recall the famous case of the too-heavy, broken, or missing hammer. What we have more difficulty remembering is the temporal significance such a lapse always had for Heidegger. (See the brilliant analyses of theoretical "backtracking" in the logic course of 1925–26 [21, sections 12, 13, and 15], mentioned in chapter two, above, analyses which however manage to get along without explicit use of the term *Zuhandenheit.*) The temporal problem is broached in the introductory remark to section 69 of *Being and Time,* "The temporality of being-in-the-world and the problem of the world's transcendence." The section opens:

> The ecstatic unity of temporality, that is, the unity of the "outside itself" in the raptures of what is to come, what has been, and the present, is the condition of the possibility that there can be a being that exists as its *"Da."* The being that bears the name *Da-sein* is "cleared." (Cf. section 28, p. 133.) The light that constitutes this clearedness of Dasein is not some sort of power or source, ontically at hand, of some radiant brilliance occurring from time to time in the being in question. What clears this being essentially, that is, what makes it "open" and "luminous" for itself, was defined prior to all "temporal" interpretation as care. In care the full disclosedness of the *Da* is grounded. Such clearedness first makes possible any sort of illumination and brightening, every apprehending, "seeing," and having of something. We will understand the light of this clearedness only when we cease searching for an implanted power that is at hand, only when we inquire into the total constitution of the Being of Dasein; that is, care; that is, the unified ground of its existential possibility. *Ecstatic temporality clears the Da originally.* It is the primary regulator of the possible unity of all the essential existential structures in Dasein.

Here once again the visualist tradition supplies ontic attestation for the ontological structure of clearing; here once again it threatens to flood the dark with its brilliant glare. But Heidegger's temporal analysis of care adds a new dimension to both the "use and disadvantage" of that tradition. *Die ekstatische Zeitlichkeit lichtet das Da ursprünglich.* How are we to understand this *temporal* clearing? By appealing to the ancient luciferous chronometers, the moon, sun, and stars? Or is there something in Heidegger's effort that explodes the metaphor and metonymy of time and light, where we do not know which is the vehicle and which the tenor? Does not the second sense of *Lichtung* come to bear precisely here, suggesting that the raptures of ecstatic temporality lighten, clear, and open the world?

To be sure, the clearing does have something to do with the finitude of time. In section 79 Heidegger emphasizes (the fifth and final reference, SZ, 408): *"Because temporality constitutes the clearedness* (Gelichtetheit) *of the Da ecstatically and horizonally, it* [clearedness? temporality?] *is always already interpretable, and therewith familiar, in the Da originally."* Yet the full elaboration of the temporal horizon of the *Da,* which would include a complete account of science as theory, waits upon an analysis of the "connection" between Being and Truth in terms of the temporality of existence (SZ, 357); that is to say, it waits upon an analysis of the temporal quality of Being in general (SZ, section 5). It is a long wait.

In the essays and treatises published immediately after Being and Time, Lichtung suffers eclipse. The "open region," "openness," "the free," and "freedom" are Heidegger's preferred ways of advancing the question of Being (Anwesenheit) and Truth (Unverborgenheit). Yet in the 1930s, perhaps during the very years Heidegger is working on the problem of Ereignis (1936–38), Lichtung begins to establish itself again as a word for the disclosure of Being. Recall the extensive discussion of the clearing in the central section of "The Origin of the Work of Art" (1935; UK, 56–60), where Lichtung and Verbergung engage in the creative struggle which is the work of art. Yet Lichtung itself manifests the character of revealing and concealing, indeed of a dual concealment or darkness. Lichtung grants the opening upon or access to beings. Yet it is not a proscenium or stage, its curtain always raised, for the play of beings. For in the clearing one being can conceal or distort another. Furthermore, the clearing itself hides behind what is present: it fails to disclose what it is we are referring to when we say of a being simply that it is. Lichtung betrays a failing, a radical silence (Versagen). It embraces beings as a whole in the same mysterious way as does the nothing. Yet if the clearing already implies Verbergung, then Heidegger needs a new word for the disclosive power of Lichtung. He finds it in Entbergung, revealing or "unconcealing" (see "On the Essence of Truth," section 7, and especially "Logos" and "Aletheia," in VA and EGT).

It cannot be denied that the clearing, as revealing/concealing, maintains visualist traits even after its eclipse. In his interpretation of Hölderlin's "Homecoming" (1943), Lichtung is related to aithēr, hence to claritas. Yet it is also related to serenitas and hilaritas, to das Heitere, a special mode of cheerful enthusiasm (hence of lichten as leichten) granted by the holy (EHD, 18). In Heidegger's interpretation of "As on a Holiday . . ." (1939), Lichtung is evoked by the mention of brightness and celestial fire. Yet Hölderlin also refers to nature as "lightly embracing" all things in its openness, its "lightening" (EHD, 56–57).

We arrive at the apparent source of the visualist tradition in Heraclitus' mysterious invocation of pyr aeizōon, "ever-living fire" (VA, 275–81). Almost invariably we interpret pyr in terms of the allegory of the cave and image of the sun in Plato's Republic. But is the metabolism of fire, which as lightning steers all things (fr. 64), to be apprehended by either vision or the mind's eye? If Heraclitus is the Obscure, questioning into the clearing, it may be because he thinks the lighting differently.

Yet what is it, again, in the visualist tradition that is to be shunned? Nothing else than the tendency to interpret vision and insight in terms of beings as a grounded whole, the tendency of metaphysics or ontotheology, bypassing the ontological difference, to place Being in service to the order of beings. In modern metaphysics that tendency is manifest in the interpretation of *perceptio* in a particular being (man) who, containing a spark of divine light, catches the light reflected by all created things. As the co-projector and receptor of such light, man is the eminent subject. In *Being and Time* Heidegger tries to redefine man, not as subject, but as questioner of Being. In his "Letter on Humanism" (1947) he inveighs against the tendency to interpret *Da-sein* as subject. *Lichtung* plays a role in his complaint.

That the "essence" of Dasein lies in its existence (*SZ*, 42) means that man becomes essentially present by *being* the *Da*, that is, the clearing of Being (*W*, 156–67; *BW*, 205). Man's understanding of Being is "the ecstatic relation to the clearing of Being" (*W*, 159; *BW*, 207). Heidegger writes (*SZ*, 212), "Only as long as Dasein is, is there [*gibt es*] Being." However, he does not mean that the *ego cogito* founds Being, that Being is "a product of man." Heidegger interprets the statement as follows (*W*, 167; *BW*, 216):

> . . . nur solange die Lichtung des Seins sich ereignet, übereignet sich Sein dem Menschen. Dass aber das Da, die Lichtung als Wahrheit des Seins selbst, sich ereignet, ist die Schickung des Seins selbst. Dieses ist das Geschick der Lichtung.

> . . . only as long as the clearing of Being comes to pass does Being pass on to man. But that the *Da*, the clearing, as the truth of Being itself, comes to pass is the dispensation of Being itself. Being is the sending of the clearing.

Surely there is no need to ask whether the "sending *of* the clearing" is *genitivus subiectivus* or *obiectivus*. Here the effort is to think the *Es gibt* of Being *as* the clearing, and to prevent the clearing from collapsing into *lumen naturale*.

In the essay "On the Essence of Truth," the genesis of which spans the 1930s and early 1940s, *Lichtung* appears only in section 9, the "Remark." (The note *as a whole*—and not simply in its first paragraph—which first appears in the second edition, 1949, seems to be a retrospective addition to the essay: note the words *Seyn, Kehre, Geschichte des Seins*, and the references back to *Being and Time* as well as to the intentions of the first eight sections of the essay.) In the "Remark" the phrase appears:

> Wahrheit bedeutet lichtendes Bergen als Grundzug des Seyns.

> Truth signifies the sheltering that lightens [or: clears] as the fundamental trait of Being.

The phrase is then repeated in a more elaborate context.

> Weil zu ihm lichtendes Bergen gehört, erscheint Seyn anfänglich im Licht des verbergenden Entzugs. Der Name dieser Lichtung ist *alētheia*.

> Because sheltering that lightens [or: clears] is proper to it, Being appears from the outset in the light of concealing withdrawal. The name of this clearing is *alētheia*.

We perceive once again the inexpugnable visualist context: *erscheint . . . im Licht*. In question is a trait of *Seyn*. Heidegger's archaism (discussed in greater detail in the next chapter) deliberately remains within the orbit of metaphysics as the distinction prevailing at any given time in the history of Being between Being and beings. Perhaps it is fitting therefore that the visualist context be maintained? "Sheltering" (*Bergen*) too is related to light, albeit in a negative way: a vintage is *geborgen* (see Heidegger's essay "Logos," *EGT*, 61–62) by being *protected* from the light. Yet there is another way to interpret the matter of *Bergen* with regard to the vintage. The grapes are gathered, the vines lightened of their burden. In heavy casks stored in dark cellars the wine itself lightens and clears. "A sheltering that lightens. . . ." What can that mean?

I had the opportunity to ask that question of Heidegger in a long conversation on the afternoon of January 31, 1976. I introduce it here—as a conclusion to the present chapter—simply because Heidegger's remarks, as always, were helpful.

Bergen has something to do with truth, but by way of negation and indirection, since *Un-ver-borgenheit* is by no means *Bergen*. How are the two related? An essential clue comes from section 6 of the essay on truth, entitled *Unwahrheit als die Verbergung*, "Untruth as concealing." The word for "concealing," then, is not *Bergen* but *Verbergen*. Hence we need *two* English words here, "concealing" for *Verbergen* and some other word for *Bergen*. Heidegger's comment: "Das ist unbedingt notwendig!"—"That is absolutely necessary!"

Among the various English words I described to Heidegger, referring to a long list of notes from the *Oxford English Dictionary*, was the word "to shelter." The word is of unknown origin, but may derive from "shield" (cf. the German *Schild*), related to the verb *schildern*, Middle High German *schiltoere*, "to describe in words, to illustrate," meaning perhaps originally to decorate a shield. The connection of "shelter" with portrayal in words was intriguing, but it was the straightforward meaning of the word that convinced Heidegger: "to shelter" is to protect from wind and rain, but also from glaring sunlight. When he heard that, Heidegger interjected: "*Das ist die Bedeutung!*"—"*That* is the meaning!"

Bergen: to shelter from the light. Yet Heidegger formulates the essence of truth and truth of essence—the fundamental trait of Being—as *das* lichtende *Bergen*, "the sheltering that *lightens.*" Or *clears.* What did *Lichtung* mean? We discussed the word *Lichtung* for some time. The upshot of that discussion was that any translation of *das lichtende Bergen* which appealed to the tradition of *lumen naturale* was unacceptable: the sheltering does not "illuminate" but actively lightens and clears. To lighten is neither to glow incandescently nor to cast light on something else; it is to reduce or remove a burden or inconvenience. Heidegger called such removal or withdrawal *den primären Sinn* ("the primary sense") of the verb *lichten* in his vocabulary. I mentioned that a number of his translators had been thinking of using the word "opening" to render *Lichtung*, recalling his use of *die offene Gegend, das Offene*, and *Offenheit* ("the open region," "the open," "openness").

> Nein, das ist nicht richtig. Offenheit ist eben das Resultat des Lichtens. Die Lichtung ist primär.

> No, that is incorrect. The point is that openness is the result of the lighting. *Die Lichtung* comes first.

I then asked whether one couldn't think of *Lichtung* as *das Eröffnende*, that which opens up something, but Heidegger remained adamant, perhaps because of the awkwardness or ugliness of the expression. His comment: *Unmöglich!* "Impossible!" I was therefore left with the translator's unenviable task—to render *Lichtung* as lighting in the sense of clearing, making less heavy or burdensome. "The sheltering that lightens." Yet the very first thing that had to be sheltered was the sense of "lighting" itself. Hence my current preference for the cognate of the French *clairière*, "clearing." In any case, the task of *thinking* the transitions of the lighting or clearing of Being (as the self-concealing granting of presence) does not grow any lighter because of my remarks here. Beings are cleared; difficulties are not.

The word "to shelter" was not without its own difficulties. They were basically two. First, to shelter, because of its relation to concealment (*con-celare:* to hide completely), seemed to suggest a kind of hide-and-seek relationship with beings. Heidegger discouraged my thinking of it in this way by insisting that not even *Verbergen*, much less *Bergen*, meant *Verstecken*, putting something out of sight. Sheltering has to do with *hüten* and *schonen*, safeguarding and protecting the mystery of Being's self-concealment. For Heidegger such sheltering is the very essence of mortal dwelling. He was therefore careful to warn me not to allow the distinction between concealment (of Being) and shelter (of the mystery) to be conflated. Important to the sense of sheltering, after all, was its relation to language—*schildern*. Heidegger referred me to the theme of "sheer naming" in Hölderlin, as developed in the last of his essays on that poet, entitled "The Poem" (*EHD*, 187ff.). In doing so he explicitly rejected the Saussurian and other structuralist approaches to naming as a relationship of signification (*signifiant-signifié*). The second difficulty was that the word "to shelter" had a subjective ring to it: it is "I" who shelters the wine in cellars, protects the sheep in folds. Is it then "I" who thinks the truth of Being? Must not such truth appear within reflection, reflexively, as in the archaic expression "methinks"? Must not *Verbergen* and *Bergen* be cogitations?

Heidegger replied in some agitation that both *Bergen* and *Verbergen* are to be thought in terms of *physis*, "als das Von-sich-her des Aufgehens"—"as the from-out-of-itself of upsurgence." He paused to talk about the word *sich*, "itself," usually a reflexive pronoun expressing a special intimacy of subject and predicate. But Heidegger meant to use the word in one of its many prepositional contexts. Beings irrupt in presence *von sich her*, of themselves, under their own power, or at least not under ours. Both *Bergen* and *Verbergen*, sheltering and concealing, point to the autonomy of presencing; they are its other side, its shadow, its (undiscovered) source. They are the question-mark on the horizon of the query, *Whence?* The upsurgence of beings into presence, *physis* as such, is reticent about revealing its origins. It loves to hide. It keeps to *itself*. Lest I still confuse the *sich* with a reflexive pronoun which would send me scurrying back to the *subject* as ultimate point of reference, Heidegger remarked that *sich* should actually be the pronoun *ihm*, as it often is in Luther and occasionally in Hegel, when he slips back into his Swabian dialect, speaking for example of a thing *an ihm selbst*. (Compare the following statement from the "Protocol" to "Time and Being" [*ZSdD*, 44]: *Das Ereignis ist* in ihm selber *Enteignis* . . . [my emphases]; and cf. *SZ*, section 7.) That which surges up of itself, *das Von-ihm-selbst-her Aufgehende*, would be (Heidegger concluded) what Goethe—though not Kant—means when he uses the word "objective," *gegenständlich*.

Although both *Verbergen* and *Bergen* are to be thought in terms of *physis*, *Bergen*, "to shelter," has the other shade of sense alluded to earlier. In the essay on truth Heidegger calls the phrase "the sheltering that lightens" *eine Sage*, a "saying," as opposed to a proposition, *eine Aussage*. *Bergen* has a special relation to *legein*, to that peculiar kind of mortal speech that lets lie before it what is already there in presence. Such "letting" is in fact a sheltering. If we can still hear in the word "shelter" the German word *schildern*, then the meaning of *Bergen* is: to shelter in fitting words, words that neither hamper nor hurry but only respond to what surges forth, lingers awhile, then slips back into the darkness whence it came.

Yet once Heidegger had mentioned *physis*, which stems from *phōs*, *phaos*, "light," had he not unwittingly slipped back into the visualist tradition? Indeed.

Or is this only partly true? *Physis* is perhaps the event we ought to invoke for that convergence of the two senses of *lichten* which would be true to the matter. Upsurgence illuminates nothing; it lightens and clears as the very presencing of beings.

The primary sense of clearing or lighting was that of making less cumbersome, more buoyant. But Heidegger suddenly spoke of it in a new way, repeating several times in an animated and even elated manner the word *vielleicht*, "perhaps," "possibly," separating the two syllables by a scarcely audible breath and raising the tone of his voice on the second, "viel-*leicht!*" And this suggests "very readily," "very *likely*." The *vielleicht*, with respect to *lichtendes Bergen*, implied the *possibility* of an openness in which what presents itself—and *perhaps* even presencing itself—can come to the fore.

Such a possibility (*Möglichkeit*) reminds me of Heidegger's interpretation of *mögen*, "to like" and "may be," *das Vermögen*, "faculty," "potentiality," or "power," and *das Mög-liche*, "the possible" or "like-ly," in his "Letter on Humanism" (*W*, 148; *BW*, 196). There *Möglichkeit* is no longer a condition of possibility in any transcendental sense but a way to designate a thinking that keeps to the element of Being. *Viel-leicht* is (perhaps) the *like-lihood* of thinking Being as the clearing. It may be, however, that such thought alights for Heidegger long before he writes the "Letter on Humanism," long before we find such thinking likely. In *Being and Time* Heidegger defines Dasein in terms of possibility-being: human existence is the specific likelihood of *Sein-können*, the possibility of disclosure or *Lichtung* as such. These transitions or metabolisms of *Lichtung* may well take us not farther away from but closer to *Being and Time*.

At all events, what holds in my memory is the elation, a harmonious commingling of *hilaritas* with *serenitas*, heard in the tone of voice and seen in the opening wide of the eyes, as though perhaps a heightening in the lungs or catch in the breath was an intimation of the *Von-ihm-her* of upsurgence—the ineluctably concealed and sheltering source of all possibility, the clearing—viel-*leicht!*

6 *Die Kehre:* Heidegger's Ostensible Turning

For Otto Pöggeler

"Instead of all the endless, baseless chatter surrounding the *Kehre,* it would be more advisable and fruitful to enter first of all into the matter designated by the word" (*LR, xviii*). Entry is made difficult by the fact that Heidegger speaks of "reversal," "turning," or "turn" in two very different contexts, while commentators have added a third context all their own.

First, Heidegger descries an *impending* turn in Western history itself as the history of Being, a turning in which the future of our technological era is at stake.

Second, he cites a *frustrated* turning in his own thought, earmarked by two familiar reversals of terms: from Being and Time to Time and Being, and from the essence of truth to the truth of essence. These two contexts are surely related, although one glimpses the relation only after a great deal of study.

Finally, a third context for the *Kehre,* introduced by scholars decades ago, characterizes Heidegger's career of thought itself as having executed a *successful* turn, from phenomenology to "the other thinking," or from existentialism to "the thinking of Being." This third context has all but swamped the first two—nothing succeeds like success. Let me therefore begin with a brief account of the impending turn in and of the technological age; I shall then refer to the attempted but frustrated reversal in Heidegger's project; upon which shall follow a plunge into the eminently successful developmentalist bog; and finally, I shall try to extricate the remainder of my chapter by reverting to that turn in the history of Being which occurs at its outermost point or *eschaton.* This last takes place, as we shall see, in and as Heidegger's confrontation with Nietzsche's philosophy.

What Heidegger advances against "the endless, baseless chatter" surrounding his ostensible *Kehre* is his thought concerning a turn in the age of planetary technology. The matter is difficult, among the most difficult in Heidegger's writings. In his fourth and final lecture to the Bremen Club in December, 1949, "Die Kehre" (*TK*, 40–43), Heidegger refers to an impending—or at least possible—turning in our experience of the contemporary world. He has already defined the "danger" impacted in the essence of technology as total occlusion of all nontechnical ways of revealing beings. Even our efforts to predict and control the hazards of technology, he says, conform to the calculative, manipulative mode of technicized thought, hence contributing to the closure. There is a chance that we will attain "insight into what is" (*Einblick in das, was ist*); yet such insight can only be freely granted as an *Ereignis* or "propriative event" of a peculiar sort. The "turning" is that impending event in which Being once again draws near to man (*prope*) and claims him as properly its own (*proprie*). The danger ensconced in the essence of technology is that Being will persist in turning *away* from its own essential unfolding and *against* its own preservation in mortal thought. The promise concealed in the danger is that a self-turning (*Sichkehren*) abides in the very danger as such: it is possible for the danger to come to light, as it presumably already has in Heidegger's thought, and for Being to turn to and into (*Einkehren*) the realm of man and beings. In short, the impending turn is a particular shape of *Ereignis* or the granting of Time and Being. It is the abrupt turning of the danger in such a way that danger itself reveals the epochal destiny of Being. The turning reveals our own epoch as one that frames beings, neglects Being, and devastates the thing. Only the flash of an eye can apprehend such an impending turn: *Einblick* is surely related to what Heidegger has earlier called *Augenblick*. The thinker's task is to train his eye on that possible momentary turning, enabling the technological hazard to turn into a kind of rescue.

In order to introduce the second context of the turning—Heidegger's abortive reversals of Being and Time to Time and Being and of the essence of truth to the truth of essence—we need only recall the matter discussed above in chapter two as Heidegger's "meta-ontological" turn. There we heard Heidegger define the "transition into meta-ontology" as an organic development of the *temporal* analysis of Being, that is to say, of the projection of the meaning of Being onto Time. He employed the word *Kehre* when describing the manner "in which ontology itself turns back and enters into the ontic metaphysical realm in which it tacitly already stands" (*26*, 201; cf. p. 41, above). Among the crucial aspects of the meta-ontological turn into Time and Being are the introduction of the notion of being as a whole (*das Seiende im Ganzen*); the experience of the nothing as the radical absence of ground; the destructuring of the history of ontology, understood now as finite interpretation or what I have been calling *frontal* ontology; and the metaphysics of truth as disclosure and concealment. Yet we have also seen how difficult it is to comprehend precisely *why* the thinking of Time and Being fails. To be sure, the failure has to do with

Heidegger's increasing discomfiture with his analyses of ecstatic temporality and especially with the tendency to understand the ecstases as a ground or transcendental horizon upon which Being is a priori projected. For the present we need to pursue only one aspect of the meta-ontological turn: the effort to think Time and Being ultimately focuses on the question of *alētheia*, truth as the interminable play of unconcealment and concealment in the clearing of Being. In other words, the reversal presaged in *Being and Time* as "Time and Being" is precisely the reversal attempted later from the "essence of truth" to the "truth of essence." The two crucial texts for this apparently later—but actually identical—reversal are the 1949 "Note" to the essay "On the Essence of Truth" and the famous "Letter on Humanism" of 1947. (See *W*, 96–97 and 159; *BW*, 140–41 and 207–08.) The former merits an especially close reading, even though in chapter five I have already referred to it.

Writing in retrospect on the "essence of truth," Heidegger in 1949 calls it a question that "arises from the question of the truth of essence." That is to say, the question of the essence of truth presupposes as its seedbed the question of the truth of essence. The word *truth* may by now be read as *unconcealment*. The word *essence* (*das Wesen*) is more recalcitrant. In the first place, and in the last place too, the word is irremediably metaphysical: from the early Middle Ages to Hegel it designates the quiddity or actuality of beings, their "whatness." Although Heidegger's reversal here cannot twist free of its metaphysical integument, Heidegger does try to think the word *wesen* as a verb rather than as a nominative. That very effort introduces movement, metabolism, ek-stasis, rapture—in short, *history*—into the question of truth. One of the three Indo-Germanic roots of the words for "to be," the *wes-* of *wesen*, suggests tarrying, lingering, and the "whiling" away of time. In Middle High German *wësen* is an infinitive equivalent to the New High German *sein*; only remnants survive in the participial forms *anwesend, abwesend,* and *gewesen,* meaning to be present, to be absent, and to have been. Yet these very participial forms betray the *temporal quality of Being* in general. Additional meanings of *wesen* that seem to have been important for Heidegger are (1) activity—*Wesen und Tun, sein Wesen treiben* suggest "doing one's thing," as Emerson says—and (2) residence or sojourn. When Luther says *sein Wesen haben* he simply means a dwelling where one holds up or settles down. *Wesen* (like *Anwesen*) hence comes to be associated with the property one owns, *possessio.* Heidegger's thinking of *wesen* resists these reifications however and emphasizes the connection with *währen,* to last or endure—not eternally, to be sure, but for the time being. In other words, the kind of thinking that we find fully developed in "The Turning" (1949) and "The Question concerning Technology" (1953) has its origins in the attempt to think "essence" verbally, historically, as the essential unfolding of the truth of Being. (See *BW*, 311–13; *Ni 4,* 140–41, n. 2.)

In the mid-1930s, after lecturing on Schelling, Heidegger adopts the archaic spelling for Being: *Seyn*. (This spelling had been introduced in the eighteenth century in order to distinguish the infinitive *to be* from the possessive pronoun *sein*, meaning "his" or "its.") By writing *Seyn* Heidegger hopes to appropriate to the question of Being the *history* of the essential unfolding (*wesen*) of truth. *Seyn* indicates the difference between Being and beings prevailing in any given epoch of metaphysics, a difference however that remains caught up in the selfsame metaphysical project of grounding beings. Yet no matter how he writes the word *Sein*, Heidegger's attempt to think Being alethiologically and essentially remains embroiled in the very language of metaphysics. The reversal of the "essence of truth" to the "truth of essence" fails to reach the clearing that lightens and conceals, and is thus hindered in its execution. In fact, Heidegger says that the reversal "remains intentionally undeveloped." Instead, Heidegger meditates on the clearing of Being *as manifested in the* Da *of* Dasein. Heidegger's thought does not slip into reverse but proceeds to abandon the "metaphysics of truth" as envisaged in 1928. Heidegger does not in the 1930s *turn away* from his initial project but *re-turns* to the intimations of Time and Being.

The above is of course Heidegger's self-interpretation. A number of scholars have rejected it and have seen fit to simplify or streamline Heidegger's account of his own ostensible *Kehre*. It is time to take the plunge.

Many German as well as English-speaking commentators have argued that in *Being and Time* Heidegger remains wholly confined within the language and methods of traditional ontology; in other words that the ontology of Dasein is merely another attempt to ground the order of beings. They suggest that Dasein is simply another word for man, and man simply another being, whose preeminence in *Being and Time* derives from the tradition of Cartesian subjectivity which Heidegger has not yet overcome. They argue that the "later" Heidegger's pursuit of Being itself, presumably beyond the horizon of beings, abandons Dasein along with all other mundane things. A mystical and mystifying contemplation of pure Being replaces existential analysis. The problem is whether such an interpretation understands at all the *difference* that makes Dasein more than an artifact or thing of nature, which indeed makes *Da-sein* the very openness that allows something like *Sein* to be addressed or heard at all.

Beda Allemann long ago effectively refuted such interpretations of the *Kehre*, proffered in this case by Otto Friedrich Bollnow and Karl Löwith. These two had argued that Heidegger undergoes a metamorphosis from "existentialist" to "philosopher of Being." Allemann replied that all such interpretations were "a misunderstanding, . . . and ultimately nothing more than a projection of their authors' own need to learn better."[1] I have argued much the same in chapter two, above, suggesting that the reversal of Being and Time to Time and Being by no means marks the end of Heidegger's search for an "ontic fundament" for ontology. I hinted that Heidegger's career of thought could as readily be described the other way around: "Heidegger-II' introduces humanity (*der Mensch*) into his texts far more liberally than does the "Heidegger-I" who analyzes *Da-sein.* I insisted that we really must twist free of the notion that there is a "Heidegger-I" who engages in ontic investigations of humanity and a "Heidegger-II" who levitates to Being. Otto Pöggeler and Friedrich Hogemann are right: "An impartial view of Heidegger's path of thought reveals that when Heidegger speaks of Being he is always also thinking of the human beings who utter the word 'is,' and that a turning from Dasein to Being cannot be some sort of exchange of the principal objects."[2] Yet I would expand their argument by saying that Heidegger is never deflected from the frontality of the relation between Being and the understanding-of-Being (*Seinsverständnis*) which Dasein *is:* Heidegger never turns his back on the hermeneutical circle in which mortals remain implicated. Thus Pöggeler and Hogemann describe Heidegger in the 1930s as taking up "in a positive manner the self-withdrawal in truth as unconcealment, or the nothing as the veil of Being, that is to say, as the unsurpassable mystery of bounded and situated truth," and this they call "Heidegger's real turning."[3] The difficulty is whether the word *Kehre* in the developmentalist sense can mean anything at all any more.

A remark by Pöggeler in another place introduces my own thesis: "Heidegger's thinking was able to turn against itself over and over again; it possessed a restlessness and a commitment to reality that many books about Heidegger lack."[4] The problem, as I see it, is not that Heidegger never deviated from a straight and narrow path, but that at every instant of his career he made more twists and turns than we can readily navigate. No wonder when we play catch-as-catch-can with "Heidegger-I" and "Heidegger-II" we wind up chasing ourselves in circles—and they are *not* hermeneutical circles! In order to clarify the reasons for my opposition to the "developmentalist" notion of the *Kehre*, I want to introduce here—even though it may seem to be special pleading—materials from a work session with Heidegger on September 29, 1975.

Our discussion centered on the Introduction to *Being and Time* as an index of Heidegger's later thought. I had already been told that Heidegger's Introduction was the last part of the book to be completed, but our conversation intensified the parallel with the Preface to Hegel's *Phenomenology of Spirit.* Heidegger said that he had kept the Introduction before him at every stage of the work in 1925–26, that he altered and updated it constantly. Even when the Max Niemeyer Verlag in Halle began to set the book in print as the eighth volume of Husserl's *Jahrbuch für philosophische und phänomenologische Forschung*, Heidegger continued to make changes in the first eight paragraphs. Behind my inquiry into the gestation of the Introduction was of course the fact that it speaks in some detail of those portions of *Being and Time* that never saw print. Section 5, "The ontological analysis of Dasein as exposing the horizon for an interpretation of the meaning of Being in general," offers enticing hints concerning the crucial problem of the relation between the temporalities of Being and of man's Being, the problem that lay near the heart of Heidegger's project in Being and Time. Section 6, "The task of destructuring the history of ontology," not only introduces us to the second half of Being and Time (which was never published, and never really composed as such) but also points us in the direction Heidegger did take after Being and Time, away from fundamental ontology and toward a prolonged encounter with the history of Being as Truth.

"Then you did have a clear idea," I asked Heidegger, "about going ahead with the book? The Introduction was to serve both parts of Being and Time, the written and the as yet unwritten?" "Aber natürlich!"—"Of course!"

I took up the less difficult question of the Destruktion first, commenting on its importance as far back as 1919–21 in the review of Karl Jaspers' Psychology of Worldviews. Heidegger affirmed that the destructuring or dismantling of the tradition was the constant theme of his lectures and seminars at Freiburg and at Marburg between 1919 and 1928, even though he published nothing on it. Heidegger mentioned that the published text of his lectures on Plato's Sophist would be particularly enlightening as regards the Destruktion. (I was not surprised to hear this lecture course mentioned: Hannah Arendt had told me about it, and it is the course she had in mind when she wrote about the rumor circulating among students in Germany in the mid-1920s that there was a teacher loose among the pedagogues, one who could perhaps teach his students how to think.)

Section 5 of the Introduction poses the more delicate problem. While Heidegger's later career may be regarded as an expansion and elaboration of the Destruktion, it is by no means clear how we are to understand the move from the nexus Zeitlichkeit des Daseins/Temporalität des Seins to the history of Being as Truth. A peculiar tension pervaded our conversation about it, as though here the danger of misunderstanding loomed large. I asked Heidegger when he began to experience doubts about working out the second half of Being and Time, that is to say, doubts about the adequacy of the "temporality of Dasein" to serve as the horizon for the question of the "temporal quality of Being in general," and doubts about the latter as the horizon for the question of the meaning of Being as such. His reply was slurred somewhat, and as usual his voice slipped through several registers, his voice alone betraying his age. The rejoinder I heard was: "Neunzehnhundertvierundzwanzig oder -fünfundzwanzig"—"1924 or 1925." But that was plainly impossible. He had just finished telling me that he had had every intention of going ahead with Division Three of Part One and with all of Part Two while preparing the first two divisions for the press—and working out the Introduction—in 1926. I wondered later, in retrospect, whether I had misheard? Perhaps he had said 1934 or '35? That at least would dovetail with our usual notions concerning Heidegger's "development" and "turn." Yet the word *zwanzig* does not sound at all like *dreissig*, and in any case I did not at that moment feel any need to ask him to repeat his answer. If I heard correctly, Heidegger was telling me that doubts about the unwritten divisions of *Being and Time* first arose while the book we possess today was being written. That would mean that they arose during the period Heidegger was lecturing on the "History of the Concept of Time" (summer semester 1925) and offering his first *logic* course (winter semester 1925–26).

The matters discussed in the first epilogue ("A") of chapter three (derived from Heidegger's 1925 time lectures) suffice to show that in a very real sense the problem of "Time and Being" antedates the first part of *Being and Time*: while the temporal quality of Being in general is quite manifest to Heidegger by 1925, we find nothing of the detailed analyses of ecstatic temporality. Heidegger himself may well have entertained doubts about his having gone "too far too soon" before *Being and Time* was "finished." The 1925–26 logic course is riddled with such doubts. The second major division of that course begins with something called "phenomenological chronology"—a term that does not appear in *Being and Time*. Phenomenological chronology attempts to thematize "the context of presence (*Anwesenheit*) and the present (*Gegenwart*)" (*21*, 206). These do not refer to space and time as forms of intuition, but to the meaning of Being in traditional ontology (*ousia, parousia*) and to the coming-to-presence (*Gegenwärtigung*) of beings in Dasein. In other words, a phenomenological chronology wants to clarify precisely that horizonal conjunction, *Zeitlichkeit des Daseins/Temporalität des Seins*. Yet Heidegger knows even now (1925–26) that temporality itself, precisely because it is his guideline, "as such always remains more or less veiled," shedding some light, but "a dim and flickering light," by which the investigation must grope its way forward. Symptomatic of its groping is the fact that here *Temporalität* appears as a name for both the temporal structure of Dasein and the temporal quality of Being in general (see section 18, *Die Temporalität der Sorge*). Heidegger himself is perfectly aware of the precariousness of his project, as the following passages illustrate:

> We have already emphasized the disadvantage of the path we are pursuing—the indeterminacy of the phenomenon of time itself, of that to which we apply the words *Temporalität* and *temporal*. This indeterminacy of orientation does not concern a merely fortuitous phenomenon. It concerns time. And to say that time is difficult to grasp amounts to a sheer platitude. No two ways about it: in the matter called "time" we cannot see our way through. . . . [237–38]
> Along what path can we succeed in elaborating this other sense of time, in order ultimately to base the temporal sense of those characteris-

tics we are calling the *Temporalien* on it? I have already indicated that on the path we are pursuing we are having to walk with our feet off the ground. . . . [243]

Sensing that his feet have found no firm foothold, groping his way forward, Heidegger is surely aware that his analyses waver between existential-ontological analysis of Dasein and exposition of the history of the notion of time in Western ontology from Aristotle to Kant, Hegel, and Bergson (see sections 19–22).

Perhaps it would have been odd had Heidegger *not* been discomfited by this mélange of fundamental ontology and history of ideas, odd had he *not* begun to doubt the feasibility of completing his project?

Perhaps Heidegger-II put in an unscheduled appearance before Heidegger-I could finish writing the first half of his major work?

Perhaps Heidegger's answer to my query—provided we heard one another aright—annihilates every current theory about Heidegger's "development" and "turn"?

We went on to talk about the final section of *Being and Time,* section 83, "The existential-temporal [*zeitliche*] analysis of Dasein and the fundamental ontological question concerning the meaning of Being in general." We read through the two compact pages, and I interrupted to ask about several enigmatic phrases.

Heidegger describes the analysis of Dasein as "one way" to pursue the meaning of Being in general, the latter being the genuine goal of his investigation. Then the following sentence appears: "Die *thematische* Analytik der Existenz bedarf ihrerseits erst des Lichtes aus der zuvor geklärten Idee des Seins überhaupt." "The *thematic* analysis of existence, for its part, *first of all* needs the light shed by the idea of Being in general *which will have been clarified beforehand*" (*SZ,* 436, my emphasis). How are we to understand that? Division One of the first part of *Being and Time* offers "a preparatory fundamental analysis of Dasein" conceived as existence and viewed in its everydayness. Division Two tries to grasp existence not only in its everydayness but *originally* and *as a whole,* as it *properly* is, grounded in temporality. But do these two divisions constitute a *thematic* analysis of existence? Or does Heidegger mean that such an analysis is yet to come? Apparently it is outstanding at the end of *Being and Time,* since it needs the already clarified idea of Being in general, whereas *Being and Time* merely searches for the horizon upon which "something like Being" can be interrogated at all. However, what has *Being and Time* been about, right from the start, if not a thematic elucidation of existence which is characterized by an understanding of Being? At the point where Heidegger seems to be indicating the future direction of his inquiry, namely, in section 83, we are in fact cast back upon its commencement.

When I said this, Heidegger nodded animatedly: "Das ist ein Hinweis auf den hermeneutischen Zirkel. Nein, das *ist* der hermeneutische Zirkel."—"That is an indication of the hermeneutical circle. No, it *is* the hermeneutical circle."

We returned to the text and read down to his formulation of "the principal problem": ". . . lässt sich die Ontologie *ontologisch* begründen oder bedarf sie auch hierzu eines *ontischen* Fundamentes, und *welches* Seiendes muss die Funktion der Fundierung übernehmen?" "Can ontology be grounded *ontologically* or does it too need an *ontic* fundament? And *which* being must perform the function of founding?" (*SZ*, 436). I recounted now the many times in *Being and Time* where "ontic testimony" is taken in an effort to "ground" the existential-ontological structures of Dasein in genuine experiences. Surely the *Daseins-analytik* takes the second option? *"Ja."* "But in your later writings," I replied, "there is no talk of *einem ontischen Fundament*—here there are no *onta* at all in question, but Being itself?"

I suppose I was thinking of Heidegger's remark at the end of his lecture "Time and Being" concerning his effort to think Being "without reference to the relationship of Being to beings" (*ZSdD*, 25). But I had always been disturbed by that expression, "Being without beings." If we set off to encounter Being itself without recourse to beings, what is to prevent our reenacting the play of metaphysics, but this time as sheer farce? And what is to become of the path cleared so laboriously in *Being and Time?*

Heidegger did not hesitate:

> Sie müssen daran denken, dass der Versuch, das Sein ohne Bezug auf Seiendes zu denken, stets ein *geschichtlicher* ist. Das heisst: in den verschiedenen Epochen der Seinsgeschichte, im Geschick des Seins, wird Sein so oder so interpretiert. *Das* ist es, was es bedeutet, Sein ohne Seiendes zu denken.

> You must remember that the attempt to think Being without reference to beings is always *historical;* that is to say, Being takes on varied significance in the different epochs of the history or sending of Being. *That* is what it means to think Being without beings.

Heidegger wanted to make it clear that his historical inquiry, his expansion of the *Destruktion*, by no means resorted to the first alternative posed at the end of *Being and Time*, the "ontological" grounding of ontology without reference to some sort of foundation among beings. (If I had studied the "Protocol" to the Todtnauberg Seminar on "Zeit und Sein" more carefully, especially pp. 35–36 of *Zur Sache des Denkens,* I would have spared myself some confusion!) It remains true of course that the foundation or fundament becomes ever more "concussible" as Heidegger proceeds: neither "temporality of Dasein" nor the "temporal quality of Being," nor the effort to ground the latter ontologically in the former, can withstand the incessant tapping of the *Destruktion*. But let me now return to the question of Heidegger's ostensible "turn," in the hope that this long digression will have convinced the reader that the convolutions of the *Kehre* are no simple matter. No, not simple, nor even duplex.

If a developmentalist "turn" were to be admitted at all, then it would surely have to resemble Pöggeler's "three-tiered" architectonic approach.[5] (The *three* stages indicates that here it is not at all a matter of a simple "binary" turning.) The first stage would begin with Heidegger's 1922–23 insight into the inadequacy of the traditional understanding of time for descriptions of factical life-experience, an inadequacy discussed above in chapter one. It is important to note that even the three-tiered interpretation presupposes some elements that will perdure through all three stages—most notably the "destructuring" of the history of ontology. Pöggeler's first stage comprises Heidegger's Marburg years and the first several years of the second Freiburg period, roughly 1923 to 1930. During this period Heidegger remains absorbed in the question eventually posed in *Being and Time*, that of the meaning of Being. The meaning of Being proves to be manifold, depending on the specific regions of being that are investigated. (That Heidegger knew something of the manifold meaning of Being well before 1923 we have seen in chapter four.) Heidegger distinguishes for example the handiness of a piece of equipment from the being at hand of an object of scientific inquiry, and both of these from human existence. Although Pöggeler and Hogemann neglect to mention the point here, we must remember that all the regions of being discussed in *Being and Time* point to the phenomenon of disclosedness (*Erschlossenheit*) and to the interplay of concealment and unconcealment in all disclosure. *Da-sein*, as disclosed or "lighted" and "cleared" in itself, is the site to which each of the meanings of Being refers; hence the meaning of Being as being *in the world* takes indisputable preeminence in this first stage of Heidegger's way. That stage culminates in what Heidegger calls the "metaphysics of truth."[6]

The second stage occupies the 1930s and 1940s, when the question of the meaning of Being develops in the direction of the question of the *truth* of Being. Heidegger is careful to identify the sense of *Wahrheit* as *Wahr, Wahrnis,* "preserve," so that the "truth" of Being is tantamount to the *history* or *destiny* of Being. Nevertheless, a residual metaphysical claim in the word *truth* troubles Heidegger's thinking during this second stage, as though there might be some standard beyond or behind history by which the truth of Being could be measured. By the mid-1930s Heidegger is employing the word *Ereignis* to name the granting of various epochs in Being's history and destiny. The "topic" of that history is the essential unfolding or occurrence (*wesen*) of the clearing of Being. Although "truth" remains the focus, Heidegger now understands his task to be the overcoming of metaphysics, including the metaphysics of truth.

The third tier of Heidegger's career rises in the years 1950 to 1964, when Heidegger "modifies" the question of the truth of Being by asking about the site or locale of Being, the *topos* of the topic. The problems of poetic language and of the essence of technology loom large; those of the "history of Being" and "truth of Being" suffer eclipse. The project of overcoming metaphysics is scarcely abandoned, yet an effort is made to leave metaphysics to its own devices. The very question of Being, and the word *Sein* itself, become increasingly problematic: the danger Heidegger sees is that *Ereignis* will inevitably be understood in metaphysical fashion as a transcendent ground for Being. He therefore tries to think unconcealment on its own terms in the apparently metaphorical language of the clearing, dwelling, sojourn, and so on, even though he is well aware that all meta-phor is meta-physical. Once again, however, it is important to recall that the clearing of Being is a theme that precedes *Ereignis*: as we saw in chapter five, it emerges clearly in "The Origin of the Work of Art" (1935) and is visible already in *Being and Time* (1927).

By now the disadvantage of all such developmentalist approaches—whatever semblance of order they provide—ought to have become apparent. Whether we subdivide Heidegger into two or three or even more parts, the problem remains that the moment we begin to think about any element of any part that element itself turns back and forth to all the remaining elements in Heidegger's thought. Heidegger began to think about these matters earlier than we ever imagine he could have, and his pondering of them lasted longer than we can ever anticipate. It is not that Heidegger never had anything to learn, not that he perched serenely beyond the vicissitudes of time. It is simply that we easily underestimate his prescience and persistence. However much we may be embarrassed by the Jiminy Cricket sentimentality of the "solitary star" of Heidegger's "single thought," the *unity* of Heidegger's career of thought remains striking. To be sure, such unity is not one-dimensional. It is not flat. Each element of Heidegger's thought turns, showing itself in sundry perspectives. These turnings seem to have had no first beginning in Heidegger's career; they certainly have no final end once we ourselves begin to turn with them.

For a number of commentators, the turning in Heidegger's career is earmarked not by an alteration in theme but by a "change of mood." Among the more sophisticated interpretations of the altered *Stimmung* of Heidegger's writing in the 1930s are two which broach the subject in terms of Heidegger's preoccupation with Nietzsche's philosophy. My own view of the *Kehre* in terms of Nietzsche and the eschatology of Being will perhaps be more convincing if I introduce it by way of contrast to the views of Hannah Arendt and J. L. Mehta.[7]

Hannah Arendt argues that Heidegger's turning or reversal is "a concrete autobiographical event" to be located "precisely between Volume I and Volume

II" of Heidegger's *Nietzsche*, that is to say, an event occurring between 1939 and 1941. Whether that ostensible event is Heidegger's "remorse" over his involvement with National Socialism or his sense of impending doom at the outbreak of the war, and no matter how pointless all such speculation concerning autobiographical events must be, Arendt is right to sense a change in tone from the lecture courses of the 1930s to the treatises on Nietzsche written in 1941. During the years 1936 to 1938 Heidegger had been hard at work on a manuscript tentatively titled *Contributions to Philosophy: "On Ereignis."* The upshot of these *Contributions* was that Nietzsche's notion of will to power had become increasingly difficult to distinguish from sheer will-to-will, that is, the essentially manipulative and destructive will of planetary technology in the epoch of nihilism. However much Heidegger's *Contributions* are refreshed by "a Sils-Maria wind" and enlivened by an *"Ecce Homo* mood,"[8] that is to say, however indebted they may be to Nietzsche, the growing disaffection from Nietzsche's metaphysics of will to power is clearly felt there. I leave behind Hannah Arendt's thesis of the "autobiographical event" in order to turn to the event of *Ereignis.* For it is here that J. L. Mehta too perceives a change of mood in Heidegger's thought.

Heidegger's *Contributions to Philosophy: "On Ereignis"* is a gigantic manuscript of extended aphorisms, somewhat in the manner of his published essay "Overcoming Metaphysics" (*VA,* 71–99). It consists of six major divisions preceded by a "Preliminary View" and a renewed discussion and "placing" of the question of *Seyn.* Heidegger describes his attempt there as a kind of "transitional thinking" (again the *metabōle!*) and *"historical* meditation" on the truth of Being. He weaves the words that form the titles of his six principal divisions into an intricate thesis statement, the key words being (1) intimation (*Anklang*), (2) interplay (*Zuspiel*), (3) leap (*Sprung*), (4) founding (*Gründung*), (5) those to come (*die Zu-künftigen*), and (6) the last god (*der letzte Gott*):

> Whatever is said here is asked and thought in the "interplay" of the first commencement and that other one; asked and thought on the basis of the "intimation" of Being in the needy state to which Being has abandoned us; asked and thought for the sake of the "leap" into Being and in order to "found" the truth of Being; asked and thought as a preparation for "those to come" "of the last god."[9]

Heidegger's "Preliminary View" to the *Contributions* describes it as a fugue rather than a system—and it is a massive fugue indeed, a Tocatta and Fugue in F Major. Pöggeler elsewhere calls it "obviously Heidegger's magnum opus."[10] Be that as it may, *Contributions* is surely a watershed for Heidegger: it is engrossed with matters of decision, *Entscheidung,* understood not in any subjectivist sense but as a historic "parting of the ways." Perhaps the most decisive departure for the book is its fundamental mood—as elusive as such things are to describe. That mood is not astonishment or wonder, not the mood that dominated the first commencement or dawn of the West; nor is it sobriety, the mood of phenomenological science and fundamental ontology; the mood is expressed in the words "horror" and "dismay," or at best "awe" and "reticence" (483), words appropriate to the epoch of nihilism. The book's point of departure is the merest *intimation* of Being, inasmuch as Being has abandoned Western man to oblivion. In the midst of all his confident machinations, modern man scarcely apprehends those intimations. Yet the first commencement of thought on Being as *alētheia* in ancient Greece "passes on to" the "other commencement," just as Heidegger will later aver of *time* that there is a *Zuspiel* of each of its dimensions to all the others (see chapter three, above). Such "interplay" requires a "leap" beyond the truth of beings to the truth of Being as presence in unconcealment. Yet human being is already cast or thrown into the openness of Being; in its very Da-sein human being is the site of Being's openness. Although it receives the name *Gründung*, related to Hölderlin's *Stiftung* (see 39, 33), the way in which Being "founds" Da-sein in any given epoch really has to do with the abyss or radical absence of grounds. Openness proves to be a clearing for the self-concealment of Being, the history of which is aberrant. And "those to come"? They are human beings who have come to accept the downgoing (*Untergang*) required of them and who, like Nietzsche's overmen, try to transform decline into a new commencement. They are seeming strangers, always a bit lost in the present, a community of solitaries—Kierkegaard, Nietzsche, Hölderlin—reflecting on the abyssal nature of the history of Being. Their principal task is to abandon the shade of the Christian "moral" God, spawned by the human need for security in salvation, for the sake of "the last god."

Here Heidegger's confrontation with Hölderlin's poetry is of decisive importance. The gods overpower man, but man surpasses them precisely insofar as he is mortal. Mortals watch the gods arrive, undergo transformation, and disappear. By their relation to death mortals are intimate with the self-concealing abyss. The gods wait upon the speech of mortals for their own names; mortals feel the abyss of the nameless on their behalf and communicate it to them. Yet even in flight the gods are never simply bygone, *vergangen;* they are as having been, *gewesen* (see 39, 94–95 and 107–8). They signal out of their remoteness and proximity something of what Heidegger calls "the last god." The last god gathers all prior godhead into its historical essence, not in a Supreme Being, but in its own ultimacy. The last god is present only in and as passing, *Vorbeigang.* To mortal *Untergang* as *Übergang,* that is, downgoing as transition, Heidegger adds the fateful passage of the gods.

I have introduced this long excursus on Heidegger's *Contributions to Philosophy* solely in order to amplify the change of mood we sense in Heidegger's writing in the 1930s. Heidegger's absorption in Hölderlin's question concerning the absence of the gods and the destitution of the Occidental world; his study of Schelling, who speculates with surgical skill on the wound that has opened in the very ground of the Christian God; his study of Nietzsche, for whom art and truth rage in utter discord; his pursuit of truth in the work of art, the site where world and earth strive; his rejection of the technological will to mastery and his surrender of science;—all these serve to make Heidegger's thought less self-assertive than it had been in prior years. The very word *Selbstbehauptung* vanishes from Heidegger's vocabulary. Yet we dare not let such a portrait degenerate into caricature. Heidegger is no pious prophet of releasement after 1938; heaven-storming Prometheus does not suddenly discover humility. If there is a change of mood of the kind I have been describing (following the lead of J. L. Mehta), then it is more subtle and certainly less abrupt than such a brief sketch must make it seem.

If in the last analysis the *Kehre* cannot be thought creatively and fruitfully in developmentalist terms, either as a change of standpoint or alteration in mood, then further thought on Heidegger's relation to Nietzsche may come to our aid. For Heidegger's reading of Nietzsche makes the usual views of his ostensible turn untenable; at the same time it enables us to revert to the possibility of a *Kehre* in the history of Being.

In his Foreword to the Nietzsche lectures and essays published in 1961, Heidegger indicates that the *Nietzsche* volumes as a whole are to grant readers "a view of the path of thought" traversed "from 1930 to the 'Letter on Humanism' (1947)" (*NI*, 10; *Ni 1*, xvi). Heidegger tells us that these lectures and essays began their long gestation in the early 1930s, along with the essays "Plato's Doctrine of Truth" (first published in 1942) and "On the Essence of Truth" (first published in 1943). In other words, Heidegger's reading of Nietzsche proceeded in tandem with his search for an *essential* thinking of the *truth* of Being; after 1929, affirms Otto Pöggeler, Nietzsche's thinking of the death of God becomes a matter of decision for Heidegger.[11] Heidegger speaks of this search in a long passage in the second volume of *Nietzsche* under the title, "The Essential Determination of Man, and the Essence of Truth" (*NII*, 193–95; *Ni 4*, 140–42). There he notes that insight into the correlation of the essence of man and the essence of truth provided the impetus for the treatise *Being and Time*. He continues: "The essence of man is determined by Being itself from the essence (understood verbally) of the truth of Being." The book *Being and Time* attempts to determine the essence of man, the *sum* of the *cogito sum*, in terms of the human being's relation to Being as such. The difficulty this attempt encountered was that modern philosophy has defined man as "subject" and all inquiries into his nature as "anthropology." "The question concerning Being as such stands outside the subject-object relation," insists Heidegger; yet the attempt to formulate the question of the essence of man (as determined in the history of the truth of Being) must refer to the language and thought of its own past. But this is the language and thought of metaphysical subjectivity. Heidegger appeals to such language and thought, indeed calling to it "for assistance, in the effort to say something entirely different." Here Heidegger offers a glimpse at the problem of the presumably "transcendental" location of the work *Being and Time* and its "fundamental ontology of Dasein." Other glimpses have been offered in the "Letter on Humanism" and *Toward the Matter of Thinking.*

In the latter (*ZSdD*, 29–32) Heidegger asks how the fundamental experience or *Grunderfahrung* of *Being and Time* may be designated. The location of its interrogation and formulations, its *Fragestellung*, was with respect to the history of Being "transcendental." As a result, *Being and Time* "in a certain sense still had to speak the language of metaphysics." Yet from the outset the aim of that work was to pose the question of the essential determination of man in the light of the question of the meaning of Being, a question which in the history of metaphysics "never came to language, but remained forgotten." Thus the fundamental experience that served as the catalyst for the question raised in *Being and Time* was the forgottenness or oblivion of Being. Heidegger's major work attempted to reawaken the question of the meaning of Being. Yet to awaken from the oblivion of Being, an awakening that is remembrance of something never thought through, one must already have undergone the experience that Heidegger calls *Ereignis*, the "propriative event" that is the proper theme of Heidegger's later work. "In the thinking of Being itself, in the thinking of *Ereignis*, the oblivion of Being as such can first be experienced." How are we to understand this? The thinking of *Ereignis* first experiences the oblivion of Being; but oblivion of Being is the fundamental experience underlying *Being and Time*. For this reason too one can affirm "that Heidegger-II is *more original* than Heidegger-I."[12] In his letter to Richardson, published as the Preface to Richardson's book, Heidegger comments on the practice of so dividing his work: "Only from what is thought under number *I* will one gain entrace into number *II*; but number *I* becomes possible only when it is contained in number *II*" (*LR*, xxiii). Here Heidegger lapses, perhaps ironically, into the archetypal metaphysical distinction between *ratio cognoscendi* and *ratio essendi*: Heidegger-II is (essentially) the condition of possibility for Heidegger-I, but we come to see this (cognitively) only by working through the productions of Heidegger-I. Perhaps Heidegger's lapsus or irony will cause us to desist from the practice of adding numerals to his name, reducing him to an object of metaphysical and technical modes of thought, and will allow Heidegger himself the last word (*LR*, xvii):

> The thinking of the *Kehre* is indeed a turn [*Wendung*] in my thinking. But this turn does not follow upon a change of standpoint or the abandonment of the question posed in *Being and Time*. The thinking of

the *Kehre* makes it manifest that I have remained by the matter to be thought in *Being and Time*, that is, that I have questioned after that aspect which was already designated in *Being and Time* (SZ, 39) by the title "Time and Being."

We are invited to consider that Heidegger's later thinking is itself "a step back" to the fundamental experience of *Being and Time*. That experience discloses itself in thought on the history or destiny of Being. With this basic experience in view, Heidegger's later thought examines the location of the inquiry, the site of the formulations, in *Being and Time*. In the second volume of his *Nietzsche* (NII, 194; Ni 4, 141) Heidegger speaks of the need to awaken "even a preliminary understanding of the *question that was posed.*" This means that we have misconstrued Heidegger's analysis of Dasein if we have taken it to be an ontology that is secured in the transcendental ground of metaphysical subjectivity. The fundament of the fundamental ontology of *Being and Time* is not the *fundamentum inconcussum veritatis* of Descartes; it does not serve as an absolutely self-secure foundation for ontological inquiry. Rather, the fundament of *Being and Time* is itself eminently concussible; neither the fundamental experience nor the formulation can serve as pillars for an edifice. Hence ceaseless "reinitiation of the analysis of Dasein belongs to the very inception of *Being and Time*" (ZSdD, 34). The preparatory, provisional analysis of human existence is utterly transitional, and the later Heidegger attempts to gain a *first* understanding of the question posed there. For it is *Ereignis* that *first* grants oblivion of Being—the fundamental experience of *Being and Time*—to thought.

Would it then be possible to conjoin in one thought Heidegger's references to the *Kehre*: the impending turn in the essence of technology, the unsuccessful reversal within his own project, described at one point as the transition into meta-ontology, and the turning at the outermost point or *eschaton* in the history of Being? Such a conjunction might look something like this: If the impending, abrupt turn in the essence of technology discloses *alētheia* as such, and if the unsuccessful reversal in Heidegger's thought itself opens on to *alētheia* as the ungroundable source of all disclosure, then these turnings come to the same; the turning at the outermost point in the history of Being must describe an arc that extends from a point prior to the beginning of Heidegger's career to its very end—and not between any two points within that career itself.

During his conversation with a Japanese colleague Heidegger responds to a question concerning the ostensible reversal in his thinking by quoting Hölderlin's "Rhine Hymn": "For as you begin, so you shall remain." He adds (US, 93):

I only know this much: because the meditation on language and Being determined the path of my thinking from early on, its discussion remained as far as possible in the background. Perhaps the basic flaw of the book *Being and Time* is that with it I ventured too far too soon.

Perhaps the *Kehre,* the turn away from forgottenness of Being to its revealing/ concealing clearing, is the attempt to catch up with the forward slippage of the matter for thought in *Being and Time,* its "too far too soon," a catching up that actually moves backward. It goes back and descends to "the location of that dimension out of which *Being and Time* is experienced" (*W,* 159). Yet this is precisely the phrase Heidegger uses to describe his reflection on the philosophy of Nietzsche. In "Nietzsche's Proclamation: 'God is dead,'" Heidegger emphasizes that his "commentary" on Nietzsche's philosophy, "in intention and scope, keeps to that one experience on the basis of which *Being and Time* was thought" (*H,* 195; see chapter eight, below). In the second volume of his *Nietzsche* he insists that his efforts to think what remains unthought in the philosophy of Nietzsche can be successful only if "the fundamental experience of *Being and Time* is thought along with them" (*NII,* 260).

Thus the *Kehre* may fruitfully be understood as a turning within the interrogation of beings as a whole in the history of Western philosophy. All intimations of truth and turning turn us *toward* the thinking of Martin Heidegger's *Being and Time.*

PART THREE
Intimations of a History of Being

7 Descensional Reflection and the Hermeneutics of History

For Michel Haar and Dominique Janicaud

> *The Goddess then, o'er his anointed head,*
> *With mystic words, the sacred Opium shed.*
> *And lo! her bird (a monster of a fowl,*
> *Something betwixt a Heideggre and Owl)*
> *Perched on his crown.*
> —*Alexander Pope*, The Dunciad *I, 287 ff.*

Metaphysical philosophy thinks the Being of beings on the basis of representa-tions grounded in reflexive consciousness. "Metaphysical philosophy" means Western thought from Plato through Nietzsche. Heidegger designates his own position in the history of the West's preoccupations with "beingness" as the end of philosophy and the inception of the task of thinking (*ZSdD*, 61–80).

Heidegger opposes thinking to metaphysics. Does he really mean to say that the great thinkers of the West have left unthought something that lay hidden at the very source of their reflections? He does. The suspicion obtrudes that such a contention is mere arrogance and presumption (*Überheblichkeit*), literally a lifting of oneself above one's fated lot—what the founders of philosophy knew as *hybris*. Nietzsche has prepared us for a more incisive attack. Could it be that Heidegger's complaint that metaphysics is characterized by oblivion of Being, along with his project of inserting past thinkers into niches of the history of this oblivion, is nothing more than a case of "German scholarship," that is to say, a peculiarly convoluted expression of will to power? Is it not indeed a most virulent effusion of will to power or will-to-will to assert that one has in the course of one lifetime grasped the "essence" of two millenia of thought?

The suspicion should be more carefully formulated. Is Heidegger's notion of the history of Being (*Seinsgeschichte*) but a latter-day variant of *Hegel's* history of spirit (*Geschichte des Geistes*)? Does it involve an interpretation of the history of philosophy from the point of view of an Absolute? Does oblivion of Being serve Heidegger as a *letztes Faktum* which shapes the history of thought with the same necessitarian frenzy that characterizes Hegel's remembrance of spirit?[1]

Karl Löwith voices the suspicion when he raises "the unavoidable question" as to whether Heidegger's notion of the *Geschick des Seins* or "destiny of Being" stamps the history of Western thought with the Hegelian—and therefore metaphysical—aspect of dialectical necessity. With Hegel that necessity takes the form of progress in consciousness of freedom. Does it with Heidegger take the form of progressive deterioration of thinking, protracted absence of Being, and prolonged nihilism? And are these forms simply inverted Hegelianisms, ultimately grounded in the same will to self-grounding certitude, the Cartesian will that Nietzsche calls impotence-to-power? Löwith's final judgment is harsh: "The 'history of Being' in accordance with which Heidegger means to appraise Nietzsche's thinking is from Nietzsche's point of view yet another 'world beyond' or meta-physics, for which 'the cock's cry of positivism' (*Götzen-Dämmerung:* Fable) remains unheard, and which has not yet been reversed into *bon sens.*"[2] Löwith does concede that Heidegger's notion of the *Geschick des Seins* differs from Hegel's *Geschichte des Geistes* in one respect: for Heidegger "Being" remains a word that "hides its secrets well," a word that safeguards its darkness and its shadow from that glaring light, that *lumen,* spawned in the Orient.

Heidegger contrasts his own stance with respect to the history of philosophy to that of Hegel in his essay, "The Onto-Theo-Logical Constitution of Metaphysics" (*ID,* 31–67). For Hegel, history is the expression of the dialectical process of thought; Hegel's own thinking cancels the apparent exteriority of this expression in the history of philosophy by showing how the dialectical process rules and advances that history. "For Hegel, the matter of thinking is Being as thought-thinking-itself, a thinking that first comes to itself in the process of its speculative development, a thinking that runs through stages of variously developed and, on that account, necessarily undeveloped forms" (34–35). Hegel understands the matter of thinking to be exercise of the power of cancellation and surpassment (*Aufhebung*), locating previous efforts of thinking in a dialectical, speculative process observed from the vantage point of the Absolute Idea.

Along with Hegel, Heidegger asks what is to be thought by our thinking: what is its matter at issue, its *Sache?* It is for Hegel that method which would guarantee the erection of a self-grounding "System of Science." Hegel's *Phenomenology of Spirit* comprises a first introduction to this system and its method. The method and the *Sache* of thinking are in Hegel's view identical, for only after the dialectical advance of and by the concept has completed itself, coming to light as in and for itself, can the *Sache* be said to have been broached at all. Not the metaphysics of Substance constitutes the truth of the matter for thinking, but the self-reflection of the Subject at the level of absolute knowledge, where both *substantia* and *subiectum* are dialectically transcended.[3]

"To enter into the strength of previous thinking" Hegel and Heidegger both deem to be the essential task (*ID*, 38). Yet unlike Hegel, Heidegger is not prepared to place other efforts at thinking in a scheme of dialectical cancellations by virtue of some sort of superior, much less "absolute," point of view; while Hegel wishes to locate what has been thought in an already thought-through plan, Heidegger announces his intention to search out the issue that remains unthought in previous philosophies. That still sounds like utter presumptuousness. Yet Heidegger insists that our suspicion "can easily be averted" if only we realize that his attempt to define the task of thinking, in light of which previous philosophers are interrogated, is itself determined by the history it questions. For this reason, Heidegger's proposed task for thinking "lies necessarily back behind the greatness of the philosophers." It is an altogether less grand affair than philosophy, since it remains merely a preparation of questions (*ZSdD*, 66). The attempt to hear what has remained unthought in the metaphysical tradition cannot be an attempt at a "yet higher systematic" than that of Hegel; rather, it is characterized by "a step back" (*ein Schritt zurück*) that aims to "set free" previous efforts of thought into their own essence (*ID*, 38–39). This liberation can succeed, Heidegger notes, only when the source of traditional thinking has been brought to light by a sustained interrogation of the tradition which deliberately moves back and down, "out of metaphysics into the essence of metaphysics" (40–41).

Nevertheless, our suspicions are not so easily quelled. By claiming to step back and down, out of metaphysics into the essence of metaphysics, and this by locating its *source*, is not Heidegger doing precisely what Hegel does in his lectures on the history of philosophy, namely, claiming to pinpoint that golden thread which runs through the broad tapestry of Western thought and lends it unity, form, and tone? Does not *Hegel's* philosophy purport to be a thinking of what is unthought in previous philosophies, a discovery of their essence and source in the absolute presupposition? The suspicion persists that by presuming to think what is unthought in prior thinking, and by locating the source of the metaphysical tradition as a whole in the separation of *logos* from *physis*—the oblivion of Being—Heidegger relegates his predecessors to predetermined niches within an interpretation as systematic and absolutist as Hegel's.

During the fifth session of the Todtnauberg seminar on "Time and Being" Jean Beaufret tries deftly to sidestep the impact of the suspicion (*ZSdD*, 51). He concedes the multiplicity of similarities between Hegelian and Heideggerian thought; yet because Heidegger "has no philosophy" as such, Beaufret argues that *ipso facto* there can be no genuine parallel with Hegel. Be that as it may,

Heidegger does have texts, and these texts do seem to betray what Michel Haar has recently called "Hegelian structures in the Heideggerian thinking of history."[4]

Michel Haar argues that both Heidegger's and Hegel's thought may be characterized in terms of *retrospection* on the history of philosophy and on what has been (*das Gewesene*) in general; in terms of a necessitous sequence of epochs in that history; and in terms of an archeology, teleology, and eschatology. There are important differences of detail in the Hegelian and Heideggerian interpretations of history, and perhaps epoch-making differences as well, but Haar concentrates on the striking similarities. What Heidegger himself celebrates in Hegel is the latter's recognition of the "convertibility" of the notions of *Being* and *History:* for Hegel as well as for Heidegger *das wesende Sein,* "essentially unfolding Being," is the coming to be of what has been, *das Ge-wesene,* and the mode of thought appropriate to it is remembrance, *Erinnerung.* In Heidegger's meditation on the truth of Being the primacy of futural, projective Dasein abates and is all but totally supressed by the haunting past of "essence," as *ge-wesen.* One might say (though Haar does not) that Heidegger takes quite literally the Greek definition of essence as *to ti ēn einai,* "that which always was in being," transforming it into the perfect tense and so letting the past invade and shape the present as "that which always has been." Yet for both Heidegger and Hegel the significance of history rests on a kind of paradox. For Hegel, history may be equated with spirit as such, just as for Heidegger Being and Being's truth are short forms for *Seinsgeschichte* and *Seinsgeschick.* The paradox for Hegel is that while history constitutes the very existence of spirit in time it remains but a *Gestalt* or "image" of spirit as it is eternally in itself. The paradox for Heidegger is that while history constitutes the essential unfolding of Being the initial source of that history remains somehow beyond or behind history (49–50). "What has been" is not a "product" or "result" of history but "an absolutely initial anteriority" (50–51). History proper is in Heidegger's view the future of an always already inaugurated past—the envisagement of *alētheia* in pre-Socratic Greece—and that past remains aloof from history proper, yielding only the barest of traces. History proper comprises a sequence of epochs of Being in which some kind of "necessity" and "lawfulness" appear to be at work. But there is the rub.

In the final session of the Todtnauberg seminar (*ZSdD,* 55–56) an attempt is made to minimize such quasi-Hegelian "necessity." The discussants insist that the epochs of Being constitute an "unconstrained sequence," one that dare not be reduced to the history of a single "Thought" on the Hegelian model. If the question be pushed, "Why is the sequence precisely the way it is?", then the only reply lies somewhere between Angelus Silesius and Goethe: *that* such a sequence has eventuated we may insist, *why* it has done so we cannot say. Yet the reply has more of the angelic Silesius than of the worldly Goethe about it:

the "Protocol" concedes that we find "something like a necessity in the series [of epochs of Being], something like a lawfulness and a logic" (cf. Haar, 49; 54). Nevertheless, that lawfulness cannot be described as the law of dialectic. Heidegger does not begin with Being in its abstract immediacy and proceed through sundry mediations to the concrete Subject in and for itself.

If we compare the four Hegelian epochs in the history of philosophy to Heidegger's four epochs of Being the similarity and the difference may become more palpable:

Hegel	*Heidegger*
1. the Oriental world	1. Greece
2. Greece	2. the Christian Middle Ages
3. Rome	3. modernity (subjectivity)
4. the German world	4. planetary technology

Heidegger foreshortens Hegel's beginning and expands his "result." His interpretation remains inveterately "Greek," although what Greece *is* cannot at all be expressed by the Hegelian concepts of immediacy or objectivity. For Heidegger sees "Greece" always within the Hölderlinian perspective of Homeric "heavenly fire" and Germanic "Junonian sobriety" (see 39, 290–94, esp. 292). If we ignore for a moment the fundamental ambiguity of "Greece," the underlying unity of the two approaches seems to emerge. While both Hegel and Heidegger leave space for a multiplicity of developments within any given epoch, both interpretations are subject to a kind of constraint. In Hegel that constraint is avowedly teleological, the realization of absolute spirit waiting upon the patient development of the concept. In Heidegger the constraint is archeological, the initial revelation and simultaneous occultation of Being releasing the entire history of Being's oblivion. The farther Western man moves from the *archē* of the Greek experience of Being the steeper his descent into forgetfulness (54). History of Being is the history of a self-enhancing forgottenness: the more cognition and self-consciousness attain to the forefront of philosophical reflection, the farther Being withdraws into the distance (*ZSdD*, 56). And if Hegel is the philosopher of *absolute* cognition and *accomplished* self-consciousness, then he must stand very near the outermost point of oblivion. What Haar calls the "cumulative logic" of Heidegger's epochs of Being—epoch understood as an *epochē* or "suspending" of Being—does not of course result in the realization of absolute knowing and consummate self-consciousness. It nonetheless does seem to conform to an inverted Hegelian "end." In fact, writes Haar, the reign of necessity in Heidegger's history of Being is *more implacable* than the rational necessity of Hegel—it is "unfathomable" and "blind" (51). One would have to have recourse to the Oriental world to find an image to satisfy it—perhaps the image of the enigmatic, frontal sphinx. Heidegger's "sending" or "destiny" of Being, whether we hear in it Judaeo-Christian strains of "dispensation," Greek pronouncements of "fate," or Near-Eastern leaden curses, contains in advance all the possibilities of history. Could such a *stricte fermeture*, asks Haar, be of any other than Hegelian ancestry?

Yet what about the *archē*, *Anfang*, or commencement of our dispensation? The sheer fact that for Heidegger there *is* a fateful commencement of our history that remains unaltered in all the history that issues from it suggests that Heidegger is even more Hegelian than Hegel. The pre-Socratic dawn remains sheltered from all dialectical depredations until eventide and even unto "the dawn to come." "The essential past of *das Gewesene* directs the future in the manner of an immutable destiny and not simply as the first term in a series of transformations" (52). Yet if that is so then Heidegger's thought is teleological after all, as we see most clearly when Heidegger claims the "consummation" of metaphysics to be planetary technology. Whether we look to the *archē* or *telos* we see "necessity" at work in Heidegger's history of Being (55). All the metamorphoses of the essence of truth (such as *energeia, actualitas, certitudo*) refer to the commencement inasmuch as they supplant one another as stages in the waxing forgetfulness of Being. All the metamorphoses refer to the *end* of metaphysics inasmuch as each paves the way for a subsequent moment: Descartes' *cogito* clears a path to the *ego volo* of Nietzsche's will to power, and modern metaphysics as a whole prepares the coming of planetary technology. Heidegger's is thus a *mauvais-télos*, writes Haar (54), in a phrase highly reminiscent of the Cartesian *malin génie*, because the end of metaphysics arises from the all but total obfuscation of Being. Correspondingly, the commencement in pre-Socratic Greece is not the poorest, most abstract moment for Heidegger, but the richest. True, the *Anfang* conceals itself in and from the beginning (*Beginn*) of the history of metaphysics. The commencement remains enigmatic. The initial revelation of *alētheia*, "a plenitude anterior to history and in some way subjacent to all [historical] development," resembles the initial revelation of spirit-in-itself in Hegel's philosophy. Haar rightly calls the resemblance "dangerous," and asks whether in Heidegger's celebration of the commencement we are not confronting another myth of the Golden Age, "a fiction of the dawn," *une fiction crépusculaire* (55).

Heidegger's archeology and teleology come to a head in the so-called *eschatology* of Being.[5] In Michel Haar's view, Heidegger's notion of an eschatology brings Heidegger closer to Hegel than any other notion; at the same time, "eschatology" divides Heidegger from Hegel irrevocably. What the Todtnauberg seminar avers of *Ge-stell* or technological "framing," namely, that it is Janus-faced or duplicitous (*ZSdD*, 57), Haar now asserts of eschatology. There is good cause to do so, since two of the three traits of *Ge-stell* apply also to eschatology:

both notions refer to the ultimate impact of Being, or Being's final coinage; and each is in some way a prototype of *Ereignis*, the granting and the propriation of Time and Being. (Whether eschatology resembles *Ge-stell* in its first sense, as a ramification of the will-to-will, is Haar's question!) At all events, Heidegger's eschatology of Being "prolongs the Hegelian enterprise" (57). The will to appropriate Western history as a whole, both the "empirical" history of civiliza-tion and the intellectual tradition, shapes Heidegger's history of Being. Heideg-gerian "remembrance" cannot in Haar's view "leave metaphysics to itself" (*ZSdD*, 25); it persists in its "interminable digestion" of the past (57–58). Even when it lets Being go, and even crosses Being through, as in *Toward the Question of Being* (*W*, 239ff.), the Heideggerian meditation preserves a residual claim that the thinking of *Ereignis* cancels and surpasses oblivion of Being. Heidegger *remembers*. And he claims to remember what the tradition has forgotten.

In what sense Heidegger's eschatology of Being can be a radical departure from Hegel's history of spirit is now our question. Two remarks from the Todtnauberg seminar, while helpful, are insufficient (*ZSdD*, 52–53). First, Heidegger's thinking in *Being and Time* (and presumably afterwards as well) remains at the level of *Sein* in Hegel's *Logic*: it does not transcend to the concept, *Begriff*. To this one would have to reply that *Being and Time* is everywhere on the search for an adequate conceptuality (*Begrifflichkeit*) for existence (*Dasein*); and furthermore that Heidegger's later thought seems to advance to the level of Hegelian "essence," *Wesen* in the form of an identifiable *Gewesenes*. The question then would be why Heidegger's notion of the essence of truth and truth of essence does not advance to either a logic of concepts or a material logic. The answer to that question brings us to the second point in the "Protocol." Hegel's dialectical thought, especially after the *Phenomenology of Spirit*, fails to reflect on the source and range of *negativity*. (This complaint we find not only in the 1962 seminar but also in the Marburg lectures of the 1920s and in the 1929 inaugural lecture, "What Is Metaphysics?" It is surely related to the complaint we hear throughout the 1930–31 lectures on "Hegel's Phe-nomenology of Spirit" [32, sections 5b, 7c, 10c, and "Conclusion"] concerning the Hegelian *Aufhebung* of finitude.) The major difference between Hegel's thinking of the Absolute and Heidegger's thinking of Being, cited in the "Protocol" but (strangely) absent from Michel Haar's account, is the *relation of man* to the Absolute and to *Ereignis*. Whereas for Hegel the thinking of the Absolute at least approximates cancellation of human finitude, Heidegger's seminar on "Time and Being" closes with thoughts on the irremediable finitude of both humanity and *Ereignis*. Such finitude dons a comic mask when the seminar participants feel constrained to remark—and to have the remark *pro-tokolliert*, and to have the "Protocol" authorized by Heidegger, who must "sign" it as though it were the Magna Carta or the Tennis Court Oath—that the dispensations of Being will not suddenly cease now that Heidegger has thought *Ereignis*. The participants need no longer fear that the world will come crashing down about their ears before they can flee Heidegger's hut to the peaceful clearing of the pine forest. With that signature firmly in place there will always be more to think about, and, with luck, time to think it in.

However, does mere mention of finitude manage to make Heidegger's (or our own) hermeneutics of history perspicuous in its limits? Is all suspicion thoroughly quashed by now? No. Formulated as a problem at the heart of hermeneutics, our suspicion asks: How can one claim to have achieved a decisive grasp on the essence and source of the metaphysical tradition as a whole and yet allow thinkers within that tradition to be heard?

We can approach the problem and release the pressure of the suspicion only if we grasp the character of hermeneutical thinking, like that of Nietzsche's thinking, as a kind of *descensional reflection*.[6] How Heidegger's hermeneutical thinking makes the descent delineates its similarities to, and differences from, Nietzschean philosophy. Such descent involves a deepened comprehension of Heidegger's concession that his own notion of a "history of the truth of Being" is itself determined by the history thereby named; that hermeneutical interrogation steps back behind the greatness of past philosophers; and that it is therefore less a thing than that to which it responds. For if all this turns out to be false humility or academic courtesy, the suspicions of Nietzsche's genealogical critique of philosophy will have said all that needs saying.

At the beginning and the end of "The Onto-Theo-Logical Constitution of Metaphysics" Heidegger focuses on this problem. He begins the essay by announcing "an attempt to begin a conversation with Hegel" (*ID*, 31). Heidegger does not begin by announcing that what Hegel thought has been canceled and surpassed in his own thinking. He closes with a reflection on the difficulty his own hermeneutical back-stepping inevitably confronts, which is that the language spoken in the "recovery of metaphysics" is itself largely cast in the metaphysical mold.

"The little word 'is'," Heidegger writes, "contains the entire destiny of Being, from the *estin gar einai* of Parmenides to the 'is' of Hegel's speculative doctrine, and up to the dissolution of the 'is' into exertions of will to power in Nietzsche" (*ID*, 66). With Nietzsche's metaphysics of will to power the metaphysics of 'is' disintegrates. Yet both Heidegger and Nietzsche are thrown into the language of the 'is': Heidegger wishes to adopt a stance towards the metaphysical tradition that is not itself metaphysical, and yet his posture is already largely determined by the language of that tradition. In the "Afterword" to his lecture "What is Metaphysics?" Heidegger concedes that the language of his lecture bears an uncomfortably close resemblance to the language of metaphysics which it wishes to overcome (*W*, 99). This coincidence of language is unavoidable, however, and the effort to think the essence of metaphysics unmetaphysically, to ask after the ground of metaphysics in a nonpropositional way, "remains in an essential sense ambiguous [*zweideutig*]" (*W*, 100). Thus, on the one hand, Heidegger accuses Nietzsche of following the guiding question of metaphysics by conceiving will to power as the "essence" of beings as a whole: the pursuit of "essence" is a metaphysical pursuit.[7] On the other hand, Heidegger himself wishes to step out of metaphysics and into the "essence" of metaphysics: the pursuit of *this* "essence" is *not* a metaphysical pursuit. The problem is merely evaded, not resolved, when we insist that Heidegger employs *Wesen* strictly in the verbal sense: the unfolding of a particular kind of thinking in the destiny of Being remains in Heidegger's judgment the *essential* matter. Further, Heidegger wishes to ask the question of the ground of metaphysics, without following its own guidelines; but the pursuit of "ground" describes the fundamental will of metaphysical *Leitfragen* itself. The ambiguity of the language of Heidegger's nonmetaphysical recovery of the metaphysical tradition is a consequence of the ineluctable ambiguity of truth as unconcealment: for concealment belongs to the way Being reveals itself.[8]

With Heidegger, as with Nietzsche, interpretation becomes "the play of truth and illusion in the duplicity of Being."[9] The *Zweideutigkeit* or *duplic-ity* of Being's concealing and revealing disclosure plays in the very language of interpretation. Just as Nietzsche shatters the language of metaphysics while speaking it; just as his relationship to metaphysics is one of liberation *and* imprisonment;[10] so too is Heidegger's hermeneutical philosophy delivered over to the language of its metaphysical heritage even as it strives to think beyond it. I should say, rather, to think *beneath* the language of the metaphysical inheritance, to enter ever more questioningly into the hermeneutical encirclement it shares with Nietzsche. For in order to escape the fatality of that kind of encirclement one would oneself have to be the circularity of the *ens causa sui* that has served as the ultimate ground of reflexive subjectivity, a ground which by Nietzsche's time has become the *circulus vitiosus deus*.[11] But to *be* this circularity would entail being in general, and, once the question of the meaning of "being" were raised, the fatal encirclement of descensional reflection could never be escaped, its frontality never circumvented.

On the basis of his insight into the ambiguity of Nietzsche's attempt to throw off the thinking and language of metaphysics, an attempt that nevertheless seeks its ground in the metaphysics of will to power, Heidegger determines to break through the language of *ratio* and propagate a language of *thinking*. It is precisely that attempt to throw off the scheme of "rational thought" which Nietzsche considered essential but futile. In *Being and Time* Heidegger calls it the "ultimate business" of philosophy to "preserve the *force of the most elemental words* in which Dasein expresses itself," and this by hearkening to the speaking of language (*SZ*, 220; 163). In his "Letter on Humanism" Heidegger writes, "The liberation of language from grammar into a more original, essential articulation is reserved for thinking and poetizing."[12] The project of liberation from grammar—which conceals ontological commitments—is founded upon this attitude of hearkening:

> If man is to find his way once again into the nearness of Being he must first learn to exist in the nameless. . . . Before he speaks man must first let himself be claimed again by Being, taking the risk that under this claim he will seldom have much to say. [W, 150; BW, 199]

To forfeit the security of *ratio*, which at the close of his first published article on Nietzsche Heidegger calls "the most stubborn opponent of thinking" (H, 147), is to open thinking to anxiety and essential ambiguity or ambivalence. Something irreversible happens to discourse: representational, propositional, evaluative, and all "necessitarian" modes go silent as thinking approaches the core of human finitude at the center of the hermeneutical encirclement.

"It is high time to break the habit of overestimating philosophy and of thereby asking too much of it" (W, 194). Heidegger's thinking wishes to ask the question of the meaning of Being more originally than metaphysics has asked it; but precisely on that account it must set aside Hegel's confidence that the perennial "love of wisdom" can now be replaced by "wisdom itself" in the form of "absolute knowledge." What Heidegger calls "thinking" does not fly so high.

> Thinking is on the descent to the poverty of its provisional essence. Thinking gathers language into simple saying. In this way language is the language of Being, as clouds are the clouds of the sky. With its saying, thinking lays inconspicuous furrows in language. They are still more inconspicuous than the furrows that the farmer, slow of step, draws through the field. [W, 194; BW, 242]

Heidegger's mixing of metaphors betrays the complexity of the "simple saying" of thinking, a complexity that has been the gadfly to his thinking from *Being and Time* (1927) to "Time and Being" (1962). Heidegger begins and ends his letter to Richardson by commenting on the difficulty of finding language for what calls for thinking. One must doggedly remind oneself that all formulations of the question of "Being and Time, Time and Being"—words such as *Geschick, Kehre,* and *Vergessenheit*—must remain multiple in meaning. "This manifold thinking demands, not so much a new language, but a transformed relation to the essence of the old."[13] It is significant that Heidegger includes among the formulations that compel manifold thinking the word "oblivion" or "forgotten-ness" (*Vergessenheit*). That was the word which earlier seemed to serve as the *letztes Faktum* of Heidegger's approach to the history of metaphysical philosophy. But descensional reflection, which sustains its being held out into the nothing in the experience of anxiety, so that it remains a thinking-within-anxiety, neither achieves nor requires the security-in-certitude of an ultimate fact. It must content itself with intimations of a history of Being devoid of *archē, telos,* and even *eschaton.* Heidegger writes:

> Thinking does not overcome metaphysics by climbing still higher, surmounting it, transcending it somehow or other; thinking overcomes metaphysics by climbing back down into the nearness of the nearest. The descent, particularly where man has strayed into subjectivity, is more arduous and more dangerous than the ascent. The descent leads to the poverty of the ek-sistence of *homo humanus.* [*W*, 182; *BW*, 231]

How then does Heidegger's history of Being differ from Hegel's history of spirit? We know that Hegel was able to track the flight of spirit from its dawn in the Orient until the high-noon of Hohenzollern Germany. Yet what has occurred since Hegel's midday has interrupted spirit's flight, grounded man, and undermined our thinking. What occurred was: Nietzsche. The divine way of unobstructed vision is closed off to Heidegger, and the way of Being descends toward that mortal region between the tragic and the satyric which calls for thinking.

8 The Last Thinker of the West

For Al Lingis

"The thesis of Heidegger's *grand livre* [that is, his *Nietzsche*, published in two volumes in 1961] is much less simple than people have generally tended to say," writes Jacques Derrida, quite justly.[1] In fact, his remark applies to *all* of Heidegger's texts on Nietzsche. Sufficient warning that any effort to explicate in a dozen pages *die Sache* of Heidegger's prolonged and intense confrontation with Nietzsche remains futile. Let this brief chapter invite and incite efforts that will demand more time and greater solicitude.

It is tempting to compare Heidegger's confrontation with Nietzsche to his companionship with Hölderlin. Heidegger himself would picture the latter as the proximity and intimacy of two pines rooted in the silent forest earth; the "neighborhood of the chanting poet" constitutes a "wholesome danger" to the thinker. Hölderlin and Heidegger: no cloud ever darkens their sky, a sky that stretches across the expanse of the clearing that is held open by the very distance that separates thinker from poet.

In contrast, Nietzsche, whom Heidegger from the outset acknowledges as *Denker* rather than *Dichter*, encroaches on Heidegger's own space. Nietzsche does not declaim from one distant mountain peak to Heidegger perched on another—an image one might fashion to characterize the conversation between great thinkers—but infiltrates and crowds close, implants doubts and eradicates convictions, whispers Heidegger's own second thoughts to him, illuminates and confounds at once. Their confrontation is stormy. Late in that *Auseinandersetzung* Heidegger confesses that he has had to take with utmost seriousness Nietzsche's message to Georg Brandes: that it is no great trick to *find* Nietzsche, the challenge being rather to learn how to *lose* him, that is, to release Nietzsche to his own place in the history of metaphysics. Yet Heidegger never really loses Nietzsche, never "locates" him, never shakes free of him, because Nietzsche never releases his grip on Heidegger. That is fortunate. The tempestuous encounter with Nietzsche prevents Heidegger from becoming what we have only now accused him of being—a bloodless shade of Hegel. The piety of Heidegger's questioning and the apparent quietism of *Gelassenheit* are everywhere undercut by the passion of Nietzschean suspicion and the rage of a descensional reflection without cease. To repeat: history of Being is not history of spirit. That is Nietzsche's primary, decisive incision; that is his deepest cut. And there is no poetic annealing, no restoration of the Absolute in hymns—

if Mozart is (as Heidegger says) "God's lute-play";

if Hölderlin plucks the lyre while God withdraws in irreversible retreat;

if Trakl, as we shall see, rescues the lyre as it slips from Hölderlin's hands and with it sings the palsied deity, the progenitor of a ruined race;

it is nonetheless Nietzsche the thinker who must inter the defunct and toneless divinity with all his instruments, Nietzsche the thinker who must fashion for the philosopher a new lyre. Less companionable than the men of music and hymn, Nietzsche nonetheless accompanies Heidegger early on and to the end.

Precisely when Heidegger first read Nietzsche we do not know.[2] But he studied the philosopher's works during his student years at Freiburg, 1909–14, especially the second, expanded edition of the *Nachlass* material published as *The Will to Power* (1906). Two decades later that text served as the source for the topics of Heidegger's lectures on Nietzsche: the will to power as art and as knowledge, from Book Three, sections I and IV; the eternal recurrence of the same, from Book Four, section III; and nihilism, from Book One. The volume also had an impact on Heidegger's early writings, not as an explicit theme for investigation, but as an incentive to philosophic inquiry in general. During his *venia legendi* lecture of 1915, "The Concept of Time in the Discipline of History," Heidegger alluded to philosophy's proper "will to power" (*FS*, 357). By that he meant the need to advance beyond epistemology to metaphysics, that is to say, to interrogation of the goal and purpose of philosophy as such. In his Habilitation thesis (1915–16) Heidegger revealed the influence of Nietzsche when he stressed philosophy's function "as a *value for life*" (*FS*, 137–38). Philosophy as such exists "in tension with the living personality" of the philosopher, "drawing its content and value from the depths and the abundance of life in that personality." In this regard Heidegger cited Nietzsche's formula "the drive to philosophize," and he praised that writer's "relentlessly austere manner of thought," a manner enlivened, however, by a gift for "flexible and apt depiction."

During the decisive Marburg years, 1923–28, Nietzsche appears to have withdrawn completely from Heidegger's central concerns, making room for Aristotle, Kant, and Husserl. Heidegger apparently wished to distance himself from the Nietzsche adopted by *Lebensphilosophie* and by the philosophies of culture, worldview, and value. As I noted at the very outset, in chapter one, his rejection of the category "life" and adoption of "existence" for his nascent analyses of Dasein had come to light already in 1919–21, the years of his confrontation with Karl Jaspers' *Psychology of Worldviews*. His spurning of the neo-Kantian value-philosophy of Wilhelm Windelband and Heinrich Rickert undoubtedly delayed Heidegger's public confrontation with the philosopher who sought the revaluation of all values. Yet throughout the 1920s Nietzsche's *style* of thought continued to captivate Heidegger. For example, in the midst of an otherwise dry-as-dust, utterly sober phenomenological account of Husserlian intentionality, categorial intuition, and the a priori, which Heidegger proffered in his 1925 lecture course on "The Concept of Time," we find the following remarkable avowal:

> Philosophical research is and remains atheism; for that reason it can afford "the arrogance of thought." Not only will it afford such arrogance, but this is the inner necessity and proper force of philosophy, and precisely in such atheism philosophy becomes—as one of the greats once said—"the gay science" [*Fröhliche Wissenschaft*]. [20, 109–10]

Phenomenology as rigorous science, *but with gaiety:* neither Husserl nor even Scheler was equal to it!

Yet there is little gaiety in the masterwork that concludes Heidegger's Marburg period, *Being and Time*. Only three references to Nietzsche's thought appear in that text; and only one of them is a substantive reference.[3] Nevertheless, as we have seen in chapter six, the "fundamental experience" of *Being and Time* and Heidegger's reading of Nietzsche are intimately related. At the close of that chapter I cited Heidegger's essay "Nietzsche's Proclamation: 'God is dead,'" to this effect: "The following commentary, in intention and scope, keeps to that one experience on the basis of which *Being and Time* was thought" (*H*, 195; cf. *NII*, 260). If that one experience be the oblivion of Being, which implies forgottenness of the nothing in which Dasein is ever suspended, then we may say that in *Being and Time* Heidegger brings the question of the death of God home by inquiring into the death of Dasein and the demise of metaphysical discourse. Among the principal motifs of *Being and Time* are: the finite, ecstatic horizon of the being that is Dasein; the interpretation of Dasein as care or possibility-being, structured temporally as existential, factical, and falling; and the being-a-whole (*Ganzsein*) of Dasein as being-unto-death (*Sein zum Tode*). However rarely cited in *Being and Time*, Nietzsche may well be the regnant genius of that work— Nietzsche, who

exposes the anthropomorphic base of metaphysical projections and the evanescence of Being understood as permanence of presence;

supplies genealogical accounts of time and eternity in such a way that the latter appears as vengeance wreaked on the former;

confronts without subterfuge human existence as irredeemably mortal, bursting with possibility yet bound to fatality;

insists always and everywhere that on this earth thinkers as well as artists must (in Ezra Pound's words) "make it new."

In writing these things I approach the core of the Heidegger/Nietzsche confrontation and encounter which dominate the 1930s, 1940s, and early 1950s in Heidegger's career of thought.

Let me now try to formulate some of the principal themes of Heidegger's published works on Nietzsche and to state what I take to be the profound and enduring impact of these themes on Heidegger's own thought. Although my presentation will not be uncritical, I will at no point ask whether Heidegger's reading of Nietzsche is "adequate" or whether Heidegger "represents" Nietzsche fairly: in the first place, Heidegger does not purport to "represent" Nietzsche, and in the second, no matter how "inadequate" his reading of Nietzsche may be, Nietzsche himself, born posthumously, retains his own style and stylo, makes his own counterthrusts, dances his own defence. I offer my aid, he laughs. Nor, alas, do I have the requisite space to indicate the importance of Heidegger's reading for contemporary confrontations with Nietzsche, especially in France, from Bataille through Deleuze and Klossowski to Foucault and Derrida.

NIHILISM AND THE END OF METAPHYSICS

With his announcement of the death of God and the collapse of all worlds "beyond," Nietzsche becomes the historian and herald of nihilism. The history of nihilism comprises the rise and fall of the highest values hitherto, values such as "purpose," "unity," "Being," and "truth." But thanks to his insight into the origins of nihilism in the very instauration of otherworldly values, that is, the identity of nihilism and moralistic metaphysics, Nietzsche also becomes the herald of "perfect" or "ecstatic" nihilism. Heidegger shares Nietzsche's suspicion that nihilism is not a recent, typically modern phenomenon; he accepts Nietzsche's judgment that the reign of nihilism is coterminous with that of Platonistic metaphysics. This epochal reign reaches its apotheosis when the horizon that once demarcated the "true" from the "merely apparent" world fades, when the true world "becomes a fable." When he pierces the horizon of "the true"—not satisfied merely to invert the Platonistic hierarchy of the sensuous and supersensuous, Becoming and Being—Nietzsche precipitates the crisis of metaphysics.

At the same time, however, by insisting on a revaluation of values, as though there might be some absolute standard (such as "life" or "will to power") by which values might be gauged and promulgated, and by treating nihilism ultimately as an affliction of which Occidental history might be cured, Nietzsche remains caught in the orbit of metaphysical thinking, trapped in passive-reactive nihilism. Samson indeed brings down the temple, but on his own head. Thus we attain a first glimpse of the irresolvable ambiguity and even ambivalence of Heidegger's reading of Nietzsche: pursuing the question of the horizon of "the true," Nietzsche nonetheless fails to pose the question of the essence of truth, *das Wesen der Wahrheit,* and fails to see that his own critique of "the true" presupposes the traditional notion of truth as *adaequatio, homoiōsis;* conceiving of his philosophy early on as the overcoming of Platonism, Nietzsche nonetheless fails to recognize the fatal kinship of revaluation with the *idea tou agathou* and thus fails to recover the tradition by means of an originary reading of the early Greek thinkers; subjecting Cartesian subjectivism and intellectualism to a scathing critique, Nietzsche nonetheless fails to draw the full consequences of his discovery that *ego volo* is but a brainchild of *ego cogito* and fails to recognize that the mere substitution of "body" for "spirit" cannot overcome representational thought; descrying the origin of nihilism in the pristine establishment of transcendent values, Nietzsche nonetheless believes that some values can be rescued from nihilism; advocating a fully developed, ecstatic nihilism, sprung from the depths of tragic wisdom, Nietzsche nonetheless fails to confront the question of the essence of the *nihil* and fails to experience the source of nihilism in the happenstance that in Western history *Being itself comes to nothing.*

The ambiguity—and ambivalence—in Heidegger's reading of Nietzsche may best be expressed in two questions. How is it possible that Nietzsche's philosophy implies nothing less than the *end* of metaphysics, and yet *is itself* a metaphysics? How can Nietzsche be called *the last* metaphysician and yet still be considered *one* metaphysician among others?

THE METAPHYSICS OF WILL TO POWER
AND ETERNAL RECURRENCE

Will to power and eternal recurrence of the same are the crucial poles of Nietzsche's metaphysics, the other key words—nihilism, revaluation, "justice," and overman—revolving about them. Heidegger insists that these two thoughts constitute a unity, that they designate what scholastic philosophy called the *essentia* and *existentia* of entities. This implies that will to power and eternal recurrence are responses to the ancient ontological question *ti to on,* in the metaphysical form, "Was ist das Seiende?", "What is the being?". They are replies to the guiding question within metaphysics (*die Leitfrage*) but not to the grounding question concerning metaphysics as such (*die Grundfrage*). The putative unity of will to power and eternal recurrence, as the essence and existence respectively of all beings, at times assumes a merely schematic, almost syllogistic form in Heidegger's lectures and treatises: If will to power is a self-willing that brooks no obstacles, then its unconditioned willing can only be a perpetual self-overcoming; any being that *is* essentially will to power can *exist* solely as eternal recurrence of the same. This schematic interpretation tends to understand will to power cosmologically (and thus metaphysically) rather than to employ it genealogically; it woefully underestimates the exhilarating and devastating import of Nietzsche's supreme and most burdensome thought—*die ewige Wiederkehr des Gleichen.* In his haste to refute Alfred Baeumler—who embraced a politicized will to power while spurning the "Egypticism" of eternal recurrence, thus proclaiming the lamentable *disunity* of Nietzsche's thought—Heidegger at times neglects the multiple perspectives of will to power and the tragic pathos of eternal return. Yet Heidegger shares Jaspers' conviction that recurrence is Nietzsche's central thought and he devotes his best interpretive efforts to it, not only during the summer semester of 1937 but also in lectures delivered in the early 1950s. However, before taking up discussion of eternal recurrence, I must elaborate somewhat on Heidegger's criticism of Nietzsche's metaphysics.

WILL TO POWER AND VALUATIVE THOUGHT

According to Nietzsche, will to power is "the ultimate fact we come down to." To Heidegger's ear *das letzte Faktum* has an unmistakably metaphysical ring. Just as Heidegger's own asseverations on the metaphysical *Urfaktum* of temporality become increasingly suspect to him after the publication of *Being and Time,* as we saw earlier in the second and third chapters of this volume, so too Nietzsche's desire to define the very essence of beings seems futile to Heidegger. (Of course, it is Nietzsche, with his genealogy of the *causa prima*—the "first cause" originating in "laziness," "weariness"—who helps to make such tendencies suspect!) Nevertheless, Heidegger eschews the genealogical employment of will to power and rejects its cosmological-biological usage. There is little left to be said, other than that will to power seems to derive from Leibnizian *vis* and *appetitus* and from the interpretations of "will" in Kant, German Idealism, and Schopenhauer. Heidegger does say all this, in spite of his warning that to trace probable dependencies and influences among thinkers is to forget their universal dependence on Being and its destiny. Only in his first lecture course, "Will to Power as Art," does will to power receive sympathetic and thought-provoking treatment. There it is seen as nothing less than an ecstatic being-beyond-oneself in the manner of human existentiality or finite transcendence. As perpetual self-overcoming, will to power is another word for *epimeleia, Sorge,* "care." As I indicated in chapter six, Hannah Arendt is right when she notes that the later lectures and essays (in volume II of *Nietzsche*) abandon this positive interpretation of will to power and equate Nietzsche's doctrine with the will-to-will that inaugurates the reign of planetary technology.[4] Whether Heidegger ever truly overcomes the schematic "cosmological" interpretation of will to power—as the *essentia* of entities—may be doubted; certainly there is no breakthrough here to fundamental problems, as there is in Heidegger's thinking of eternal recurrence.

The negative balance in Heidegger's account of the metaphysics of will to power is chiefly due to the role of value thinking (*Wertdenken*) there. Heidegger's allergic reaction to Nietzschean "revaluation of all values" derives partly, as I have noted, from his own rebellion as a student and young teacher against the influential neo-Kantian *Wertphilosophie* of his mentor, Heinrich Rickert. Throughout his career, Heidegger inveighed against the philosophy of value as a debasement of Kant's philosophy. Although Nietzsche seems to have recognized the necessity of overcoming Platonistic valuation as such, Heidegger faults him for retaining confidence in "values" themselves, indicts him for the unfounded hope that this lame duck of Kantian-Cartesian subjectivism, this insipid residue of secularized Christianized *aretē*, could rescue Occidental humanity from its own essential history—nihilism. In value thinking Heidegger sees the major obstacle to Nietzsche's advance beyond metaphysical modes of thought. The project of revaluation deflects and distracts Nietzsche from the questions of Being, truth, and the nothing. Nietzsche comes closest to those questions in his thought of eternal recurrence.

ETERNAL RECURRENCE, TIME, AND DOWNGOING

Nietzsche's sundry communications of eternal recurrence, in *The Gay Science, Thus Spoke Zarathustra, Beyond Good and Evil,* and various unpublished sketches, convince Heidegger that eternal recurrence is not so much a dogma as an experience in and of *thinking*. It has to do, not so much with the *existentia* of beings (as the treatises published in volume II of *Nietzsche* tend to assume), as with "existence" in both Jaspers' and Heidegger's senses. In the summer semester of 1937 Heidegger struggles to confront the full import of Nietzsche's tragic insight into Becoming and his Dionysian affirmation of it.

The previous semester's course on will to power as art had focused on the opposition—indeed, the "raging discordance"—between art and truth. Art, the creation of transfigurative semblance, proved to be worth more than truth for the enhancement of life. Such enhancement occurred in what Nietzsche called "the grand style," the enraptured style that conjoined under one yoke the rule of form-giving law and the anarchy of originary chaos. Nietzsche's discovery of the yoke, the most life-enhancing thought and most powerful dissemblance, fashioned in the raging discord between art and truth, was given the title "eternal recurrence of the same." Heidegger insisted that this thought had something—perhaps everything—to do with the question of Being and Time, Time and Being.

Standing in the "gateway of the Moment"—not simply observing the gateway from the side, as does the dwarf, who makes everything too easy for himself—Zarathustra is cast into *time*. The figure of Zarathustra thus serves as an image of perspicuous, resolutely open Dasein. The "eternity" of eternal recurrence is not that inappropriate nonfinite time which, according to *Being and Time* section 65, is derived from finite time proper, but the moment (*der Augenblick*) of insight and decision. On the threshold of the moment of time Zarathustra affirms that all transition (*Übergang*) toward the overman (*Übermensch*) ineluctably requires downgoing (*Untergang*).[5] Zarathustra's contempt for the "last man" and his disgust with humanity in general, his nausea, are confronted and overcome in the thought of recurrence—although what "overcoming" now may mean becomes a capital question, one that cannot be resolved by a polite reference to "self-overcoming." Zarathustra's convalescence consists solely in thinking this thought—although the thought itself, as the most powerful dissemblance, at times seems to be a ditty cranked out on a barrel-organ, a child's entertainment offering sheer distraction from the harsh realities of historical existence. In Heidegger's view, all depends on the actual work, *die Wirk-lichkeit*, of the thinking itself. All depends on fashioning the lyre that will sustain the tension of discord, the tension of the Heraclitean bow (Yeats calls it life-in-death, death-in-life), the tension that will hold the melody of mortality.

Neither Nietzsche nor Heidegger are unduly optimistic about the success of such work. Nietzsche has Zarathustra describe himself as a cripple on the hither-side of the bridge that leads to redemption from revenge. In his final lectures and essays on Nietzsche, Heidegger persists in posing the crucial question of such redemption. All his earlier preoccupations culminate in the question, "Who is Nietzsche's Zarathustra?" With a view to the thought of eternal recurrence, this question translates to the query, "What is Called—and What Calls for—Thinking?"

The decisive work—thinking recurrence—takes place, according to Heidegger, in the section of *Thus Spoke Zarathustra* entitled "On Redemption." There the spirits of vengeance, gravity, and ressentiment, themselves the propitiating spirits of otherworldly metaphysics and morals, are perceived as arising from the frustration of man's will in the face of time's irreversibility. Before the facticity of the "it *was*" the will stands helpless. It is not merely that the ephemeral character of Becoming paralyzes the will, nor that transience gives rise to the castrating nostalgia for the *ewige Weibliche*. What is truly crippling is

the sheer intransigence of the past,
the intractability of the *fait accompli*,
the lapidary impassivity of what used to be.

Rather than will nothing at all, the harried will wills the nothing: hence the ennervating delirium of passive nihilism. Rather than affirm the ordinance of

time, the will conjures a counterwill to fulminate against time and its *"Es war"*:
hence the movable feast of rancor and revenge.

Redemption from the spirit of vengeance, the transformation of reactive
nihilism into ecstatic nihilism, and the transfer of allegiance from the Crucified
to Dionysos require that the will declare of the past, "Thus I willed it, I will it so
now, and thus shall I will it forever!" Willing the eternal recurrence of the same
reconstitutes the "it was" as a "so be it," dissolves the impassivity of the past in
the potent solution of its present willful act. Thus man "administers the proof"
that the contingencies of the past conform to what will to power itself wills; thus
humanity earns "the right to claim" that the happenstances and hazards of the
past are its own doing; thus the past is transmuted into perpetual future by a will
that "continually remains presence-to-self."[6]

Heidegger doubts the efficacy of such willing to perform the redemptive work
of eternal recurrence. "Thus I willed it!" declares the will. What is the source of
such a declaration? It asseverates something of the past in the present. Can what
it avers of the past be affirmed in the gateway of the Moment, where time looms
before me and then recedes over my shoulder to a remote eternity? Or must such
a declaration proceed from the side, in the dwarf's perspective, as a (now)
transparent ruse? Reconstituting the "it was" as a "so be it"—is that not to
subordinate *Sein* to *Sollen*, and not to *Wollen*, in the manner of the most supine
Platonism? To dissolve the impassivity of the past in the activity of a willful
present—is that not to embrace the traditional metaphysical preference for
activity over passivity? What sort of "proof" would convince the genealogist
that contingency has been successfully converted into will? Has not the ditty of
proofs been played out? What sort of *droit de prétendre* will transform the victim
of chances into the demiurge of destinies? And when the past is transformed into
perpetual future by a will that remains perpetually present to itself, is not the
metaphysics of presence, that is to say, the ontology based on the understanding
of Being as permanence of presencing (*Beständigkeit des Anwesens*), merely
confirmed in its dominion? The paradoxical assurance that the will's perpetual
presence to self is a perpetual sacrifice of self, an infinite self-overcoming, does
not convince: "perpetual sacrifice" offers up the same old lamb over and over
again, and it no longer fools gods or men.

All these doubts about "redemption"—about what one might call the *deca-
dence* of redemption—trouble Heidegger. They culminate in his charge that
Zarathustra's teaching on redemption fails to liberate metaphysical man from the
spirit of vengeance:

> Does such thinking overcome prior reflection, overcome the spirit of
> revenge? Or does there not lie concealed in this very *stamping* [cf. *The
> Will to Power*, no. 617]—which takes all Becoming into the protection of

eternal recurrence of the same—a form of ill will *against* sheer transiency and thereby a highly spiritualized spirit of revenge? . . . What is left for us to say, if not this: Zarathustra's doctrine does not bring redemption from revenge? We do say it. Yet we say it by no means as a misconceived refutation of Nietzsche's philosophy. We do not even utter it as an objection against Nietzsche's thinking. But we say it in order to turn our attention to the fact that—and the extent to which—Nietzsche's thought too is animated by the spirit of prior reflection. [VA, 121–22; Ni 2, 228–29]

Thus Heidegger does not close the question of Nietzsche's place in the history of metaphysics. Who *is* Nietzsche's Zarathustra? Zarathustra is the advocate of the circle of life and suffering; redemption from the circle is not his proper brief. Zarathustra espouses the goal of overman; he dare not confuse himself with the goal. Zarathustra recognizes all transition to be a downgoing; he dare not quit the doorway of the moment of time. In short, the work of eternal recurrence, as the work of *thinking*, remains to be done.

THE LAST THINKER OF THE WEST

How can Nietzsche be called the *last* metaphysician and yet still be considered one metaphysician among others? If Nietzsche were wholly absorbed by the "guiding question" of metaphysics, completely oblivious to its "grounding question"; if he had thought purely and simply in terms of values, merely inverting the "above" and "below" of the Platonic hierarchy; if his analysis of nihilism had remained but a phase in the history of nihilistic metaphysics; how then could Nietzsche have exhausted the possibilities of metaphysical inquiry, of representational and valuative thought, and how could he have envisaged the event of metaphysics *as* nihilism? If the "last name" in the history of metaphysics "is not Kant, and not Hegel, but Nietzsche,"[7] then *how* is *Nietzsche* able to draw a line under his own name and so call an entire tradition to account?

From the outset of his confrontation with Nietzsche, Heidegger accords him the status of a thinker; that is, one who ponders the essence of metaphysics itself. In "What Calls for Thinking?" Heidegger designates him, not the last metaphysician, but "the last thinker of the West," *der letzte Denker des Abendlandes* (WhD? 61; cf. H, 94). The word *letzt* could mean several things:

Nietzsche the *most recent* thinker, *le dernier cri*?

Nietzsche the *ultimate*, that is, the supreme and superlative thinker?

Nietzsche the *final* thinker, that is, the thinker of finality, after whom no one is to be expected, after whom the West as such, or thinking itself, or both of these together, can no longer be what they once were?

This third understanding of the word *letzt* would of course place in jeopardy the claim of any contemporary *to be* a thinker. . . .

Nietzsche's impact on Heidegger's thought is second to none. In "What Calls for Thinking?" Heidegger deliberately couples Nietzsche's name with that of Aristotle, a telling conjunction when one remembers the cardinal position of Aristotle in awakening the question of Being. The Heidegger/Nietzsche encounter occurs across a long series of shared sites—junctions, crossroads, intersections and interceptions, underpasses and ambuscades. To cite a few:

Nietzsche's definition of a strong will as one that knows how *not* to will (*SII*, 987–89) is an unsung precursor of Heidegger's *Gelassenheit* and "commemorative thinking";

Zarathustra's cry, "Be true to the earth!" is heard again in Heidegger's pledge to the earth of the Fourfold and in his initiation of mortals to their mortality (see chapter ten, below);

Nietzsche's role, assisting Kant, Schiller, Schelling, and Hölderlin in awakening in Heidegger a sense of the primacy of art and the artwork in the question of Being, becomes clearly visible when will to power as art is proclaimed the "necessary point of departure" for Heidegger's inquiry into Nietzschean thought;

Nietzsche's critique of metaphysics helps to propel Heidegger beyond the incipient "meta-ontological turn" of his own thought—from "ontology of Dasein" to "the metaphysics of truth"—in the years immediately following the publication of *Being and Time;* and, most generally,

Nietzsche implants the suspicion that an entire epoch of thought and belief has inevitably succumbed, that what we piously call "tradition" is for the most part a product of anxiety in the face of thinking.

Beyond piety, yet still within anxiety, I ask again what Heidegger means when he calls Nietzsche *den letzten Denker des Abendlandes.* Is Nietzsche (1) the most recent, current, and topical of thinkers; is he (2) the ultimate and superlative thinker; or is he (3) the final thinker of the evening land? The first is too innocent for Heidegger, the second too edifying. Both in any case would actually be said otherwise in German. Only the third (and *last*) is risky enough, outrageous enough, literal enough, to suit Heidegger's estimation of Nietzsche. If at times nothing seems new under the sun of Heidegger's history of Being, it is because he too needs to protect himself from Nietzsche's newness. Thus Heidegger's thinking *counter to* Nietzsche remains always in service to a thinking *to encounter* him. *Auseinandersetzung* remains subtended by an *Entgegendenken,* confrontation by an encounter.

On the eve of his lecture series on Nietzsche, Heidegger defined the task of his own thought as one of bringing Nietzsche's thought "to a full enfolding" (*EM*, 28). The confrontation and encounter with Nietzsche, nascent in Heidegger's student days and still vital in the conversations of his last years, remained crucial for Heidegger—for knowing who he was and what he was to do.

All of which brings us now to the question of the *results* of Heidegger's history of Being. Can descensional reflection transcend mere intimations to hard and fast results that would be relevant for the technological age in which we live?

9 Results

For Richard Rorty

result, verb: *To arise as a consequence, effect, or conclusion from some action, process, etc.; to end or conclude in a specified manner. [Adaptation of Latin result-are, "to spring or leap back," formed on* re+saltare.*]*
—Oxford English Dictionary

Result: . . . This labor of spirit to know itself, find itself, this activity is spirit, the life of spirit itself. Its result is the concept it grasps of itself; the history of spirit the clear insight that spirit willed all this in its history.
—Hegel, Lectures on the History of Philosophy

Result: . . . Belief in the categories of reason is the cause of nihilism. . . . Final Result: . . . It is always and everywhere the hyperbolic naiveté of man, positing himself as the meaning and standard of value for things.
—Nietzsche, The Will to Power, no. 12 B

In the second volume of his *Nietzsche*, Heidegger argues that Nietzsche's "revaluation of all values" tries to win *results* from the history of nihilism and that it therefore remains nihilistic—in the sense of passive, reactive, or incomplete nihilism (*NII*, 60; cf. 85–90). The very will to a new valuation, the compulsion to rescue beings as a whole and establish positive results for their history, is a metaphysical—hence nihilistic—will: it betrays a kind of thinking that Nietzsche ought to have overcome, a "value thinking" that is too busy calculating results to confront the *nihil, das Nichts.* Heidegger himself eschews valuative-calculative thinking. In his "Letter on Humanism" he derides the elevation of beings to "values" as the most noxious of nihilisms (*BW,* 228). However, does Heidegger's thought too hope to establish results in and for the history of philosophy, precisely in its constant appeals to primordial beginnings and irrevocable ends? Is its circling about "origins" and "outcomes" in service to some transcendent standard, hence forgetful of the ontological difference? Is its yearning for results yet another instance of metaphysical nostalgia? And if the histories of metaphysics and nihilism do coalesce, as both Nietzsche and Heidegger claim, would not Heidegger's thought be nihilistic?

The final section of Hegel's *Lectures on the History of Philosophy* bears the title *Resultat*, "Result" (20, 454). The "result" of Hegel's history may be understood in two very different ways, either as the conclusive *concept*, spirit in and for itself, which would be the attained goal and absolute end of the history of philosophy, or as the ongoing *deed* or activity of thought, "eternally producing its opposite and eternally reconciling itself to it," which would be absolute postponement of the end and result. Most interpreters, especially in England and America, have adopted the first interpretation. At the same time countless commentators have raised the question I have been pursuing throughout these intimations of a history of Being, namely, that of the relation between the Hegelian and Heideggerian views of history. The guiding suspicion has been that Heidegger's "history of Being" is a mere inversion—not a radical deconstruction—of Hegel's "history of spirit." Replacing the itinerary of remembrance would be the entropy of oblivion-of-Being; but the fated or predestined character of such oblivion, its historical *necessity*, would render oblivion as absolute as Hegelian recollection. The result would be that Heidegger's thinking of history cannot shatter the ontotheological constraints it is everywhere on guard against, and that in this respect his efforts come to nothing—they constitute one more episode in the history of passive nihilism. Heidegger himself tries to quell this suspicion, as we have seen, by insisting that his thought executes a step back "out of metaphysics into the *essence* of metaphysics" (*ID*, 38–41). Yet is that not an Hegelian claim, one that ties *archē* to *telos*, guaranteeing secure results? Does the stepping back genuinely surrender all counterfeit finalities or does it cling to conclusions—results? Does it continue to confront the nothing that makes its own interpretation transitional, "metabolic," finite? If not, there is no way it can recover from the embarrassment of an exaggerated sense of self-importance. In philosophy that illness is terminal.

Richard Rorty faults Heidegger with a fatal overestimation of the importance of philosophical work in general.[1] He would agree with John B. Yeats, who asserted that "all contemplative men were in a conspiracy to overrate their state of life."[2] Rorty finds it ludicrous for Heidegger to suggest "that our present troubles are somehow due to the Plato-Nietzsche tradition . . . , that our fate is somehow linked to that tradition" (258). "Who but a philosophy professor, after all, would think that the drama of twentieth-century Europe had some essential relation to the *Vollendung der Metaphysik?*" (251).

If we consider the first act of that drama, the First World War, reviewing Sidney Bradshaw Fay's classical analysis of its immediate and distant causes—the struggle for world markets, the colonial rivalries, the fateful early alliances, the xeno-phobias flourishing on propaganda and the popular press, the circus of Kakanian (Austro-Hungarian) government, the nightmare of Russian plans for general mobilization, the bizarre Willy-Nicky telegrams—it all seems a part of that anonymous *adversity* that Merleau-Ponty perceives at the heart of our political life, more a nexus of ineluctable and incomprehensible stupidities than anything one could define as "subjecticity," "will-to-will," "calculative thought," or *"Ge-Stell."*[3] Yet might not trade warfare, mobilization, *Realpolitik,* and all the rest, even the unbelievable bungling, conceal "some essential relation" to the way Europeans think and have thought; and would it be utterly ingenuous to believe that the history of metaphysics has had at least "some essential relation" to such thought? One of the most astute observers of events leading to the Great War— Robert Musil, in *Der Mann ohne Eigenschaften*—would surely cite as one of the immediate causes the failure of the *Parallelaktion* to found an "International Committee for Precision and Soul." (Such a committee doubtless would have formulated the question of the meaning of Being!) As for our "present troubles," as Rorty cites them, "the strip mines of Montana, the assembly lines of Detroit, and the Red Guards of Shanghai," they doubtless have more to do with the given material and social forces of production, or with structures of sublimated gratification, than with "forgetfulness of Being" (252).

Heidegger is aware that the very *question* of Being is anomalous, that to raise it is to appear overweening and professorial. But the thought of Being as refusal, withdrawal, closure, and oblivion, insofar as it evokes a critique of unbridled manipulation and exploitation of beings by an insatiable will-for-more—does that thought leave Anaconda and General Motors altogether untouched? True, such a thought has no vote at stockholders' meetings; but if that is our standard, I wonder how much Dewey tempers their doings? Rorty argues that "Heidegger's weakness is that he cannot escape the notion that philosophers' difficulties are more than *just* philosophers' difficulties. . ." (258). While I thrill to the jaded tone, I cannot help thinking of the way in which our most up-to-date medical handbooks reproduce Descartes' *Traité de l'homme* in all methodological and conceptual essentials; one does not have to be a Jungian to realize that Descartes' difficulties are now everybody's headache. Is Descartes simply an exception? John Dewey's own plea for *reconstruction* in philosophy attests to the possibility that philosophers' difficulties—if the philosophers are more than academicians and the difficulties more than quibbles—may be everyone's problems, whether everyone knows it or not. And especially when no one knows it.

Rorty repudiates the "hope" that Heidegger invests in *Denken*—in a moment we will see Jacques Derrida refer to that same "hope"—because he takes it to be not only risible but also ominous in its political implications:

> Heidegger's hope is just what was worst in the tradition—the quest for the holy that turns us away from the relations between beings and beings (the relations, for example, between the ghastly apparatus of modern

technology and the people whose children will die of hunger unless that apparatus spreads over the rest of the planet). *Tout commence en mystique et finit en politique*. . . . [256]

Heidegger's preoccupation with "the holy" is indeed discomfiting. I too get dizzy in the "mirrorplay of the Fourfold," which is a bit like being "Lost in the Funhouse." Yet it is wrongheaded to confuse Heidegger with holy pictures. For him the holy has to do with the daimonic, the *nothing* which finite transcendence must confront in anxiety.[4] Even so, *das Nichts*, as a substitute for the holy, will hardly satisfy Rorty's complaint. He wants results. For the children's sake. I too want these results, and so does Heidegger. Yet Heidegger is not convinced that the spread of the ghastly apparatus *will* save the children. True, he has nothing more efficacious to suggest. Pursuing the thought of Being (better: the thought of *alētheia*, revealing and concealing) rescues us from no painful quandaries; it in no way promises relief from the complications of technology and the frustrations of politics.[5]

Because however the planetary reign of technology constitutes in Heidegger's view the single most significant result of the history of Being, the scope of the present discussion ought to be expanded somewhat. A careful reading of Heidegger's "The Question concerning Technology" is surely called for; but I will here allow the discussion to take the direction Rorty has chosen. In a paper entitled "Heidegger against the Pragmatists," an early version of a chapter planned for a forthcoming book on Heidegger, Rorty pursues the question of Heidegger, technology, and politics. The fifth section of the paper, "Pragmatism as the Poetry of Technology," contrasts Heidegger's sense of the danger in technology to Dewey's celebration of technological progress. While Heidegger can only hope—as we saw in chapter six—that the essence of technology as a totalizing mode of revealing will some day turn mankind toward revealing as such, Dewey more pragmatically hopes for the liberation of mankind from toil and the universalization of leisure. My own view of the chances for liberation from toil waits upon a decisive refutation of Sartre's analyses of the economy of scarcity in his *Critique of Dialectical Reason*. While other-directed Americans, borne on the crest of Riesman's "second revolution" and reveling in an economy of abundance and consumption, can readily dismiss scarcity as the mere birth pangs of *homo oeconomicus*, I am dubious about an abundance that remains so unevenly distributed and so tenuous even where it seems secure. As for leisure, I declare myself a latter-day Thorstein Veblen, albeit without the requisite talents. Nevertheless, my dissatisfaction with (Rorty's) Dewey does not imply complete satisfaction with Heidegger.

Whether the hazard or the promise of technology consists in "a destiny of revealing" is too high-flying a question for me to answer. But flying high often seems a form of escape. The question of technology is after all one of and for the human community; if not merely mortal in its provenance, it is surely mortal in its effects. And when all is said and done it is clear that Heidegger offers little constructive insight into matters of human community. Even though Rorty is careful not to allow the "they self" to be interpreted as though it were a chapter in Ortega's *Rebellion of the Masses*, one is still left with either the dreariness of public life in *Being and Time*, the more disturbing "deeds which found the state" of the 1930s, the cautious resistance or intransigent silence of the 1940s and 1950s, and the self-serving interviews of the 1960s. As Rorty insists, there is no good reason why Heidegger should not affirm a Deweyite conception of authentic communal Dasein with its groups of finite creatures joined in a common endeavor without eternal guarantees. Unfortunately, as commentators like Schwan, Harries, Pöggeler, and Arendt agree, Heidegger in the 1930s was far more likely than Dewey to reopen secret negotiations with Eternity (posing as Results in History) in order to seek such guarantees. The old undigested potato dumpling of the Schillerian-Hegelian *Staatsidee*.

Nevertheless, while I have no sympathy for the latter, no stomach for it, Dewey's "bourgeois liberal democracy" hardly seems substantial enough for our own ravenous times and places. It is easy to laugh at Heidegger's nostalgia for Greek pastorale. It is harder to laugh over our own bourgeois illiberal pejorocracy, utterly enthralled as it is by its mythic "Frontier" past, its Puritan confidence in the identity of wealth and grace, its Lone Ranger approach to political conflict, and its Yankee Doodle Dandy sense of finitude and restraint. Like Rorty, I would prefer to live in a world that is being systematically reshaped in order to provide human beings with enough to eat. I am less convinced than he that our present world essentially *is* such. Like Rorty, and unlike Hannah Arendt and Heidegger, I am ready to propagate the democratic *civitas pelegrina* among the stars, if not to paint Coke signs on the moon; I am ready to board Kubrick's stunning spaceships, if not Pynchon's sterile ones or Kilgore Trout's seedy ones. Yet I am not as sanguine as Rorty about Dewey's curious amalgam of science-fiction and the adventure of Christian civilization. The most judicious recent account of the results of that adventure I take to be Stanley Elkins's *The Living End*. It is certainly possible that the saving power has risen behind Heidegger's back, in the pragmatic USA, but that would only mean (reading Hölderlin's as a speculative proposition) that North Armorica is also the site of the gravest danger, the danger that Heidegger in "What Calls for Thinking?" refers to as "devastation."

The devastation of hectic thoughtlessness is of course not restricted to the Western Hemisphere, and Rorty is correct when he insists that Heidegger is the last one who could claim that he has gotten history right. While I cannot share Rorty's dew(e)y optimism, I do share many of his suspicions about Heidegger's politically undifferentiated condemnation of technology. However, I would shift those doubts from the realm of epistemological skepticism to the historical theme of nihilism in our public life and our technological and economic structures and institutions. And my suspicions would try to become interrogations.

It may well be that Heidegger—thinking of technology and the *nihil*—remains as trapped in destructive nihilism as any of us. When he declares to the editors of *Der Spiegel* that "only a god can rescue us now," is it courageous acceptance of our common fate or capitulation before the task of twentieth-century political life on earth? Is it a halfway romantic yearning for salvation, a culpable blindness to those interests whose investments feed technology and so propel its essence? When he denies that any current political system has the least inkling of what the technological will-to-will has in store for humankind, is it unclouded insight into what is happening in both Germanies, in China and India alike, in Cuba as well as in the wretched lands of the *junta*? Or is it a refusal to recognize genuine differences among political systems, a refusal that tacitly serves one particular system and so remains "German Ideology"? When he condemns contemporary art and literature in the West for their "homelessness," insisting that all things "essential and great" must be rooted in a "homeland," can that be anything more than the last vanishing wisp of romantic nationalist nostalgia, that is to say, incomplete nihilism? For must not "homelessness" be the site of Heidegger's own intimations? Finally, when he denies philosophy any role at all in efforts to alter "the world situation," is it clear-sighted perception of the end of philosophy, a candid recognition of limits, or is it merely a negation of illusory totalizing alternatives, and thus passively nihilistic to the core? The "silence" of the "other kind" of thinking: does it hold secret converse with Hölderlin and let all the rest drop, in what Nietzsche calls a "Buddhism of the deed"?

I mean none of these questions rhetorically. Neither can I answer any of them quickly and so put them aside. It may be that none of the questions refers any more to Heidegger than to myself. Such questions do make a difference, not merely for the future of Heidegger's thought but for the present of our own. They are *pragmatic* questions, however precipitous they may be. They are questions, as I think Rorty's paper shows, for Heidegger *and* (not *against*) the pragmatists.

But let me return now to Rorty's earlier paper, "Overcoming the Tradition: Heidegger and Dewey." For Rorty's fullest statement of his complaint against Heidegger (I have abridged it here) ends with an important claim:

> Heidegger's attachment to the notion of "philosophy"—the pathetic notion that even after metaphysics goes, something called "Thought" might remain—is simply the sign of Heidegger's own fatal attachment to

the tradition: the last infirmity of the greatest of the German professors. . . . No matter how much Heidegger seems to have overcome
our professional urge to compete with the great dead philosophers on
their own ground, no matter how much he may try to distance himself
from the tradition (not to mention his fellow professors), he is still
insistent that the tradition offered us "words of Being." He still thinks
that the place where philosophy was is the place to be. He thinks that to
cease thinking about what Plato and Kant were thinking about is to be
diminished, to lose hold of what is most important, to sink into darkness.
If he were true to his own dictum that we should "cease all overcoming,
and leave metaphysics to itself," he would have nothing to say, nowhere
to point. *The whole force of Heidegger's thought lies in his account of the
history of philosophy.* [256–57]

The complaint must be amended somewhat. Heidegger does hold that the
tradition offers us "words of Being." Yet these turn out to be bare traces, hints
that the tradition preserved in spite of itself, leaving them unthought. Hence
Heidegger's ceaseless preoccupation with and criticism of the tradition. It is not
that "the place where philosophy was is the place to be." That place is gone: no
one realizes that more clearly than Heidegger, not even the hero of reconstruction in philosophy. Nor is it a question of the fear "to cease thinking about what
Plato and Kant were thinking about." Heidegger's fear is that we have not yet
really begun to think with them. What *were* Plato and Kant thinking about?
Can we be sure it makes no difference, that we can dispense with them, before
knowing what they were about?

Rorty's claim, however, is correct. The whole force of Heidegger's thought
lies in his account of the history of philosophy—as the history of Being as
presencing (*Anwesen, ousia*), named but not thought in the history of metaphysics. Yet the force of Heidegger's thought is deflected by two powerful
ambiguities. First, the tradition is rooted in the meaning of Being as presence,
Vorhandenheit, Anwesenheit, and so on, yet the tradition nowhere thematizes
these; Heidegger's own relation to the tradition is therefore ambiguous, in the
sense that his interest lies precisely in what the tradition did *not* think. Second,
the fundamental experience of *Being and Time*—oblivion of Being and the
finitude of Dasein—compels Heidegger's hermeneutics of the tradition to be
both radically destructive (that is, dismantling and subverting) and constantly
aware of its own limitations in language and in thought, due to its long gestation
in the tradition. Even the young Heidegger knows, as Richard Rorty and John
Dewey do not seem to know (perhaps it would be Un-American to know it),
that all courageous and forthright decisions to abandon metaphysics result in
naive reduplications of its patterns of thought. The passion to be original, to

start from scratch, to roll up our sleeves and attack our "present troubles," dissipates itself in second-hand and third-rate replays.

Jacques Derrida has not simply decided to quit the House of Being and let it fall to ruin; he wavers between the call to preserve the tradition and the need to escape it. However, such wavering is not indecision but strategy, a strategy that animates all his work. The need to escape the tradition is impressed upon Derrida by Nietzsche, who throws the histories of spirit and Being into turmoil precisely by locating them in the context of the history of nihilism. If Derrida has a word to oppose to Spirit and Being it is *différance*, which is not a concept, not a term reducible to the metaphysics of presence. Yet Derrida is wary of this word as well, which he intentionally disfigures, alters in the writing, in order to prevent its becoming a name.

> There will be no unique name, not even the name of Being. It must be conceived without *nostalgia*; that is, it must be conceived outside the myth of the purely maternal or paternal language belonging to the lost fatherland of thought. On the contrary, we must *affirm* it—in the sense that Nietzsche brings affirmation into play—with a certain laughter and with a certain dance.[6]

It is precisely "nostalgia"—one thinks of Camus' critique of Husserl's transcendental phenomenology: *"Cette nostalgie d'unité, cet appétit d'absolu"*[7]—that Derrida sees in Heidegger's quest for Being, "the quest for the proper word and the unique name."[8] He also calls it "Heideggerian hope"—one thinks of Richard Rorty's "such a faint, modest, and inarticulate hope" (256). Derrida extinguishes that hope by tracing the play of simulacra or signs in "the text of metaphysics." He jots notes in the margins. Just as the simulacra of the text efface themselves, so too is Derrida's work self-effacing yet distracting, marginal yet penetrating, silent yet obtrusive. One of the consequences of his thought is the dislocation of all talk about "epochs" and "outermost points" in the "history of Being" by which one would establish unequivocal, eschatological, apocalyptic results. Nevertheless, the following passage cannot suppress the claim that *différance* is "older" than the history of Being (or: "'older'" in quotation marks!), and cannot avoid mention of the present "age" (without markings):

> Perhaps we must try to think this *unheard-of* thought, this silent tracing: namely, that the history of Being (the thought of which is committed to the Greco-Western logos), as it is itself produced across the ontological difference, is only one epoch of the *diapherein*. Then we could no longer

even call it an 'epoch.'. . . . Thus, in a particular and very strange way, différance [is] 'older' than the ontological difference or the truth of Being. In this age it can be called the play of traces.[9]

The Heideggerian text cited most often in Derrida's "Différance" is "The Anaximander Fragment" (1946; EGT, 13–58). One should not be deluded into thinking that this text is "representative" of Heidegger's views on the history of philosophy: a remarkably different view would result if one were to study "the existential origin of history in terms of the historicity of Dasein" (SZ, section 76), on the one hand, or "The End of Philosophy and the Task of Thinking" and "Hegel and the Greeks," on the other. It may well be that "The Anaximander Fragment" is the *least* typical of Heidegger's essays on the history of philosophy.[10] Yet much of what I have discussed so far—the questions of Heidegger's thirst for results in the history of philosophy, nihilism, the overestimation of philosophy, the possible abandonment of the House of Being for the play of traces—arrives at a critical juncture in this essay.

Near the outset of "The Anaximander Fragment" the following passage appears:

> But what entitles antiquity to address us, presumably the latest late-comers with respect to philosophy? Are we latecomers in a history now racing toward its end, an end which in its increasingly sterile order of uniformity brings everything to an end? Or does there lie concealed in the historical and chronological remoteness of the fragment the historic proximity of something unsaid, something that will speak out in times to come?
>
> Do we stand in the very twilight of the most monstrous transformation our planet has ever undergone, the twilight of that epoch in which earth itself hangs suspended? Do we confront the evening of a night which heralds another dawn? . . . Will the land of evening[11] overwhelm Occident and Orient alike, transcending whatever is merely European to become the location of the more originally destined history that is coming? . . . What can all merely historiological philosophies of history tell us about our history if they only dazzle us with surveys of its sedimented stuff; if they explain history without ever thinking out, from the essence of history, the fundamentals of their way of explaining events, and the essence of history, in turn, from Being itself? [EGT, 16–17]

I cite this passage—which consists entirely of questions—at length because it focuses on the hermeneutical problem of history as such, on the vast span between antiquity and modernity (beginning and end, the respective "places" of initiators and latecomers), and on the vaguely felt possibility that the future may disclose something concealed and "unsaid" in and about the very beginnings. Heidegger descries the twilight of a new epoch, although he knows that it is twilight of evening, an evening facing a night. A scenario of hope, but also of hazard. He ventures to hope (or to hazard) that the new dawn will somehow re-enact or perhaps enact for the first time the dawn of Ionia, the original illumination (as Hegel would say) of the *Abendland*. Beginning and end would somehow converge, then vanish:

> The antiquity pervading the Anaximander fragment belongs to the dawn of early times in the land of evening. But what if that which is early outdistanced everything late; if the very earliest far surpassed the very latest? What once occurred in the dawn of our destiny would then come, as what once occurred, at the last (*eschaton*), that is, at the departure of the long-hidden destiny of Being. The Being of beings is gathered (*legesthai*, *logos*) in the ultimacy of its destiny. The essence of Being hitherto disappears, its truth still veiled. The history of Being is gathered in this departure. The gathering in this departure, as the gathering (*logos*) at the outermost point (*eschaton*) of its essence hitherto, is the eschatology of Being. As something fateful, Being itself is inherently eschatological. . . .
>
> If we think within the eschatology of Being, then we must someday anticipate the former dawn in the dawn to come; today we must learn to ponder this former dawn through what is imminent. [*EGT*, 18]

What could be the object of such an eschatology? The last things—the ultimate results? Can we really expect to find in our cybernetics and cyclotrons, our world trade and global wars, simulacra of *dikē*/*adikia*, "order" and "disorder"? And if we do find convergences, does it mean anything more than that we are bound to read into an ancient text the preoccupations of our own time? Can Heidegger truly be trying to think eschatology the other way round—to think *genesis* and *phthora*, coming-to-be and passing-away "according to the ordinance of time," as somehow informing our own frenzied world? Can it be more than the rhetoric of pedagogy when he asserts that Anaximander is *ahead of* rather than *behind* us? Once history has been turned around in such fashion, how are we to know whether we are coming or going? Matters are apparently worse than Rorty even suspects.

Heidegger invites our ridicule. Yet as we smirk, particular segments of the Anaximander fragment begin to disturb us, especially the phrase *kata to chreōn*, "according to necessity," which nowadays sounds more like a leaden curse than a hymn to spirit. (And which sound would be closer to Anaximander's sense?)

To Heidegger, *chreōn* signifies the "usage" according to which beings emerge from unconcealment, linger awhile in presence, then disappear in order to leave space for others; another name for the usage is "the jointure of order," by which presence is "handed over" (cf. *hē cheir*, "hand") to beings, but which itself never becomes present; hence a third name, "the self-veiling essence of Being" (49–52). The usage and jointure of order (*dikē*) leave only traces in the text of metaphysics. When the Being of beings is called *actualitas* (a futile effort to render Aristotle's *energeia*), the granting of presence slides unobtrusively yet irremovably into the realm of what is taken for granted—present beings. The event of presencing itself withdraws: necessity becomes the lidless eye of spirit or the blind impetus of billiard balls, becomes theology, then classical physics and history. The two last yield results in the areas of technology and scholarship, although they do not touch the mystery:

> Man has already begun to overwhelm the entire earth and its atmo-
> sphere, to arrogate to himself in forms of energy the concealed powers of
> nature, and to submit future history to the planning and ordering of a
> world government. This same defiant man is utterly at a loss simply to
> say what *is*; to say *what* this *is*—that a thing *is*. [*EGT*, 57]

In Heidegger's view the implacable will-to-will of modern technology and the oblivion of Being spawned in ancient times are two sides of the same coin—better, two readings of the Gestaltist's perceptual puzzle. By tracing the outlines of the first he is led to the second; by meditating on the second he claims insight into the essence of the first. His inquiry into Anaximander employs histo-riographical and philological tools, measures out the historical distance. Yet genuine engagement with the fragment occurs in another way: "Curiously enough, the saying first resonates when we set aside the claims of our own familiar ways of representing things, and ask ourselves in what the confusion of the contemporary world's fate consists" (57). The "familiar ways of representing things" are those taken by the scholarly discussion of Anaximander, the tradi-tion of "Presocratic" philosophy, and our understanding of the history of ideas as what lies behind us, available as results for research. To inquire into contempo-rary confusions, however, rather than rely on tried and tested academic sup-ports—that is a risky undertaking whose principal presuppositions, namely, that contemporary problems and the ancient inscription or palimpsest stem from the same source, and that the source will show itself more or less undisguised in each, can in no way be validated.

"Eschatology of Being" nonetheless embraces both presuppositions: the *logos* or gathering at the outermost point or *eschaton* is a gathering for *departure*. The departure involves the long-concealed fate of Being, the "essence" and provenance of Being as such, which now vanishes, "its truth still veiled." And yet if the epoch of Being closes upon its own secrets, reticent to the end, whence the confidence that once was will show itself again? Whence the putative identity of the two dawns in our present dusk? How are we to anticipate "the singularity of the dawn in the singularity of what is coming," when what is to come first of all is the closure of night? Does such anticipation foist its own obscurities onto Anaximander? Dawn and dusk both bestow twilight, but twilight is an ambiguity, not an identity; and it is Heidegger himself, as we shall see, who warns us not to try to turn night into day (VA, 151). Or does Heidegger mean that it is *the reticence of Being* itself, the pervasive ambiguity then as now, which we are to experience? If that were the case then all results in the history of philosophy would become utterly tenuous; the history of Being as withdrawal would recoil on every effort to interpret both dawn and dusk. Would such recoil frustrate all historical meaning, disperse the hardwon results of all historiological toil?

Hannah Arendt suggests that the secret of Heidegger's "anticipation of the former dawn in the dawn to come" is actually that in "The Anaximander Fragment" there is "no place for a 'History of Being'. . . ; Being, sheltered in its concealment, has no history."[12] Again: "Being, in its enduring withdrawal," because it is absent, has "no history in the realm of errancy," that is to say, the realm of human history.[13] The result would be what we heard Michel Haar claim earlier, in chapter seven, namely, two histories, a secular and a sacred; it would make of Heidegger not so much the secretary to Being ("Thinking says what the truth of Being dictates") but its inspired high-priest ("The poetizing essence of thinking preserves the sway of the truth of Being"). Ingenious as Hannah Arendt's account is, and as troubling as its consequences undoubtedly are—since the division into two histories would simply ape the Platonic *chōrismos* and thus collapse into incomplete nihilism—it falters in that according to Heidegger Being *reveals itself* within our sole history, if only through traces, *as* withdrawn; errancy is the only history we have, and the thinker of "the truth of Being" safeguards those traces of presencing as intimations of the history of Being. "Truth" (*Wahrheit*) has no other sense than the "preserve" (*die Wahr, Wahrnis*) of those traces (H, 321; EGT, 36). In this "historic dialogue between thinkers" no one is privy to the Word, no one is secretary by appointment, and all the high-priests, like Zarathustra's pope, are "retired." Nevertheless, the problem of our proximity to the preserve, to those traces that have to be identified, deciphered, and interpreted, looms as gigantic and insoluble as ever. For traces, preservations, are *results*.

There is no doubt that in later years Heidegger grew more cautious about interpreting the truth of Being (a phrase he stopped using in the 1950s and 1960s), and especially about asserting identities in its history between an unknown future and an undisclosed past. His role for example in the Heraclitus seminar conducted by him and Eugen Fink in 1966–67 is almost exclusively a cautionary one: Heidegger reminds Fink and the participants again and again that the 2,500 years that separate them from Heraclitus are truly impassable, that there is no path to the world Heraclitus knew except the bumpy and interminable *via negativa*. The thesis of "Hegel and the Greeks" is every bit as modest: while for Hegel the Greeks have "not yet" discovered the full identity of substance and subject, for Heidegger the Greeks' experience of *alētheia* has "not yet" been sufficiently pondered by us. Yet Heidegger never abandoned his conviction that these thinkers are of vital importance, that in spite of the great strides made by the philological sciences such thinkers still have everything to tell us, and that they dare not be relegated to the status of antique curios which from our advanced position we can observe with mixed curiosity and condescension.

But now to conclude, state results. It is surely pathetic to believe or hope that at the end of metaphysics some sort of "other thinking" will effect any real change in the world. Hollywood cowboys will still vie for the Presidency—and they will win. We will continue to learn the names of newborn nations from reports on infant mortality rates. The odd thing is that while Heidegger entertains no hope of dramatic change, he still insists that thinking—as a *possibility*—is the most important thing we possess. In "What Calls for Thinking?" (*WhD?*, 161) Heidegger writes:

> Thinking—more precisely, the attempt and the task to think—is now approaching an era when the high demands which traditional thinking believed it was meeting, and claimed it had to meet, become untenable. The way of the question "What is called thinking?" lies even now in the shadow of this inadequacy, which can be described in four statements: (1) Thinking does not bring knowledge as do the sciences; (2) Thinking does not produce usable practical wisdom; (3) Thinking solves no cosmic riddles; (4) Thinking does not endow us directly with the power to act. As long as we still subject thinking to these four demands, we shall overrate and overtax it. Both excesses prevent us from returning to a no longer customary modesty and from persisting in it, amid the bustle of a civilization that clamors daily for a fresh supply of the latest novelties, and daily chases after excitement. And yet the way of thinking, the way of the question "What calls for thinking?", remains unavoidable as we go into the coming era.

Perhaps that too is pathetic. Yet it would be piteous to suppose that simple abstention from thought and neglect of Nietzsche, Parmenides, and all the rest would make our world more intelligent and intelligible. Here Heidegger, ornery and paradoxical as he may be, is right: when it comes to our ways of thinking, the past is omnipresent insofar as we are ignorant of it, and it is our future whether or not we inquire. The past is anything but passed.

If that is so, however, then all hopes of "overcoming" the tradition must be surrendered. Heidegger has attempted this through his "step back." For Derrida the *Schritt zurück* becomes a leap rather than a mere step, not Kierkegaard's leap of faith but a bound beyond the cloying piety of the House of Being, a leap in dance, a *saltus* of Nietzschean affirmation. Insofar as Heidegger's intimations of a history of Being tend to seek necessary results by fixing on origins and ends, that history falls prey to the suspicion that it is but one more effort to rescue and restore the past, to find the concept and perform the deed, an effort ensconced in the history of reactive nihilism, dreaming all the old dreams. When Heidegger's thought is most pious and insistent, least light-hearted and ironic, when it takes itself abominably seriously, Nietzschean/Derridean laughter is a welcome corrective. Yet the *resaltus* of deconstruction has its own limitations and dangers: the play of disciples can become self-indulgent, the "yes" of their ecstatic nihilism can become the hee-haw of the jackass (cf. *Thus Spoke Zarathustra*, IV, "The Awakening"). We are caught between *tierischem Ernst* and asinine hilarity.[14]

"'Results' are given only where there is reckoning and calculation," notes Heidegger (*NII*, 85; *Ni 4*, 48). More fitting than reckoning with results is that modicum of philosophy to which Whitman refers in his "Backward Glance O'er Travel'd Roads": "I think I have at least enough philosophy not to be too absolutely certain of any thing, or any results." More fitting than calculation of results where the history of philosophy is concerned is the renewed leap back, whether it be back to Plato or Kant or Dewey, whether it be sober (as Heidegger insists) or with levity (as Derrida suggests), back-tracking, double-checking, interrupting the endless conversation with an occasional question.

PART FOUR
Intimations of Mortality

10 Mortality, Interpretation, and the Poetical Life

For Joan Stambaugh and J. L. Mehta

Toward the end of his article, "Nietzsche's Proclamation: 'God is dead,'" Heidegger notes the sense of danger in Nietzsche's thought and the anxiety he communicates to his readers. Yet Heidegger would not divert us from the danger or shelter us from the anxiety. For what is at stake in such anxiety is the very matter or "sake" of thinking: thinking itself dwells in anxiety, and must sustain that dwelling with care. The "later" Heidegger rejoins the "early": "Anxiety in the face of thinking is . . . anxiety in the face of anxiety" (*H*, 246).

In his article, "The Critique of Subjectivity and Cogito in the Philosophy of Heidegger," Paul Ricoeur writes: "The basic difference, perhaps, between the later Heidegger and Heidegger I would be that the self no longer finds its authenticity in freedom unto death, but in *Gelassenheit*, which is the gift of the poetical life."[1] Ricoeur formulates carefully what many others have argued in a cruder fashion, namely, that Heidegger's later preoccupations with *Sein* abandon the "existentialist" trappings of *Dasein* and of anxiety in the face of death in favor of the more high-minded contemplation of Being and the *language* of Being. Against Ricoeur cautiously, and against those cruder formulations polemically, I would like to argue that *Gelassenheit* is already at work in the analysis of anxious Dasein in *Being and Time* (1927), and that anxiety in the face of death remains central to *Gelassenheit* (1959) and to the thoughtful-poetical life. Though the second half of the argument will receive fuller treatment here, some comment on the role of *Gelassenheit*, "releasement" or "letting-be," in the analysis of Dasein is needed.

As I understand it, the crucial problem of Heidegger's hermeneutics of Dasein, in which the disclosure of Dasein's primordial finitude is to be secured, is *to let death be*. Letting *finitude* come to light invokes the problem of *letting-be as such*. *Gelassenheit* is precisely that hermeneutical project of achieving a mode of thought and language beyond any sort of representational, valuative, or manipulative consciousness, all of which in their will to power obscure that dimension in which the finitude of Dasein plays. In *Being and Time* Heidegger selects the phenomenon of anxiety in the face of death as the one whose phenomenological description and hermeneutical pursuit will display the elemental character of Dasein as care. Because anxiety is a remarkably individualizing phenomenon, the description of it must banish the idle talk, whimsical curiosity, and tranquilized bustle characteristic of Dasein's everyday modes of behavior, and allow Dasein to stand in the simplicity of its Being-there. Yet precisely on that account the ontological explication of anxiety confronts enormous difficulties in bringing the phenomenon to language and communication. At the very heart of the experience of anxiety lies an excruciating silence, in which words *about* anxiety tumble over one another and issue hollow sounds. This is true even when the "professor of philosophy" speaks most coldly and abstractly, without visible signs of fear and trembling.[2] In "What is Metaphysics?" Heidegger describes the crisis into which discourse is thrown in the experience of anxiety in terms we first heard in chapter two: "Anxiety robs us of speech." *"Die Angst verschlägt uns das Wort"* (W, 9; BW, 103). *Verschlagen* means to strike dumb, to deprive of breath, to distract from a path of thought, to board-up and shut-away. Anxiety strikes us dumb. "Because beings as a whole slip away, so that just the nothing crowds round, in the face of anxiety all utterance of the 'is' falls silent." One can speak of anxiety at all only by *releasing* oneself into the nothing, that is, by becoming free from "those idols everyone has and to which he is wont to go cringing" (W, 19; BW, 112). Idols—that means: words. A phenomenological description of anxiety—in the face of death, thinking, and itself—must therefore be an anxious description, one that experiences its radical finitude, its being-towards-an-end, its metabolism, in its every word. The death of Dasein is anticipated when the nothing in which its interpreting is suspended returns the echo of a burst of laughter to every one of interpretations's words. The death of Dasein is anticipated not so much in chit-chat at funerals as at the writing desk.

In section 40 of *Being and Time* Heidegger argues that Dasein's flight from its own understanding of Being, a flight from the shadowy presence of its finitude into the cheerful light of its everyday preoccupations, *because it is a fleeing in the face of itself,* inadvertently discloses something of its fundamental Being. Dasein's "falling" away from itself trails clouds of its inglory: that on which Dasein opens as it averts its glance and pursues evasion, namely, being-in-the-world as such, can be phenomenologically interpreted. "More primordial than man is the finitude of Dasein in him" (KPM, 207). It is the primordiality of the alienation that enables Dasein to flee in the face of itself, of the dimension which in the experience of anxiety opens and closes with lightning-like speed, that gives Time and Being to interpretation. Thus anxiety is not an experience from which Dasein needs redemption. Quite the reverse. Anxiety is Dasein's opening onto its ownmost way to be, an opening that only needs to be cultivated and secured from forgetfulness. For anxiety is that experience which underlies *all* disclosure and *every* possibility of interpretation, including, arguably, those of "joy" or "profound boredom." *Being and Time*, section 40:

> Here the disclosure and the disclosed are existentially selfsame, in such a way that in the latter the world has been disclosed as world, and being-in as a possibility-being that is individualized, pure, and thrown. This makes it clear that with the phenomenon of anxiety a distinctive disposition has become a theme for interpretation. [SZ, 188]

In the description of the phenomenon of anxiety Heidegger's existential analysis reaches that crucial point where disclosure and the being disclosed converge. It is here that the hermeneutical circle is decisively joined, and Heidegger's thoughtful descent into it achieved. Thinking *is*, only insofar as it is thinking-within-anxiety, determinedly open to anxiety in the face of death. This remains the case even when it receives "the gift of the poetical life."

In *Hermann und Dorothea* Goethe remarks that neither the wise nor the pious can let death be: the wise man drags death back into life by teaching us how to handle its consequences, while the pious one exults his way past death, celebrating it as the threshold of a more perfect health and well-being. *Beiden wird zum Leben der Tod.* "For both, death becomes life." But metaphysics is both wise and pious: for it death means life, just as night means day. I suspect that in the history of metaphysics—which is always the history of morals—subtlety of conceptual manipulation and violence in the handling of death are proportionally related, the one increasing in step with the other. Conceptual transparency thickens with the opacity of death, since death violates every transparency; conceptual manipulation must therefore resort to violence and repression. What should it mean then to let death be? In "What Calls for Thinking?" Heidegger announces that his thinking wants to let the blossoming tree remain in the meadow where it stands, to let it lie before us by taking heed of it (*WhD?*, 18). Yet how are we to understand that much earlier pronouncement in *Being and Time*, to the effect that hermeneutical thinking must let *death* stand as it appears? What sort of resolute openness would this thinking require?[3]

Man is the being that lives, speaks, and dies: so the Greeks understood him. Yet man is also *to deinotaton,* as the second chorus of *Antigone* says, the most terrible being, "terrible in the sense of the overpowering power which compels . . . true anxiety" (*EM*, 114). However, man's power confronts obstacles: his force goes out to meet the overpowering power of the whole of being. Not man but Being is overpowering: man exercises force on the overpowering, and so is "violent in the midst of the overpowering." Although he must be designated as being-in-the-world, man is the being that is least at home among beings; humanity is made to dwell in the unfamiliar and to exercise power in the face of appearances. Such exercise of power Heidegger calls *interpretation.*

> Only when we grasp that the use of power in language, in understanding, in forming and building, helps to . . . bring-forth the act of force which lays out paths into the surrounding power of beings, only then will we understand the uncanniness of all violence. [EM, 120–21]

The outcome of man's violence against the acknowledged overpowering may be called *Gelassenheit.* The exercise of power in language, especially the language of poetizing-thinking, actualizes the Being (or presence) of a thing and makes it effectively real: the exercise of power in language is the "effecting" of the thing (EM, 122). When the poet utters the word "sea" as though that word were spoken for the first time, his work of art brings that being to presence and lets it shine. However, in order to call the being to presence, in order to utter the word at all, the poet or thinker must *respond* to the encroachment of the thing. He and his power are at the mercy of the overpowering power of being as a whole—in this case, of that being Melville's Ishmael calls the "ungraspable phantom of life," which is "the key to it all." Man's every utterance therefore hangs on the edge of an abyss: such is the anxiety of all art, and indeed of all language, which in the vertigo of its most mighty naming stands always on the brink of nothing. Emily Dickinson, number 1563:

> By homely gift and hindered Words
> The human heart is told
> Of Nothing—
> "Nothing" is the force
> That renovates the World—

The violence of interpretation which makes mortals most powerful is also that which makes their Being most enigmatic and precarious, inasmuch as there is one uncanny and overpowering thing under whose aspect all interpretation turns mute. "All violence shatters against one thing. That is death. . . . It is not only when he comes to die, but always and essentially, that man is without exit in the face of death" (EM, 120). "Anxiety" brings together in one word an experience of the violence of interpretation and of death. This confluence Heidegger calls *mortality.*

The kind of language suited to letting-be, which aims its violence at its own tendency to forget its fatality, Heidegger calls mortal gesture or bidding, *das Geheiss.* In an article given the unadorned title "Language," Heidegger describes the event of language in the statement, *"Die Sprache spricht"* (*US*, 20; cf. 147–48). Language speaks. By emphasizing the first term of this apparently violently tautologous assertion, Heidegger denies that it is man who speaks. His denial would affirm that man speaks genuinely only insofar as he listens and responds to the speaking of language. Who then is man? Man is the mortal. In his essay, "The Thing," Heidegger writes:

> Mortals are human beings. They are called mortals because they can die. To die means to make death as death possible. Only man dies. . . . Death is the monument of nothing, that is, of that which is by no means "existent" but which comes to presence nonetheless, even as the very secret of Being itself. As the monument of nothing, death is the hideaway of Being. We call mortals "mortal," not because their life on earth ends, but because they make death possible as death. The mortals are who they are, mortals, being present in the hideaway of Being. They are the essential relation of presence to Being as Being. [*VA*, 177; cf. *US*, 22–23]

This passage elucidates several issues:

1. The hermeneutics of language and the language of hermeneutics both require that interpretation open itself determinedly to intimations of the mortality of Dasein, the mortality of *Mensch*.

2. Only man, conceived as primordially finite Dasein, exists in that dimension of Being which discloses all things and Being *as* Being. Only man is present to the nothing where Being itself hides. Only man can die. Only man: neither god nor beast, nor an amalgam of the two, that is, the philosopher.[4]

3. The name Heidegger offers to designate the presencing of beings, and of Being as Being, is the "nothing." It is the region in which Being hides. This mortal region into which man finds himself thrown, and the way in which man must preserve that region, are further elaborated in a passage from the essay "Building Dwelling Thinking":

> Mortals are human beings. They are called mortals because they can die. To die means to make death *as* death possible. Only man dies, and indeed he dies continuously as long as he remains on the earth, under the sky, and in the face of divinities. If we name the mortals, then we think the other three along with them, although we do not reflect upon the unity of the four. We call this unity *the Fourfold*. Mortals *are* in the Fourfold insofar as they *dwell*. But the fundamental trait of dwelling is protective cultivation [*das Schonen*]. Mortals dwell in a way that protectively cultivates the Fourfold in its presencing. [*VA*, 150]

I make the following observations:

1. Being able to die, which means sustaining an openedness to the anxiety of mortal disclosure, is called "dwelling." .

2. Dwelling means care and cultivation of the way in which earth, sky, divinity, and mortality itself come to presence and/or withdraw.

3. Such cultivation waits upon mortals—those who alone are able to die—and is itself fourfold:

(a) Mortals dwell on the earth by rescuing it from all forms of exploitation. The fundamental form of exploitation is the careless violence of any interpretation that flees from "that thing" against which all interpretation shatters. Exploitation is the opiate of thinking. To rescue the earth from the slumbering violence of interpretation means to "let it be free in its own coming-to-presence." To rescue the earth means to fulfill the task of Nietzsche's thinking: *"Bleibt der Erde treu!"* "Remain true to the earth!"

(b) Mortals dwell under the sky, writes Heidegger, insofar as they welcome the light of day and receive the dark of night and do not try to transform the one into the other.

(c) Mortals dwell on the earth under the sky insofar as they await divinities, which they can neither concoct nor command. Indeed, as the *Beiträge* insist, godhead is experienced in its ultimacy as passage (*Vorbeigang*).

(d) Mortals dwell insofar as they protect and cultivate intimations of their mortality, and this by letting them be:

> Mortals dwell insofar as they conduct their own essence, which is that they make death as death possible, into the usage of this possibility, in order that it be a good death. That mortals come to meet the essence of death in no way means that they make death, as empty nothingness, their goal; nor does it mean that they are to becloud dwelling by gaping toward its end. [VA, 151]

What Heidegger here recounts is in fact the full unfolding of Zarathustra's *Untergang*: "That your dying be no blasphemy against man and earth, my friends: that is my plea to the honey of your soul."[5] Dwelling then means: to let the earth be free, to receive the glowing and darkening sky, to await divinities, to encounter mortality—and to reflect on the unity of the Fourfold by confronting without subterfuge the nothing. Yet confrontation with the nothing is the task already undertaken—though surely not completed—in *Being and Time*.

Reflection on the possibility of Dasein's death requires a transformed relation to language. Only in the bidding gesture does the mortal let language speak, and the gesture that wraps itself in folds of silence so as not to frighten the world away, the most faithful gesture, is poetizing thought. Poetizing is mortal dwelling and is essential building because its thinking listens to the overpowering speech of language. Poetizing "does not soar beyond or surpass the earth, in order to leave it behind or hover over it; poetizing first brings man to earth, onto the earth, thus bringing him into dwelling" (VA, 192). Accustomed as we are to a poetry that most often leaps up to behold rainbows, the conjunction of poetizing and dying seems bizarre and even contradictory. Or at least in bad taste. Yet Heidegger, like Hölderlin, denies that the wings of poesy are designed to transport mortals to imagined idylls; he affirms that poetry enables man to dwell *auf dieser Erde*.[6] Goethe too offers examples of poetic thinking that dwells on the earth.

The essential affinity of poetry and mortality is enigmatically portrayed in the first scene of the second part of *Faust*, lines 5505ff. A herald announces poetic images mystical and ghostly, images he cannot grasp, and whose significance he therefore cannot explain. Through the crowd of images a glittering coach draws near; it carries a youthful driver and his master. The driver challenges the herald—who may be the poet himself—to name and describe the two allegorical figures of the coach. Responding to the challenge, the herald describes the driver as a charming and seductive youth; his master seems a wealthy and magnanimous king, so worthy that he defies description. The driver then reveals the identity of his master: it is Plutus, god of plenty, who is also (although the clever youth does not say so) king of the domain of the dead. The "extravagant youth" himself is *Poesie*. Wealth-and-death (Plutus, Hades) advances in the coach of poetry, although poetry is by no means simply his vehicle. Poesy affirms:

> My riches too reveal no end;
> For I am Plutus' fairest friend.
> I liven and cheer his feast and dance;
> Whate'er he lacks—that I dispense.

Turning to the god of the underworld, the youthful driver demands:

> Don't I steer nicely wherever you say?
> Am I not there when you point the way?

Plutus freely concedes that Poesy is to him a kindred spirit:

> You are spirit of my spirit.
> You act upon my every whim,

Are richer than I myself have been.
I am grateful that your service I command,
Greenest of branches in my garland.
To all a true word I commend:
My beloved Son, in you am I well content!

Here Plutus is designated only as dispenser of wealth. Yet for the ancients, as Goethe knew well, the earth yields her fruits to mortals from underground, in proximity to the kingdom of death. Death rules the domain of images into which the heraldic poet is thrown. The original herald, the original bearer of the magic wand or *rhabdos*, is Hermes, conductor of souls to the underworld and namesake of the descensional reflection of hermeneutics. Like Poesy, Hermes is wily and seductive; he signifies and leads; he devotes himself to wealth-and-death. Such is "the gift of the poetical life."

Poetizing-thinking speaks more softly but ultimately more powerfully than the assertory, calculative lingo of science and technology—if not as silently as poetry itself. Thinking *must* make assertions: Heidegger makes what he himself calls "the naked assertion" that the poem offers access to what is originally achieved in language (*US*, 16). Heidegger's thinking within anxiety makes a strenuous call for the gentle cultivation of the poetic word. Not only does mortality speak in a language that thinks within anxiety, but speech also mortalizes in that same language: language is not thought's vehicle of escape from anxiety but its anxious opening onto mortality. Heidegger's "naked assertion" is itself a mortal gesture. Inasmuch as interpretation has shattered against "that thing," all assertion becomes gesture. Mortality itself is that horizon always present but ungraspable—the interminably open yet finite horizon of mere intimation—and interpretation can only devote itself to the Sisyphan task of letting it *be*.

11 Strokes of Love and Death

For Jacques Derrida

Historians will call them contemporaries. Martin Heidegger was born a scant two-and-a-half years after Georg Trakl. As young men both read intently the novels of Dostoevsky and the lyric of Hölderlin. Nietzsche enthralled them. Both were caught up in fierce discussions about the purpose of art in the age of *Menschheitsdämmerung,* an age when not only gods and idols but European man himself "was submerging in the twilight . . . , into the night of decline . . . , in order to emerge again in the waxing twilight of a new day."[1]

Yet it is hard for us to think of Trakl and Heidegger as contemporaries. Trakl died of an overdose of cocaine

Deep is the slumber in darkling poisons [156]

at the age of twenty-seven; Heidegger died during the eighty-sixth year of life, so that it was difficult to isolate a medically definitive "cause." In 1914, while Heidegger was preparing his Habilitation thesis on medieval philosophy, Trakl stood appalled by the rout of the Austrian troops at Grodek. The *Habilitationsschrift* appears today in a volume of Heidegger's "early" writings; "Grodek" was the last poem Trakl wrote. After completing his doctoral work and Habilitation, Heidegger taught three generations of students in Germany, dominating European thought for at least that many decades. Trakl scarcely had time to secure to himself contemporaries; the name "Heidegger" for example meant nothing to him. But Trakl's name meant much to Heidegger, even during his student years before the War.[2] It is above all the personal significance of Trakl for Heidegger that strikes us as strange yet undeniable—though one may ask whether a poet ever signifies or sings in an impersonal way.

Nothing seems more anomalous at first than Heidegger's admiration of Trakl. Consider the bizarre oval portrait of the poet taken about 1910: hair parted aslant down the middle and pomaded flat against the skull, eyes glazed in shadow, nostrils flared, lips set in an expression of grim expressionlessness, neck and shoulders bare, pallid flesh white on black.[3] Two portraits of Hölderlin dominated the wall to the left of Heidegger's worktable in Freiburg, a silhouette of the twenty-year-old (original in the Stuttgart Landesbibliothek) and Louise Keller's famous sketch of the devastated seventy-two-year-old; but no portrait of the peculiar, precocious devastation Trakl embodied—ascetic sensuality, naked yet anesthetic—graced his walls. Whence the attraction to Trakl? Perhaps Trakl was but a reminiscence of the one who in Heidegger's eyes was the poet of poetry. For Trakl "took up the lyre that slipped from Hölderlin's hands" (Klaus Mann) and glided "hölderlinisch into an infinitely blue stream of fatal attenuation" (K. Pinthus). Hölderlin's voice resounds in many of Trakl's verses:

> Der dunkle Plan scheint ohne Massen . . .
> ["Melancholie des Abends," 20]
> Und Brot und Wein sind süss von harten Mühn . . .
> ["Der Spaziergang," 24]
> Und in heiliger Bläue läuten leuchtende Schritte fort . . .
> ["Kindheit," 98]

Yet it is belittling to both thinker and poet to speculate on the "attraction" of the one for the other. Trakl's voice is more compelling than that, and Heidegger's devotion not so easily won. Rainer Maria Rilke recalls hearing that voice and describes his reaction to it in four words: ergriffen, staunend, ahnend, und ratlos.[4] The progression is significant: transfixed by Trakl's poetry, astounded, discerning but intimations of meaning, feeling utterly at a loss, Rilke tries to enter its mirrored space, brilliant but inaccessible. Ratlos, he asks Ludwig von Ficker, "Who can he have been?" Heidegger's response to Trakl's voice (though not to the question as to who he may have been) appears in "Language in the Poem: A Discussion [or: Placement] of Georg Trakl's Poem" (US, 35–82).

By hoping to situate Trakl's poetry within the space opened by a "single unsung poem," and by claiming to hear "the one dominant tone of his poem," Heidegger appears to want to transcend all limits in order to penetrate and occupy Trakl's world.[5] Yet the outcome of Heidegger's endeavor is acknowledgment of the irreducible multiplicity of meaning in Trakl's lyric, the site of which remains unterwegs, in transition, transfixing but never fixed; so that discussion of its place is always out of place if it fails to listen in the way Hamlet heeds his father's ghost—"Hic et ubique? then we'll shift our ground.—" Within the crystalline space of Trakl's lyric Heidegger elucidates myriad themes and images: der Fremdling, the stranger and wanderer in search of the earth; Untergang-Übergang, the (Nietzschean) trajectory of his search; "apartness" (Abgeschiedenheit), a tentative name for the terminus of that trajectory; der Schmerz, the pain that nourishes the flames of spirit; das Abendland, the land of evening, a still undiscovered country, as the site of Trakl's lyric. Only one among such themes and images impresses itself upon me here, at the end of these *Intimations:* the generation of mortality, struck by love and death.[6]

"Strokes of love and death": *Schlag der Liebe, Schlag des Todes.* What do the words *Schlag, schlagen* mean? Hermann Paul's *Deutsches Wörterbuch* lists six principal areas of meaning for *der Schlag;* for the verb *schlagen* it cites six "proper" senses and ten "distant" meanings. Deriving from the Old High German and Gothic *slahan* (from which the English word "slay" also derives) and related to the modern German word *schlachten,* "to slaughter," *schlagen* means to strike a blow, to hit or beat. A *Schlag* may be the stroke of a hand, of midnight, or of the brain; the beating of wings or of a heart. *Schlagen* may be done with a hammer or a fist. God does it through his angels and his plagues; a nightingale does it with his song. One of the most prevalent senses of *schlagen* is to mint or stamp a coin. *Der Schlag* may therefore mean a particular coinage, imprint, or type: a horse dealer might refer to *einem guten Schlag Pferde.* It is by virtue of this sense that *Schlag* forms the root of a word that is very important for Trakl, *das Geschlecht.* Paul lists three principal meanings for *Geschlecht* (Old High German *gislahti*). First, it translates the Latin word *genus,* being equivalent to *Gattung: das Geschlecht* is a group of people who share a common ancestry, especially if they constitute a part of the hereditary nobility. Of course, if the ancestry is traced back far enough we may speak of *das menschliche Geschlecht,* "humankind." Second, *das Geschlecht* may mean one generation of men and women who die in order to make way for a succeeding generation. Third, there are male and female *Geschlechter,* and *Geschlecht* becomes the root of many words for the things males and females have and do for the sake of the first two meanings: *Geschlechts-glied* or *-teil,* the genitals; *-trieb,* the sex drive; *-verkehr,* sexual intercourse; and so on. All three shades of meaning haunt Trakl's poetry. *Geschlecht* may suggest the human race as such (as in *Traum und Umnachtung,* 149–57), or that part of it that dwells in cities (as in "Der Abend," 179); in "Helian" (80–84), a glowing figure of the sun and the generative year, *Geschlecht* clearly has the sense of the generation that passes, as the son "steps into the empty house of his fathers" (82; cf. "Verwandlung des Bösen," 124); while elsewhere (as in "Passion," 139) the word reflects its third sense:

> . . . Dunkle Liebe
> Eines wilden Geschlechts.

> . . . Darkling love
> Of a wild generation.

Heidegger employs the words *Schlag, schlagen,* and *Geschlecht* throughout his major article on Trakl.[7] He first writes *Schlag* and *schlagen* (in the form *ver-*

schlagen—recall the phrase *die Angst verschlägt uns das Wort*) while interpreting Trakl's line, "The soul is a stranger on earth" (143). Such a line seems to betray the Platonistic view that the soul, a stranger on earth, is *im Sinnlichen . . . dahin nur verschlagen*, driven off-course and rudely cast upon the shoals of the sensuous world; here on earth she (rather, "it," since *ein Fremdes* is neuter) lacks *den rechten Schlag* and so is miscast. However, Heidegger resists that Platonistic interpretation by reading *fremd* ("strange") as the Old High German *fram* (cf. the English "from"), moving forward and away, being underway, a movement that nevertheless remains *auf Erden*, "upon the earth." Heidegger observes laconically that Trakl's "Springtime of the Soul," of which this line is a part, mentions no other possible abode for the soul in some past or future circumstance. The wanderer soul sets out in search of its own homeland, where it must dwell.[8] In which direction? *In den Untergang hinab* (*US*, 42; cf. Trakl, 101). The wanderer soul, the stranger, goes down in search of the earth—Thus, we recall, began Zarathustra's *Untergang*—in "rest and silence." What sort of rest and silence? Heidegger does not falter: *In die des Toten*, the tranquility of those struck in death.

In Heidegger's discussion of Trakl's lyric the word *Schlag* next appears in the phrase *der Schlag der* verwesten *Gestalt des Menschen* (*US*, 49; "Siebengesang des Todes," 134): the coinage or imprint of the decomposing form of man, the type of man whose essence has abandoned him. But "Oh, how ancient is our *Geschlecht*" ("Unterwegs," 96), as old as the *animal rationale* of philosophical anthropology, as old as the Christian ontotheology such anthropology serves. Of course, the genus (animal) is more troublesome to the tradition than the specific difference (rational). Of what sort is man's animality? At the end of that tradition Nietzsche says that man is the *noch nicht festgestellte Tier*, "the as yet undetermined animal."[9] Heidegger comments (*US*, 45–46):

> The assertion does not at all mean that man has not yet been "confirmed" as a fact. He has been so confirmed, all too decisively. The phrase means that the animality of this animal has not yet been brought to a firm ground, brought "home," brought to the indigenous character of its still-veiled essence. Occidental-European metaphysics since Plato has been wrestling to gain such a firm definition. Perhaps it wrestles in vain. Perhaps its way into the "under way" is still obstructed. The animal that has not yet been defined in its essence is modern man.

Perhaps it wrestles in vain, utterly unable to liberate itself from the framework of the *animal rationale*. Perhaps the *unterwegs* remains inaccessible to it: *unterwegs* here means "the way back down," the *katabasis* "out of metaphysics," the downgoing unto mortality. In his "Letter on Humanism" (1947) Heidegger argues that while metaphysics does think of man in terms of *animalitas* it never succeeds in confronting with equanimity "our appalling and scarcely conceivable bodily kinship with the beast" (*W*, 157). It prefers to span what seems the greater distance to God. Yet in the historic ascent from rationality to subjectivity man bypasses his essence (ek-sistence). Such passing by, such oblivion, yields "the decomposing form of man." Georg Trakl seeks and finds an image to counter it: *ein blaues Wild*, an animal untamed but fragile, deep azure in hue, that haunts the forest rim at dark. It is associated with the poet's sister (73, 184) and with the poet himself, shivering on the threshold of his dead father's house (124) or treading the dark paths of passion (139), associated too with the path of the sun and the celestial year at summer solstice (163). *Ein blaues Wild:* Heidegger hears it as a name for the *mortal* who wanders with the stranger down to their native soil, the earth.

Trakl contrasts *ein blaues Wild* and the decomposing, degenerate, accursed *Geschlecht* of humanity. The third section of *Traum und Umnachtung* begins, "O des verfluchten Geschlechts" (155), "O of the accursed race!" Heidegger now asks (*US*, 50):

> By what is this *Geschlecht* struck, that is, cursed? The Greek word for curse is *plēgē*, the German word *Schlag*. The curse of the decomposing *Geschlecht* consists in the fact that this ancient *Geschlecht* has been dispersed in the discord of *Geschlechter*. Within such discord each of the *Geschlechter* seeks the unchecked tumult of individualized and utter savagery. Not the twofold as such, but discord, is the curse. From the tumult of blind savagery, discord casts the *Geschlecht* into abscission and imprisons it in unchecked individuation. So ravaged, so severed in twain, the "fallen *Geschlecht*" can on its own no longer find its way into the right *Schlag*. It can find its way only as that *Geschlecht* whose twofold nature wanders forth out of discord into the gentleness of a confluent twofold. That *Geschlecht* is "foreign," and it follows the stranger.[10]

Wildheit, Vereinzelung, Aufruhr, zerschlagen: I recall the European *Geschlecht* in late summer of 1914, when all the lights across the Continent expire one by one. An Austrian medic enters a barn where ninety wounded lie in heaps and there is no doctor and not enough morphine; the following day he balks at mess and cries *So kann ich nicht weiterleben!* and they take his weapons from him and lock him in the basement of a psychiatric ward. After several days the drugs that might have gone to a dozen wounded go into him. Several days after that a wealthy philosopher-mathematician who had anonymously supported the poet arrives with hopes of meeting him, but by November 6 Trakl is three days in the grave. Ludwig Wittgenstein writes to von Ficker: "I am shattered, though I didn't even know him." I think too of another medic and close observer of the Austrian wounded and dead during the Great War:

> The first thing that you found about the dead was that, hit badly enough, they died like animals. Some quickly from a little wound you would not think would kill a rabbit. They died from little wounds as rabbits die sometimes from three or four small grains of shot that hardly seem to break the skin. Others die like cats; a skull broken in and iron in the brain, they lie alive two days like cats that crawl into the coal bin with a bullet in the brain and will not die until you cut their heads off. Maybe cats do not die then, they say they have nine lives. I do not know, but most men die like animals, not men.[11]

Humanity: the as yet undetermined animal: until struck irremediably in death. In his last poem Trakl hears the "savage keen" of soldiers' "shattered mouths" (193).

Zwiefache, Zwiefalt, Zwietracht, Entzweiung: I think of another kind of struggle, not of nation against nation but of a twosome, a kind that is halved; it may be the raging discordance of art and truth, or the primal strife or world and earth; or it may simply be the race of man and woman, whom Trakl calls *die Liebenden,* the lovers. They embody the *Sanftmut einer einfältigen Zwiefalt,* as even a hasty sketch of their appearance in Trakl's poetry attests. Theirs is the mild time of gentle embrace (30, 179). Raising roselike eyelids under the shadow of a tree (105), breathing sighs among its branches (46), blond and beaming lovers cast darkling looks and in some obscure conversation come to know one another as man and woman (95, 144). Lovers glow afresh in winged things (24), embracing delicately with longing arms (95), suffering "more gently" (117). In "Joyous Spring" (22) the breath of lovers flows "more sweetly" through the night as they blossom toward their stars: the lovers' upsurgence in the poem mediates between two starkly contrastive lines, the first an outcry of what Nietzsche would call "Schopenhauerian pessimism,"

> Wie scheint doch alles Werdende so krank!
>
> How sickly seems all Becoming!

the second a hardwon Dionysian affirmation, the subdued response to the more joyous but also crueller spring,

> So schmerzlich gut und wahrhaft ist, was lebt.
>
> So painfully good and true is what lives.

Yet the shadow side of the lovers is never far in Trakl's poetry. They are imprisoned in disclosure (*wahrhaft*) by their very being (*ist, lebt*); they die "on their way across" (165). Their periodic resurrection is an earthly one, bound to its origins. Hence the prayer the poet utters in response to the "Nearness of Death" (73):

> O die Nähe des Todes. Lass uns beten.
> In dieser Nacht lösen auf lauen Kissen
> Vergilbt von Weihrauch sich der Liebenden schmächtige Glieder.

> Oh, the nearness of death. Let us pray.
> This night, on pillows still warm,
> Yellowed by incense, lovers' delicate limbs unravel.

The incense is reminiscent of lines that are vital to Heidegger's discussion of Trakl (*US*, 77–80), from the latter's "Abendländisches Lied" (133):

> O, die bittere Stunde des Untergangs,
> Da wir ein steinernes Antlitz in schwarzen Wassern beschaun.
> Aber strahlend heben die silbernen Lider die Liebenden:
> *Ein* Geschlecht. Weihrauch strömt von rosigen Kissen
> Und der süsse Gesang der Auferstandenen.

> Oh, the bitter hour of downgoing,
> When we gaze on a face of stone in black waters.
> But beaming lift the silver lids of lovers:
> *One* Geschlecht. Incense streams from pillows of rose
> And the sweet song of those resurrected.

Essential to the earthly resurrection is that its radiance not dispel the shadow. In Trakl's poems the shadow is cast by three figures: woman, brother, and sister.

Blessings of harvest are associated with woman (cf. "Frauensegen," 11), her blossoming womb and the fountain of her breast (24). However, in the second stanza of "The Accursed" (113–14) she embodies "plague," the curse of humankind as such; a tangle of scarlet snakes writhes in her tunneled womb; a child lays his brow in her hand. Yet in the third stanza of that poem woman is transfigured. *Resedenduft* now enwreathes her (cf. "Verwandlung," 60), the fragrance of mignonette or *reseda odorata*, a plant employed in folk medicine against fevers of infection and plague, administered with the incantation *reseda, morbos reseda*, heal, heal the sickness! Woman: source of the *plëge* or *Schlag*; yet also the source of cure. Both sources well up in the figure of "Sonja" (115). Her predominant qualities are *Sanftmut* and *Stille:* "gentle" is said of her three times, "quiet" four times. Yet the source of the confluent twofold in Sonja is itself a wound:

> Wunde, rote, niegezeigte
> Lässt in dunklen Zimmern leben.
>
> Wound, red, never shown,
> Lets live in dark chambers.

"So painfully good and true is what lives." Beautifully and gently Sonja smiles as the hand of the dead reaches into the child's mouth: the roselike sighs of the lovers grow mute upon the mouth of Elis (92).

Elis is that child, the brother who has died young (129) and so become holy (81). Elis sings the gentle song of childhood (134), the more silent childhood of the dead (129). He appears as the initial victim of plague, crying the plaint of women at the crisis of birth (107, 132), and as one still unborn—not so much already dead as still awaited—in any case, utterly apart, *abgeschieden* (cf. "Elis, 93, and "Gesang des Abgeschiedenen," 170–71). Yet the presence of the youth who is absent, the figure in which he haunts the poet, is called *die Schwester*. She is the counterpart of Elis (cf. *die Jünglingin*, 172), of the stranger and wanderer soul (cf. *die Fremdlingin*, 186), and of the monk (cf. *die Mönchin*, 177, 185). It is for Trakl's Elis as it is for Musil's man without qualities: the word *sister* is "heavy with indeterminate longings." Her profile is not so easily adumbrated.

The sister combs her blond hair (23) and plays a Schubert sonata in the next room (96). She speaks companionably with ghosts in the garden (29). She haunts an isolated forest clearing at noon amid the silence of animals (142), her mouth whispering in the black branches (25). Her white face (81, 189) stares forth strangely in "someone's evil dreams" (58), while her own sleep is troubled (78) by stormy melancholy (192). She appears as a beaming youth in autumn amid black corruption (104). A flaming demon (154) with eyes of stone (157), then a pallid figure with bleeding mouth, revealing a silver wound, she murmurs, "Prick, black thorn" (187). Her lunar voice reverberates through the night of the spirit (131). Her image emerges from the blue depths of the mirror, plunging the brother into darkness, as though he were dead (151): she is perhaps a child in the summer garden whom he violates (152, 48). But when all collapses she greets the bleeding heads of fallen warriors—shadow of the Valkyries (193). Trakl dedicates the first of his "Rosary Hymns" to the sister (73). There he associates her with evening and autumn, the southerly flight of birds, and *ein blaues Wild.* He marks her slight smile, the melancholy above her brows: .

> Gott hat deine Lider verbogen.
> Sterne suchen nachts, Karfreitagskind,
> Deinen Stirnenbogen.

God twisted the lids of your eyes.
Stars seek at night, Good Friday's Child,
The arc of your brow.

Enough! Flood of images! What philosopher could snatch thought from the inundation?

Most astonishing about Heidegger's dialogue with Trakl is that he seeks no rescue from that flood: images whelm whatever formulas are launched in his own "placement."[12] One of the images that strikes Heidegger's eye—as it does that of Yeats's "Minnaloushe"—is that of the moon. The brother treads "lunar paths" in search of the one who died young or is yet to be born; he is entranced by "the lunar voice" of the sister. Heidegger recollects the way ancient Greek lyricists speak of the moon and stars (*US*, 48–49); in the context of abscission, the confluent twofold, and *selēnē*, who as Semele is the mother of Dionysos, I now recall something else.

At Agathon's drinking party Aristophanes wipes his nose and begins his encomium to Eros. He opens by explaining "the nature of man," *den Schlag des Menschengeschlechts*, which originally consisted of three *Geschlechter* (*genē*), male, female, and androgynous. The male sex descended from Helios, the sun. The female sex arose from Gaia, the earth. The third sex was truly lunar, for it had as its parent *selēnē*, the moon, "which participates in both sexes" (Plato, *Symposium*, 190b 3).

Curious things are happening already. The two sexes we recognize as palpably true-to-life are "descended from" the sun (male) and the earth (female). Yet how does the earth father her children? How does the sun bear and nurse his? The only sex that makes any sense is the moonstruck androgynous. However, Aristophanes does not pause to make comic capital out of that; indeed he warns Eryximachus not to try to make a joke of his speech, since he is altogether serious. However that may be, Aristophanes recounts the familiar story of the hybris and nemesis of the androgynes and of Zeus's solomonic wisdom.

> Now, when the work of bisection was complete it left each half with a desperate yearning for the other, and they ran together and flung their arms around each other's necks, and asked for nothing better than to be rolled into one. So much so, that they began to die of hunger and general inertia, for neither would do anything without the other. . . .
>
> Fortunately, however, Zeus felt so sorry for them that he devised another scheme. He moved their pudenda (*aidoia*) round to the front, for of course they had originally been on the outside—which was now the back—and they had begotten and conceived not upon each other, but, like the grasshoppers, upon the earth. So now, as I say, he moved their

members round to the front and made them propagate among themselves, the male begetting upon the female. . . .

So you see, gentlemen, how far back we can trace our innate love for
one another, and how this love is always trying to reintegrate our former
nature, to make two into one, and to bridge the gulf between one human
being and another.[13]

The nature of humankind, or at least the *Schlag* of that third of it whose
descent Aristophanes can properly trace, is to be a *symbolon* (191d 4), a coin
split down the middle, each half consigned to one of two friends; that coin
devotes the rest of its days to the search for its fitting partner, jagged edge
exposed, stirred by the tumultuous Empedoclean passion to become whole
again. Through such passion it hopes to heal the plague or *Schlag* of having been
severed in twain, of having fallen into the discord of unchecked individuation,
which so easily degenerates into the savage recklessness of Anaximandrian
adikia. The salutary passion of which man is the symbol is called Eros. Stroke of
love.

Yet it is but one *Schlag* that mints humanity, murderous and amatory. How are
love and death to be thought together? We are prepared to answer that question.
We hum along bravely as Tristan and Isolde sing their Liebestod duet or we
allude to matters psychoanalysis is said to have settled long ago. We are too well
prepared. Yet even the most avant-garde efforts to intertwine in thought the
themes of love and death fail to escape or even recognize ancient habits of
representation.[14]

Are we really to look to Heidegger and Trakl for instruction in this matter?
According to more than one recent French philosopher, the Dasein of Heidegger's *Being and Time* is altogether sexless. Heidegger himself took the life of
Aristotle as exemplary for his own, a life that ostensibly consisted of being born,
working, and dying—notwithstanding what medieval gossips recount concerning Aristotle and Phyllis. According to ardent biographers, Trakl had an
incestuous relationship with his younger sister. ("We have invented incest," say
the Last Men, and they blink.) Neither Heidegger nor Trakl seems a fitting
mentor. For Trakl the sister remains a terrifying embodiment of generation and
corruption, a reflection of both benediction and reproach. An intense ambivalence toward woman permeates his verse. As for Heidegger, precious little is
said in his work concerning matters of love. The things relating to human
sexuality that Heidegger communicates to his Marburg students after the publication of *Being and Time*—to the effect that the term Dasein is "neutral" (one
almost reads "neutered"), that it subsists prior to "factical dispersion" in the
body and the body's two sexes, so that embodiment for Dasein is merely one
"organizational factor" among others[15]—only exacerbate our suspicion. In

"What Is Metaphysics?" Heidegger does refer to the joy experienced in a beloved human being, but it is a "joy in the presence of Dasein—not in the mere person" (*W*, 8; *BW*, 101), a presence that remains ethereal, estranged, ghostlike—in a word, transcendental-metaphysical. Although Heidegger recognizes metaphysics' flight from embodiment for what it is, and although Nietzsche convinces him that Dasein is "some body who is alive,"[16] he does not exhibit the role that the lived body plays in ek-sistence, does not make manifest the body *as* ek-sistent. As a result, "nearness to Being" remains exposed to the misinterpretation that it is an angelic hovering, dreamy and disembodied, among the outermost spheres. It remains for Jean-Paul Sartre, Maurice Merleau-Ponty, and a range of others to clear a stretch of the descensional path on which we are *unterwegs*.[17]

Yet the long passage we read some pages back, on the discord of the *Geschlechter*, the severance of humankind, and the "gentleness of a confluent twofold," perhaps gives the lie to my present complaint. In his dialogue with Trakl, Heidegger looks for that *Sanftmut einer einfältigen Zwiefalt* that might transform and regenerate the decomposing *Menschengeschlecht*. He tries to follow the stranger who wanders ahead in search of gentleness and unity. In which direction? Again the answer comes: *In den Untergang* (*US*, 51). Trakl celebrates the gentleness of couch and grave, which are for him a kind of childhood; such gentleness he limns as the figure of Elis, the youth long departed, whose memory the brother sings.

But we balk. Such "singing" should regenerate a decomposing race? The hymn to a dead boy, withered before blossoming? We are incredulous. Yet Elis is a true child of the moon, concealing in himself "the gentle duality of the sexes" (*US*, 55), addressed throughout Trakl's poetry in both masculine and feminine forms, not so much dead (as we have seen) as yet to be born. The spirit of Elis incorporates a new *Schlag des Geistes* (*US*, 66). "Spirit" now means the flame that feeds on persistent, gentle pain, the pain of severance, which gathers the race to the site of its dwelling. Heidegger calls such a spirit "the essence of mortals." That is what Trakl sings. It is what Heidegger tries to think, as a friend who listens to the stranger who died young. In that way he becomes a brother to the stranger and thereby to the sister. Brother and sister embrace in *ein Geschlecht*, gently, as mortals. This is what Heidegger calls "the dominant" tone of Trakl's lyric. "The unity of *the one Geschlecht* flows from that *Schlag* which gathers in unification the discordant twofold of *Geschlechter*, out of apartness . . . , into the more gentle twofold" (*US*, 78). Trakl sings the "sending of that *Schlag* that forcefully casts— and that means rescues—the race of man into the essence that remains reserved for it" (*US*, 80). What essence is that? To be the race that is homeward bound, on the way back down to its earliest origins, sublunary earth.

More than incredulous now, indignant, we dredge up names for that kind of song or thought. "Dreamy romanticism," Heidegger says, anticipating his critics. Others will say: If not an outright invitation to incest, hence subversive of the basic pillar of exogamous civilization, of culture as such, then a sublimated wish-fulfillment of the repressed regressive fixated primary choice of love-object, psychic infantilism, and in either case unwholesome and reprobate. And others: A flagrant example of alienated atomized impotent and narcissistic petit-bourgeois utopism. Still others, less eloquent, will sneer: What do you expect from poets and philosophers? We are all too well prepared.

Yet how would it be if, for all our talk of Eros and Thanatos, the single *Schlag* of love and death has not yet come home to us? Such a question is not meant as an invitation to reduce one to the other, as traditional ontotheology has always done, love being the kiss of death, and death the kiss of peace; it is meant as an injunction to let the innate power of both coin our thoughts on man and woman. One thing is certain: as long as "man" remains the shuttlecock of metaphysics, batted back and forth between *animalitas* and *ratio*, such thinking cannot succeed. Neither can it succeed by means of the anthropological sciences which in their effort to emancipate themselves from metaphysics forget the origins of their most beloved presuppositions. Nor finally will it succeed at some popular level where the sciences of man carry no weight and philosophy and poetry are scorned: our cemeteries sprawl far from town beyond the outermost tramline and our loves in photo mags with staples through their bellies.

What is that? What is the *distance* that keeps us safely out of reach of both?

Perhaps it is time to take a second look at the forgotten sources of our thoughts on man and woman, in texts such as the following:

> Of beings, some are forever and are divine; others harbor being and nonbeing. The beautiful and divine, according to its own nature, is always the cause of what is better in whatever harbors it; whereas what does not harbor that which is forever shares in being (and nonbeing) and in the worse as well as in the better. . . . Since the nature of such a genus [that is, the *Schlag* of living beings] is incapable of being forever, what is generated is always the only way it can be. . . . Hence, there is forever a genus of humans . . . , and since the source of the genus is the male and the female, it is for the sake of generation that male and female are in the respective beings. . . . And male comes together and mingles with female in the work of generation; for this is something that concerns both in common.[18]

According to Aristotle, men and women share the fate of dwelling in the lower cosmos, below the circle of the moon, under the ecliptic of the sun. They are hence subject to periods of fertility and frigidity, *genesis* and *phthora,* the raptures of finite time. Considered as individuals, men and women do not last forever. Only when they are viewed as a "genus" that "generates" a likeness of itself do men and women partake in the lasting. Their being cast in the mold of love is both a symptom of the incapacity of their upsurgence to endure forever and the ironic realization of the way they forever are. In Aristotle's eyes that way possesses a grandeur that radiates to the rims of the stars and is reflected back again. Why and how in the development of Christian ontology that view must change, why Hegel must in the end deride generation as *schlechte Unendlichkeit* (*Enz,* section 370), why it is that Eros must be poisoned, whereupon instead of dying he degenerates to vice (Nietzsche, *SII,* 639), why the shapes of man and woman must dwindle to the "decomposed figure of humanity," are questions that still need to be asked. Answering them may demand a new kind of thinking, a kind I can only hint at here.

At the outset it may be enough to dwell on the fact that for all our readiness to confront Eros and Thanatos we have virtually nothing to say to them—whereas they have a long tale to tell us. Let our response to them therefore be coined in *Gelassenheit,* a kind of thinking that combines traces of twofolds so as to form a third, "foreign" strain, itself beyond the dialectics of activity-passivity, willing-notwilling, advancing-waiting. Little wonder if the foreign strain that wrests phenomena from concealment solely in order to grant their inalienable obscurity and that strikes a critical pose before every monument of traditional wisdom while resolving to remain open to it should wear a lunatic aspect; children who have abandoned their innocence gladly, suspicious of their own preparedness to cloak all things with words but encouraged to let suspicion be as well, children of the long night, but under stars. At the end of their nocturnal conversation about *Gelassenheit* the teacher says, "For the child in man, night remains *die Näherin der Sterne*" (G, 71), the gentle seamstress who lets the stars, inconceivably remote, grow near.

> Sterne suchen nachts, Karfreitagskind,
> Deinen Stirnenbogen.

Good Friday's children have by now become the children of care (*Kar-,cura*), the generation struck by love and death.

In the preceding chapter I suggested that the principal effort of Heidegger's *Being and Time* and of much of his later work is to let death be. *Schlag des Todes.* Now I am asking whether the same kind of thinking may induce men and women to let one another be. *Schlag der Liebe.* Men and women—let one another be? Should they turn their backs on one another? That was tried before,

Aristophanes says, and not even Zeus could make it work. For men and women *Gelassenheit* means something else, something like "a gentle confluence of the twofold," befitting mortals of both molds.

> Now, supposing Hephaestus were to come and stand over them with his tool bag as they lay there side by side and suppose he were to ask, Tell me, my dear creatures, what do you really want with one another?
>
> And suppose they didn't know what to say, and he went on, How would you like to be rolled into one, so that you could always be together, day and night, and never be parted again? Because if that's what you want, I can easily weld you together, and then you can live your two lives in one, and, when the time comes, you can die a common death and still be two-in-one in the lower world. . . .
>
> We may be sure, gentlemen, that no lover on earth would dream of refusing such an offer, for not one of them could imagine a happier fate. Indeed, they would be convinced that this was just what they'd been waiting for—to be merged, that is, into an utter oneness with the beloved. [*Symposium,* 192d–e]

Men and women, joined as mortals, give one another whatever "man" can be. If not a minor theme after all, it is still in a minor key. Its dominant tone is no heroic coupling by which desire would be drained utterly and the Other appropriated once for all. No preestablished harmony, no dream of perfect complementarity, no oblativity, no fraud. For the ancient mode is tragic. And tragedy is "from the dawn." Though generations may banish these intimations of mortality, both Trakl and Heidegger, untimely contemporaries, try to relearn them. They inscribe them in an ancient genealogy—"In ein altes Stammbuch"—in the disconcerting neutral form:

> Wieder kehrt die Nacht und klagt ein Sterbliches
> Und es leidet ein anderes mit.
>
> Again night comes, something mortal keens,
> And an other shares the pain.

Notes

INTRODUCTION

1. "Je sens la mort qui me pince continuellement la gorge ou les reins. . . ." Quoted in Maurice Merleau-Ponty, "Lecture de Montaigne," in *Signes* (Paris: Gallimard, 1960), p. 254.

2. Otto Pöggeler, "Neue Wege mit Heidegger?" in *Philosophische Rundschau*, XXIX, 1/2 (1982), 42. See also Werner Marx, "Die Sterblichen," in Ute Guzzoni, ed., *Nachdenken über Heidegger: Eine Bestandsaufnahme* (Hildesheim: Gerstenberg, 1980), pp. 160–75; and especially *Gibt es auf Erden ein Mass?* (Hamburg: F. Meiner, 1983), soon to appear in an English translation published by the University of Chicago Press.

CHAPTER 1

1. Karl Jaspers, *Psychologie der Weltanschauungen*, 6th ed. (Berlin: Springer, 1971). Apart from a few minor changes in the second edition (1922), the exclusion of the Foreword to the third edition (1925), and the inclusion of the Foreword to the fourth edition (1954), the sixth edition reproduces the first—even to its pagination. I have cited this most recent edition because of its availability to the present-day reader. Citations appear in the text as: (*J*, with page number).

2. Martin Heidegger, "Anmerkungen zu Karl Jaspers' *Psychologie der Weltanschauungen*," in *Karl Jaspers in der Diskussion*, ed. Hans Saner (Munich: R. Piper, 1973), pp. 70–100. Cited in the text by page number (in parentheses). Apart from information supplied by Professor Saner, to the effect that Heidegger's essay was "originally thought of as a review" (see Saner's note, p. 100), the exact history of the text remains unknown. My own enquiries have established that Heidegger dropped plans to publish the piece shortly after sending the typescript to Jaspers in June, 1921. Communications surrounding this unpublished review sparked a cordial relationship between the two thinkers during the 1920s; their friendship did not, however, survive Heidegger's involvement in the NSDAP in 1933–34. To the best of my knowledge, neither man ever commented publicly or expressed anything in writing on Heidegger's Jaspers article. See my discussion of the Heidegger-Jaspers relationship in the *Journal of the British Society for Phenomenology*, XII, 2 (May 1978), pp. 126–29.

3. We know very little about the origins of *Being and Time*. Hans-Georg Gadamer notes that its "original form" was a lecture delivered to the Marburg theologians during 1924; see his "Martin Heidegger und die marburger Theologie," in *Heidegger*, ed. Otto Pöggeler (Cologne: Kiepenheuer & Witsch, 1969), p. 169. But the original form of some of the most fundamental ideas of *Being and Time* precede this lecture by three to five years. Two of the years 1916–21 Heidegger spent on the Western Front. Hence the years

1919–21, during which Heidegger worked on his review of Jaspers' book, become even more important in the chronology leading to *Being and Time*. None of this, however, is meant to cast doubt on the importance of the Marburg lectures (1923–28) in the genesis of *Being and Time*, which the published volumes of the Heidegger *Gesamtausgabe* have already demonstrated.

4. Jaspers entered a handwritten note in his copy of the second edition, saying that he could not revise the book "without writing it all over again" (100). See note 19, below.

5. In his Appendix (note one), Heidegger is highly critical of Jaspers' "Introduction" (especially its third section, "Systematic Basic Thoughts," which a new edition "might well drop") for failing to perform this preliminary work.

6. It would be quite another task—but an important one—to see how Heidegger's later essay, "Die Zeit des Weltbildes" (1938), now appearing in *Holzwege*, pp. 69–104, recoils directly on Jaspers' work: "That the world becomes an image results from the very same process by which man becomes the Subject among beings." Cf. H, 85, and note 9, 98–103.

7. According to Heidegger, neither the "understanding" of *verstehende Psychologie* nor the problem of the "historical," which is to say, neither of the problems that derive from the work of Dilthey, are adequately treated in Jaspers' work. Cf. the Appendix to Heidegger's review (99–100, note three).

8. The "limit situations" are not discussed until the third chapter of the book (J, 229ff.). Heidegger suggests in his Appendix (note two) that this chapter be brought forward to the beginning of the book, in order that the second and first chapters might "emanate" from this material.

9. For Heidegger's later criticisms of Nietzsche in this regard, see his *Nietzsche*, I, 573–74.

10. On the "how," see SZ, section 71. (I am indebted to Thomas Sheehan for this reference.)

11. On *Vorhandenheit* see SZ, sections 21 and 64.

12. Cf. the existential structure of the *sich vorweg*, in SZ, section 41.

13. In section 42 of *Being and Time*, *Bekümmernis* appears as an ontic mode of *Sorgen*, related to *Besorgen* (cf. p. 197). The two root words are closely related in meaning: see Hermann Paul, *Deutsches Wörterbuch* (Tübingen: Max Niemeyer, 1966) pp. 374a and 611a. The Jaspers review points forward only in the vaguest way to those structures of *Sorge* so painstakingly analyzed in the preparatory analysis of Dasein's everyday existence in the First Division of *Being and Time*. In this early essay (93) Heidegger speaks of the self as having "self-worldly" relations (*selbstweltlich*) (cf. SZ, section 5), "with-worldly" relations (*mitweltlich*) (cf. SZ, section 26), and "environmental" relations (*umweltlich*) (cf. SZ, section 15). No further details appear.

14. Heidegger speaks of the *historisch* unfolding of my having-my-self, preferring this word to *geschichtlich*. Later, in *Being and Time* and in subsequent writings, he reserves *historisch* for things relating to the discipline of history and prefers *geschichtlich* as a more original kind of "historizing." Although he names past, present, and future in the Jaspers review, he does not yet call them *ecstases* of time, nor does he mention *Zeitlichkeit* or *Zeitigung* at all. See chapter three for further discussion of "temporality."

15. Cf. *Verfallen* in SZ, section 38.

16. For the following I am indebted to Otto Pöggeler, "Neue Wege," esp. pp. 57–58, and to Otto Pöggeler and Friedrich Hogemann, "Martin Heidegger: Zeit und Sein," in Josef Speck, ed., *Grundprobleme der grossen Philosophen* (Göttingen: Vandenhoeck & Ruprecht, 1982), V, pp. 48–86. An essential sourcebook is Pöggeler, *Der Denkweg*

Martin Heideggers, second edition (Pfullingen: G. Neske, 1983), soon to be published in English translation by Humanities Press and Macmillan. I am grateful to have had Pöggeler's writings—and his letters—before me as I write.

17. See Thomas Sheehan, "Heidegger's 'Introduction to the Phenomenology of Religion,' 1920–21," in *The Personalist,* LX, 3 (1979), 312–24.

18. Cf. *Being and Time,* sections 39–40, 45, 50, 61 and, above all, 63, "The hermeneutical situation gained for an interpretation of the meaning of the Being of care, and the methodological character of the existential analysis in general." See also chapter two, below.

19. These remarks (from 1954) are reproduced in the current edition (the sixth, 1971). Both these and those appearing in Jaspers' Foreword to the third edition (1925) may be taken as a direct response to Heidegger's critique of the first edition. Because the third edition is all but unobtainable today I shall offer a translation of its Foreword here:

The new edition reproduces the second without changes. I would like to make a few purely personal remarks as to why a reworking of the text would have been out of place.

One possible result of such a reworking would have been an entirely new book. At the time I wrote, having become aware of worldviews as moments or dimensions in the one true worldview which embraces the whole in an indefinite manner and never explicitly, I tried to formulate my thoughts on the basis of intuition and to communicate them without a great deal of deliberation. The particular matters that came to be presented this way still seem to me to be true; I could not present them any better, but only differently. Since I have long been engaged methodologically in risking the second step—a logically defined clarification of the modern consciousness of existence—it seems all the more natural to me to leave my youthful undertaking in its initial form. At that time there was a secret ideal expressed in the general stance of the book, in the very manner of its analyses, without my knowing or willing it. I acknowledge this secret ideal without reservation as present to me now. Yet the limits that are fixed in the very nature of such a presentation demand that the identical content appear in sundry forms. I am laboring at a new configuration, and it would be false for me to achieve it merely by reworking a text already at hand. As a result of my work I have become another person so far as knowledge and logical form are concerned, although not in my basic attitudes. I prefer to leave my earlier effort untouched, in the hope that after its attempt at a psychological clarification and undergirding of philosophical existence I can produce a logical, systematic one.

The other possible result of such a reworking would have been that the book suffer damage. Because it has flaws—in structure, in methodological observations, in historical digressions, thus in the kinds of things that must be regarded as inessential in the light of the book's goal—I would have wanted to correct them on the basis of my present perspective. Weak lines or pages might have been struck, many formulations might have been altered, and, above all, the things that are missing might have been adduced and the systematic character of the whole entirely redone without touching particulars. But that would have resulted in a two-headed monstrosity. The book would have suffered—and for the sake of merely extrinsic and tangential correctness.

The impact of Heidegger's criticisms and of the publication in 1927 of Heidegger's *Being and Time* may be seen in Jaspers' three-volume *Philosophie* (Berlin: Springer, 1932). In this work Jaspers comments on the centrality of the question of Being for contemporary philosophy (*I, ix*); he refers to Being and to Dasein in his more detailed account of death (*II, 220ff.*), which is itself brought forward and made the primary "limit situation" (*II, 201ff.*); and he introduces an account of "anxiety," *Angst* (*II, 225ff.*).

20. Heidegger's analysis of guilt (*Schuld*) owes much less to Jaspers than does the analysis of death. It seems probable—although no explicit evidence emerges from the review—that Jaspers' preoccupation with "genuineness" and "authenticity" (*Echtheit, Eigentlichkeit*) (cf. *J, 35–39*) exerts an influence on Heidegger's use of both notions—perhaps the most problematic notions in Heidegger's *Being and Time*. Heidegger's *Eigentlichkeit*, structurally related to *Jemeinigkeit* and nonethical at least in its intention, cannot be identified with Jaspers' *Echtheit*. Yet Heidegger also imports (from Jaspers?) the concept of *Echtheit* into his analysis (cf. *SZ*, 146 and 148).

CHAPTER 2

1. I am thinking for example of the final pages of the "Letter on Humanism," of "On The Essence of Truth," section 3, of "Time and Being" (*ZSdD*, 12ff.), and of "The Thing" and "Building Dwelling Thinking" (both in *VA*) in their entirety.

2. A detailed comparison of *Basic Problems*, section 19, and Jacques Derrida's "*Ousia et Grammé*" seems to me to be absolutely essential, since section 19 constitutes Heidegger's own note to a footnote in *Being and Time*. A translation of Derrida's article by E. S. Casey appears in *Phenomenology in Perspective*, ed. F. J. Smith (The Hague: M. Nijhoff, 1970), pp. 54–93.

3. My readers may be astonished that such doubts come so soon. But when I asked Heidegger during my last conversation with him, on January 31, 1976, precisely when he began to have serious doubts about being able to complete Division Three of *Being and Time* Part One, he replied, "1925 or 1926." But those are the years when Divisions One and Two were still underway. Heidegger-II put in an appearance before Heidegger-I could write his magnum opus! Perhaps he had already put in an appearance in 1919, as I have suggested in chapter one, in order to expose Jaspers' lack of clarity concerning the "founding act." (My conversation with Heidegger is recounted in greater detail in chapter six, below.)

4. I have already recorded something of the doubts that assail Heidegger during his lectures of 1927 and 1928, doubts concerning his "temporal interpretation" of Being as such. In *Basic Problems* he complains about the lack of a "perfect mastery of the phenomenological method," about an inability to unravel the complex structures his own temporal interpretation has uncovered (*24, 439*). To be sure, when he refers to the "phenomenological method" he is thinking of section 7 in *Being and Time* and of his own interpretation of phenomenological reduction, construction, and destruction (cf. *29–32*). And in the 1928 *Logic*, after a fascinating comparison of Leibnizian microcosmic Monads and Heideggerian world-situated Dasein, he expresses an unwillingness to pursue the question of the extent to which "the interpretation of Dasein as temporality can be grasped *universal-ontologisch*" (*26, 271*). For it is a question he "cannot decide," a question "still altogether obscure" to him (*ibid.*).

5. That Heidegger never abandons the question of the finitude of Time is evinced by the final paragraph of the Todtnauberg Seminar protocol, which records—all too elliptically—the concluding discussion on the finitude of *Ereignis* and of the "Fourfold." The discussion employs the terms "end, boundary, the own—to be safeguarded in the own," and defines *das Eigene* as "what is one's own," *Eigentum* (*ZSdD*, 58).

6. See "Being and Truth, Being and Time," in *Research in Phenomenology*, VI (1976), 151–66, especially 165.

7. These words point toward the central hermeneutical admonition of *Kant and the Problem of Metaphysics*, to wit, Heidegger's insistence that "precisely the elaboration of the intrinsic essence of finitude, an elaboration required by, and conducted with a view to, the grounding of metaphysics, must as a matter of principle itself remain finite and can never become absolute" (*KPM, 229*). But the words also point back to the 1925–26 logic course, where Heidegger speaks of the nature of "presuppositions" in philosophy. He writes: "Every philosophical problematic has something behind its back which, in spite of the supreme transparency which that problematic might possess, it cannot attain. For it possesses its transparency precisely from the fact that it doesn't know about the presupposition" (*21*, 280).

8. That the "capacity for transformation" cannot be satisfied with one grand pirouette toward Being (i.e., the *Kehre* as usually interpreted, the conversion to Being) is suggested by the following passage: "Meta-ontology is possible only on the grounds and in the perspective of the radical ontological problem, and is at one with it. The very radicalization of fundamental ontology compels the designated transition of ontology to emerge from ontology itself [*aus dieser selbst hervor*]" (200).

9. Cf. Heidegger's remarks on what he calls *der existenzielle Einsatz* (177).

10. Heidegger continues to probe the enigma of the withdrawal of beings as a whole in his 1929–30 lectures at Freiburg University. (These lectures, published in 1983 as volume 29/30 of the Gesamtausgabe under the title *Die Grundbegriffe der Metaphysik: Welt—Endlichkeit—Einsamkeit*, reached me only when the present book was at proof stage: hence this regrettably brief note.) Here he analyzes the fundamental mode of attunement which we call "boredom," *die Langeweile*, literally the protracted "whiling" away of time. He endeavors to trace this mood—so tantalizingly reminiscent in its effects to the fundamental disposition of *anxiety* in *SZ*—back to the *"unified universal-horizon of Time"* (218). Yet without success: "With this reference to the horizon of Time we gain nothing" (219). For such mere references do not penetrate the entire dimension of problems which Heidegger had been grappling with long before he published *SZ*. "What does it mean to say that Time is the horizon?" It is clear that such a horizon must encompass beings as a *whole*. Yet Heidegger's analysis (see §32) can do no more than erect the paradox of *Binden/Bannen*: the horizon of Time both binds and bans Dasein to and from beings as a whole, both captivates and catapults it, both fascinates and banishes it. Heidegger is unable to elucidate this power of time *to ban* beings as a whole. His reference to the *Augenblick*, while crucial to the issue of the finitude of Dasein, does not serve to illuminate the temporal character of the "moment." It is perhaps in this 1929–30 lecture course that we witness the ultimate failure—actually the default—of the analysis of ecstatic temporality. It may be a task for contemporary thinking to *recover* that analysis, to pursue it in the directions of both everydayness and finite existence. For the metabolism of time confronts Dasein in all its quotidian involvements, all the while it is under way to something insurmountable.

11. Barcelona: Editorial Anagrama, n.d., p. 80.

12. In *Philosophy and Phenomenological Research*, XXX, 1 (1969), 31–57. See especially Part IV, on Heidegger.

13. In *Speech and Phenomena and Other Essays*, etc., trans. David B. Allison (Evanston: Northwestern University Press, 1973), p. 145.

14. Ibid., pp. 138 and 145.

15. *SI*, 1011. See D. F. Krell, "Der Maulwurf: Die philosophische Wühlarbeit bei

Kant, Hegel und Nietzsche," in *boundary 2*, IX, 3 and X, 1 (1981), "Why Nietzsche Now?", 155–84.

16. *"Ousia* and *Grammé,"* in Smith, p. 93. But there are other, very different, far more modest statements. Cf. Dominique Janicaud, "Presence and Appropriation," in *Research in Phenomenology*, VII (1978), 69–71.

CHAPTER 3

1. For this second division of the course there is no manuscript in Heidegger's hand; the text is based on the corrected (but undated) Simon Moser *Nachschrift.*

2. See *24*, 334–35 and 358–59, the two places where Heidegger would have to have commented on it. On p. 334 Heidegger mentions the word "suddenly" in its relation to the "now," but he completely ignores the matter of *ekstasis.* Heidegger does discuss the word "suddenly," *exaiphnēs*, fifteen years later in a lecture course on Parmenides (see Gesamtausgabe volume 54, *Parmenides* [Frankfurt am Main: V. Klostermann, 1982], p. 223). Although the context here involves *time* (see esp. section 8b), it is no longer the *ecstatic* temporality of *existence* that draws Heidegger's attention, no longer the *Augenblick*, but "incipient upsurgence," *das Anfängliche.* (See also pp. 113–14 on the sense of time as "commencement," *Anfang.*)

3. The intriguing remarks on presence in "The Anaximander Fragment" (*EGT,* chapter 1), remarks which have captivated Derrida—cf. "Différance"—are as much as we have.

4. See the *Hinweis* to "Time and Being," *ZSdD*, 91.

5. See C. T. Lewis and C. Short, *A Latin Dictionary* (Oxford: Oxford University Press, 1879). The *Oxford English Dictionary* contains the following—misleading—remark in its entry on the verb "to exist": "The late appearance of the word is remarkable: it is not in Cooper's *Latin-English Dictionary* (1565), either under *existo* or *exto.*" Yet the noun "existence" appears much earlier than that, for example in Chaucer and in the *Roman de la Rose.*

6. We are fortunate in now having English translations—excellent ones—of these two courses: *The Basic Problems of Phenomenology*, by Albert Hofstadter; and *Metaphysical Foundations of Logic*, by Michael Heim; both published by Indiana University Press (Bloomington, 1982 and 1984, respectively). Indiana also published Theodore Kisiel's fine translation of the 1925 *Zeitbegriff* lectures in 1985.

7. The reference reminds us how indebted Heidegger's analysis of "ecstatic temporality" is to Henri Bergson—infinitely more so than to the time-consciousness analyses of Husserl. In the projected central portion of his course on the "History of the Concept of Time" Heidegger proposes to explicate the three "principal stages" of that history: Aristotle, Newton and Kant, and Henri Bergson. See *20*, 11.

8. See Otto Pöggeler and Friedrich Hogemann, p. 73, and elsewhere. Heidegger's *Beiträge zur Philosophie: "Vom Ereignis"* is discussed further in chapter six below.

9. Derrida raises a troubling question when he wonders whether the distinction between "original" and "ordinary" Time is specious, whether it is itself the expression of a metaphysics of presence or proximity, indeed a metaphysics tainted with a moral-ethical prejudice which favors the "authentic" over the "inauthentic." Yet Derrida fails to engage in (1) a careful analysis of ecstatic-horizonal Time, (2) an analysis of the Time of *Ereignis*, as *Reichen*, and (3) detailed consideration of the starting-point of *Being and Time* as finitude, to which he nevertheless does allude. It is with the question of finitude that Heidegger's analysis of Dasein in terms of the question of the "meaning" of Being initiates

an epochal—better, an eschatological—turn in the history of metaphysics. "Finitude of Time" remains the missing keystone, one that must be sought in Heidegger's thinking of *Ereignis*. For Derrida's questions, see "*Ousia* and *Grammé*," esp. pp. 88–90.

10. See chapter eight for further discussion of transition and downgoing, *Übergang* and *Untergang*.

11. "Le sentiment d'éternité est hypocrite, l'éternité se nourrit du temps." In M. Merleau-Ponty, *Phénoménologie de la perception* (Paris: Gallimard, 1945), p. 484.

12. See the entire discussion in section 19 of the *Grundprobleme*. See also the references to *metabolē* in "Vom Wesen und Begriff der *Physis*," *W*, 319, 355 and 358. I am indebted to Walter Brogan for this second reference.

CHAPTER 4

1. For a list of these courses see W. J. Richardson, *Heidegger: Through Phenomenology to Thought*, pp. 663–64.

2. Franz Brentano, *Von der mannigfachen Bedeutung des Seienden nach Aristoteles* (Hildesheim: G. Olms, 1960, a photographic reproduction of the first edition, Freiburg im Breisgau, 1862), pp. 1–2 for this and the following. I will cite the text by page number in parentheses.

3. Perhaps this is too harsh: the lists from Theta 10 and Zeta 1, as well as that of Delta 7, to which Zeta 1 refers, are indeed variants of the list Brentano chooses. It is not so much a question of how the various lists may dovetail as of how the content of any given list is to be interrogated.

4. Brentano here is presumably following Adolf Trendelenburg, *Geschichte der Kategorienlehre* (Berlin: G. Bethge, 1846), p. 167. Cf. also pp. 187–89.

5. Brentano's understanding of analogy differs significantly from that of Trendelenburg, which stresses the mathematical origins of analogy as proportionality. See Trendelenburg, pp. 149 ff.

6. Cf. Aristotle, *Met.* Beta 3, 998b 22 and Eta 6, 1045a 36; and *Nic. Eth.* I, 4, 1096a 23.

7. *Met.* Epsilon 4, 1027b 20 and Theta 10, 1051b 3ff. Brentano also refers to *Cat.* 5, 4a 37 and *De interp.* 9, qu. v.

8. See his *Kategorienlehre*, pp. ix–xi. However, Trendelenburg is not so much anti-Hegel as he is polemical against Karl Rosenkranz and Karl Ludwig Michelet, the "Friends of the Immortalized." Himself committed to a philological-textual approach—his book is dedicated to Immanuel Bekker and Christian August Brandis of the Berlin Academy—Trendelenburg inveighs against the absolutization of three-stage dialectic which, he says, "quite often has its sole ground in the need for psychological comfort, because it promises the easiest path to a panoramic view of the whole."

9. These remarks are based on Brentano's reading of *Met.* Epsilon 4, which follows the analysis in Trendelenburg's *Kategorienlehre*, pp. 167 and 187–89. Much later in his career Brentano reduces "being in the sense of the true" to an "improper sense" of being, which by now merely means *thing*. See Brentano's own *Kategorienlehre*, edited from the *Nachlass*, by A. Kastil (Leipzig: F. Meiner, 1933), p. 13.

10. See *FS*, 57ff. esp. 62 and 65–66, from which the following material derives.

11. F. Brentano, *On the Origin of Ethical Knowledge* (1889), p. 76, cited by Heidegger, *FS*, 62.

12. Edmund Husserl, *Logische Untersuchungen* (Tubingen: Max Niemeyer, 1921) II/2, 123–24. In a sense, the ideal of *totale Deckung* corresponds to Brentano's 1889 position:

in sections 38–39 Husserl speaks of an identity of *Sein* and *Wahrheit*, in which Being expresses both the being true of "acts" and the true being of their "objective correlates." "Evidence" expresses the unity of Being and truth. But all that is merely to introduce the problem of sensuous and categorial intuitions and of "the possibility of complete adequation" (p. 147).

13. Jean Beaufret has done this in his *Dialogue avec Heidegger, vol. I, Philosophie grecque* (Paris: Editions de Minuit, 1973) pp. 117ff.

14. The quoted phrase is from Hans-Georg Gadamer, "Marburger Erinnerungen," in *Alma Mater Philippina* (Marburg am Lahn: Universitätsbund e.V., Winter Semester 1973–74), p. 24. Gadamer corroborates what Pöggeler and Hogemann have already told us concerning the importance of *factical, historical* life-experiences in *process*. "No matter what he was teaching," writes Gadamer of Heidegger, "whether Descartes or Aristotle, Plato or Kant, the central issue was always his analysis of the most original experiences undergone by Dasein, experiences he liberated from the concealments of traditional concepts." Gadamer's principal example (in "Martin Heidegger und die Marburger Theologie," reprinted in Pöggeler, ed., *Heidegger*, pp. 170–71) is the course on Aristotle's *Ethics* which I have just mentioned. *Phronēsis* was a mode of knowing that did not fall back on objectification for support; it involved knowledge not of a scientific character but of "the concrete existential situation." Thus Aristotle himself offered a means for overcoming the predominant Greek interpretation of the truth of beings as *Vorhandenheit*. Nevertheless, Gadamer does not record the precise meaning of *alētheia* for Heidegger in the context of *phronēsis*, and *alētheia* is the crucial issue.

15. At *SZ*, 215, line 6, Heidegger refers to Brentano as having drawn attention to Kant's acceptance of the traditional notion of truth as correspondence. As far as I know, there are no further references to Brentano in *Being and Time*.

16. On this "double leitmotif" see the excellent account of Walter Biemel, *Heidegger* (Reinbek bei Hamburg: Rowohlt, 1973), p. 35. English translation by J. L. Mehta (New York: Harcourt Brace Jovanovich, 1976), p. 25.

17. See Heidegger, "Vom Wesen und Begriff der *Physis*," in *Wegmarken*, pp. 317, 329–30, 340, 353, and 370–71. Cf. "Aletheia," in *EGT*, 111–15. Jean Beaufret (*Dialogue*, p. 121) follows Heidegger by calling Aristotle's task *peri tas archas alētheuein* (*Nic. Eth.* VI, 3, 1141a 17), which Beaufret translates as " . . . to enter into the open until we finally can see the place from which all the rest takes its departure and which rules ceaselessly over everything."

18. I am indebted to Kenneth Maly for the following insight.

CHAPTER 5

1. See John Sallis, "Into the Clearing," in *Heidegger: The Man and the Thinker*, ed. Thomas Sheehan (Chicago: Precedent, 1981), pp. 107–15.

2. Recall however that Heidegger had already separated the word [*Da sein*] in the Jaspers review of 1919–21. See p. 15, above.

3. See Sigmund Freud, *Gesammelte Werke*, VIII, 214–21.

CHAPTER 6

1. Beda Allemann, *Hölderlin und Heidegger*, second, expanded edition (Zürich and Freiburg-im-Breisgau: Atlantis, 1956), p. 72n.

2. "Martin Heidegger: Zeit und Sein," in Speck, p. 76.

3. "Martin Heidegger: Zeit und Sein," in Speck, p. 76.

4. "Neue Wege," p. 47.

5. Pöggeler relates that Heidegger himself favored such a "three-tiered" interpretation of his career over the I-II dualism. My account of the three tiers expands upon Pöggeler's, yet I believe he would accept my additions and even my reservations. For all that follows see Pöggeler and Hogemann, p. 77.

6. See Parvis Emad, "The Conception of Logic as the Metaphysics of Truth in Heidegger's Last Marburg-Lectures," in *Research in Phenomenology*, IX (1979), 233–46.

7. See Hannah Arendt, *The Life of the Mind*, 2 vols. (New York: Harcourt Brace Jovanovich, 1977–78), II, 172ff., and J. L. Mehta, *Martin Heidegger: The Way and the Vision* (Honolulu: University of Hawaii Press, 1976), chap. 8; cf. Mehta, *The Philosophy of Martin Heidegger* (New York: Harper & Row, 1971), chap. 2, which reprints chap. 8 of *The Way*. I have discussed Arendt and Mehta in greater detail in my "Analysis" to Volume IV of Heidegger's *Nietzsche* ("Nihilism"), *Ni 4*, 272–76.

8. Otto Pöggeler, "Heidegger und die hermeneutische Theologie," in E. Jüngel, J. Wallmann, and W. Werbeck, eds., *Verifikationen: Festschrift für Gerhard Ebeling zum 70. Geburtstag* (Tübingen: Mohr-Siebeck, 1982), 475–98. Section II of Pöggeler's paper provides a detailed account of Heidegger's *Beiträge zur Philosophie*. Numbers in parentheses in my text refer to this section of Pöggeler's essay.

9. "Die hermeneutische Theologie," p. 482. The German text reads: "Was gesagt wird, ist gefragt und gedacht im 'Zuspiel' des ersten und des anderen Anfangs zueinander aus dem 'Anklang' des Seyns in der Not der Seinsverlassenheit für den 'Sprung' in das Seyn zur 'Gründung' seiner Wahrheit als Vorbereitung der 'Zukünftigen' 'des letzten Gottes.'"

10. See Pöggeler and Hogemann, in Speck, p. 49.

11. Otto Pöggeler, *Philosophie und Politik bei Heidegger* (Freiburg and Munich: Karl Alber, 1972), p. 25.

12. W. J. Richardson, *Heidegger: Through Phenomenology to Thought*, pp. 630–32.

CHAPTER 7

1. In Heidegger's view *letztes Faktum* is the term that betrays the metaphysical character of Nietzsche's philosophy of will to power. See *NI*, 417 (*Ni 2*, 156); *NII*, 114 (*Ni 4*, 73); and all of chapter eight, below.

2. See Löwith, "Heideggers Vorlesungen über Nietzsche," in *Merkur*, XVI (Stuttgart, 1962), pp. 72–83, esp. pp. 74 and 83.

3. Compare Heidegger's critique of Husserl in *ZSdD*, 69ff. and in *LR*, xiv–xv.

4. Michel Haar, "Structures hégéliennes dans la pensée heideggérienne de l'Histoire," in *Revue de la Métaphysique et de Morale*, 85, 1 (January-March 1980), 48–59. The page references in parentheses in the following paragraphs refer to this issue of the *Revue*. See also Dominique Janicaud, "Savoir philosophique et pensée méditante: Penser à partir de Hegel et de Heidegger aujourd'hui," in *Revue de l'enseignement philosophique* (February-March 1977), pp. 1–14. Janicaud anticipates Haar's question (see esp. pp. 6 and 8) by emphasizing the essentially positive "contiguity" of the Hegelian task ("Conceptualize that which is") and the Heideggerian ("Think that which holds itself in reserve"). Janicaud's essay should be kept in mind during our discussion of "Results" in chapter nine, below, inasmuch as its focus is "the destiny of rationality" in the era of science and

technology. See now also his *La puissance du rationnel* (Paris: Gallimard, 1985). Finally, for an excellent account of Hegel/Heidegger, see Robert Bernasconi, *The Question of Language in Heidegger's History of Being* (Atlantic Highlands, NJ: Humanities, 1985), chapter one.

5. I will consider the most important source of Heidegger's eschatology, "The Anaximander Fragment," in chapter nine, below. We have already seen something of the possible origins of that thought—reflected in Heidegger's 1920–21 lecture course, "Introduction to the Phenomenology of Religion"—in the first chapter of this book. Something of its attractive power we have perhaps experienced toward the close of chapter six on the *Kehre*. The very *danger* of this thought is thought-provoking in the extreme.

6. "Descensional reflection" appears in relation to the Platonic philosophy in D. F. Krell, "Socrates' Body," *The Southern Journal of Philosophy*, X, 4 (Winter, 1972), p. 451; the formulation first appears in connection with Heidegger and Nietzsche in Krell, *Nietzsche and the Task of Thinking* (Doctoral Dissertation, Duquesne University, 1971), ch. IV, from which the present chapter in part derives. See also D. F. Krell, "Descensional Reflection," in John Sallis, ed., *Philosophy and Archaic Experience: Essays in Honor of Edward G. Ballard* (Pittsburgh: Duquesne University Press, 1982), pp. 3–12; and "Hegel Heidegger Heraclitus," in John Sallis and Kenneth Maly, eds., *Heraclitean Fragments: A Companion Volume to the Heidegger/Fink Seminar on Heraclitus* (University, Alabama: University of Alabama Press, 1980), esp. sections 3 and 4.

7. See *EM*, 15; *NI*, 448ff.; *NII*, 36ff.; and "Nietzsche's Proclamation: 'God is dead,'" in *H*, 218–19.

8. I cannot develop this fundamental matter here. But see *SZ*, 221–22, on the equiprimordial relation of Dasein to truth and untruth, and "Vom Wesen der Wahrheit," *W*, 93: "The hiding away of what is concealed, as well as errance, belong to the primordial essence of truth."

9. See Jean Granier, *Le problème de la Vérité dans la philosophie de Nietzsche* (Paris: Éd. du Seuil, 1966), III, 2, esp. pp. 532ff.

10. See Eugen Fink, *Nietzsches Philosophie* (Stuttgart: Kohlhammer, 1960), pp. 179ff.

11. Nietzsche, *Jenseits von Gut und Böse*, no. 56, in *SII*, 617; and Heidegger, *NI*, 320–21.

12. *W*, 146. Cf. Nietzsche, who asserts that "thanks to the unobtrusive dominance and direction of similar grammatic functions," philosophy belongs in the province of grammar (*JGB*, SII, 584). Nietzsche ironically exalts grammar as "The People's Metaphysics" (*Die fröhliche Wissenschaft*, SII, 222) and designates grammar the most stubborn of idols: "I fear we will not be rid of God, because we still believe in grammar." (*GD*, SII 960.) He demands, finally, "Should not philosophers rise above *belief* in grammar?" (*JGB*, SII, 600.)

13. *LR*, *xxiii*. Heidegger repeated his words in a 1969 television interview: cf. Richard Wisser, ed., *Martin Heidegger im Gespräch* (Freiburg im Breisgau: K. Alber, 1970), p. 77.

CHAPTER 8

1. *Éperons: les styles de Nietzsche* (Paris: Flammarion, 1978), p. 60. Derrida's discussion of Heidegger/Nietzsche on pp. 59–102 of *Éperons* is more subtle and suggestive than his earlier remarks in, for example, *De la grammatologie* (Éd. de Minuit, 1967), pp. 31–33, "La structure, le signe et le jeu," in *L'écriture et la différence* (Éd. du Seuil, 1967), pp. 412–13, or "Les fins de l'homme," in *Marges de la philosophie* (Éd. de Minuit, 1972), pp. 161–64.

2. For the following see my "Analysis" to *Ni 1*, 245–47.

3. See *SZ*, 264, lines 15–16; 272 n. 1; and, the key reference, to Nietzsche's "On the Advantage and Disadvantage of History for Life," 396, lines 16ff.

4. Her attempt to explain the change in terms of some sort of personal remorse is highly dubious, however. See Hannah Arendt, *The Life of the Mind*, II, 172–78, and chapter six, above.

5. The word *Übergang*, we recall, united the metabolic "now" in Aristotle's treatise on time and the *metabolē* of fundamental ontology itself. See chapter three, above, and my "Analysis" in *Ni 2*, 276–78.

6. The quoted phrases in this last sentence—indeed, the entire paragraph—are from Jean Granier, *Problème de la Vérité dans la philosophie de Nietzsche*, pp. 572–73.

7. Eckhard Heftrich, "Nietzsche im Denken Heideggers," in *Durchblicke*, ed. Vittorio Klostermann (Frankfurt am Main: V. Klostermann, 1970), p. 349.

CHAPTER 9

1. See Richard Rorty, "Overcoming the Tradition: Heidegger and Dewey," in *Heidegger and Modern Philosophy*, ed. Michael Murray (New Haven: Yale University Press, 1978), pp. 239–58 (now appearing in Richard Rorty, *Consequences of Pragmatism* [Minneapolis: University of Minnesota Press, 1982], pp. 37–59). (I shall cite the text as it appears in Murray, with page numbers in parentheses.) Heidegger plays a more positive role in the article than my presentation of it here suggests. Heidegger's thought plays an even more positive role—however covert and nonthematic it may be—in Richard Rorty, *Philosophy and the Mirror of Nature* (Princeton, N.J.: Princeton University Press, 1979). Not only in the third part of the book (on hermeneutics and philosophy as "edification") but also in the two earlier "deconstructive" parts (on the mind-body problem and on traditional epistemology) Heidegger emerges as an essential impulse for Rorty's entire project. See, for example, pp. 5–6, 12, 157n., 159n., 162–63, 393–94, and elsewhere.

2. William Butler Yeats, *The Autobiography* (New York: Macmillan-Collier Books, 1965), p. 43. Rorty comments (p. 251): "One of Heidegger's strongest feelings . . . is that ages, cultures, nations, and peoples are supposed to live up to the demands of philosophers, rather than the other way round."

3. Maurice Merleau-Ponty, *Signes*, p. 304; see also pp. 298–303, which I regard as one of the most thoughtful statements of the predicament of twentieth-century politics.

4. See once again 26, 211 n., cited in chapter two, above. This note is one of the earliest references in Heidegger's work to the holy. Yet even the later lectures and essays on Hölderlin have to do with the *absence* of the holy, which may by no means become the object of a "quest"; and the essays of the 1950s invoke divinities solely as an index of departure, a measure of humanity as mortal.

5. Rorty's fears concerning Heidegger's politics are not well articulated in his article. But see in the same volume (Murray, pp. 304–28) Karsten Harries, "Heidegger as a Political Thinker," the most dispassionate and balanced discussion I have seen, and one of the most insightful. Curiously, what Harries finds objectionable is not Heidegger's "hope" but his despair, his "inward migration" after the Second World War. (Rorty might reply that such flight from political life seeks refuge in professional philosophy, so that Heidegger's hope and despair are complementary: only the German professor, in a desperate act of compensation, could confuse philosophy with "present troubles.") Harries defines Heidegger's essential insight into history, namely, that "our destiny is governed by the history of metaphysics, which conceals a finally futile search for

security," (pp. 327–28), then argues: "Only this linear view of history leads Heidegger to his despairing analysis of the present age as so deeply fallen that all attempts to criticize and reform are already caught up in that fall" (p. 328). Harries sees in this "linear" view the "antipluralistic side of Heidegger's thought," his "implicit idealization of unity at the expense of plurality" (p. 327), such idealization transforming "authenticity" into either an authoritarianism or an unmitigated individualism. As desperate as such a linear view may be, and as pluralistic as I (an unstinting admirer of William James) would like to be, the rough beast of technology seems to mesmerize all political systems, East and West, North and South, and to paralyze or neutralize in advance all effective political action. The beast craves pools of energy, and the world is dragged on its leash.

6. Derrida, "Différance," in Speech and Phenomena, p. 159.

7. Albert Camus, Le mythe de Sisyphe (Paris: Gallimard, 1942), esp. pp. 32, 63, and 69–70.

8. Derrida, "Différance," p. 160.

9. Derrida, "Différance," p. 153.

10. This is argued in Hannah Arendt, The Life of the Mind, II, 188.

11. Land des Abends, Abend-land, the West or Occident, literally, the evening-land. Heidegger's own remarks on evening, night, and dawn in the present passage may have been influenced by a passage at the conclusion of Nietzsche's Thus Spoke Zarathustra, Part One (see SII, 614; NI, 336): "And that is the great midday when man stands at the midpoint of his path between beast and overman, when he celebrates his way to evening as his supreme hope: for it is the way to a new morning."

12. Hannah Arendt, The Life of the Mind, II, 192.

13. Hannah Arendt, The Life of the Mind, II, 194.

14. However, I do not wish to imply that there is anything self-indulgent or inane about Derrida's double-readings of Heidegger. See, for example, his recent "Envoi," in Actes du XVIIIe Congrès des Sociétés de Philosophie de Langue Française (Strasbourg, July 1980), published in Paris by J. Vrin, pp. 5–30. Translated as "Sending: On Representation," by Peter and Mary Ann Caws, Social Research, 49, 2 (Summer 1982), 294–326. For more "results" in Derrida's work, with regard to Hegel and Heidegger, see "Ousia et Grammé," Marges de la philosophie, pp. 38–39 (Smith, p. 58), and "Hors Livre," in La Dissémination (Paris: Éd. du Seuil, 1972), pp. 9–67.

CHAPTER 10

1. In Manfred Frings, ed., Heidegger and the Quest for Truth (Chicago: Quadrangle Books, 1968), p. 74.

2. See the complaint—and appreciation—of Albert Camus, Le mythe de Sisyphe, p. 40.

3. Compare the use of the term Entschlossenheit, as "a distinctive mode of Dasein's disclosedness" (SZ, section 60), and as an active power of decision, a will not to will, in Gelassenheit, pp. 58–59. Entschlossenheit is the thrown project of a Dasein that is silent, reticent, and determined to cultivate anxiety as disclosure; it is the effort to resist all interpretations that would "resolutely" handle anxiety, since in the case of anxiety all handling becomes the thoughtless violence of suppression and flight. Ent-schlossenheit is un-closure, hence "resolute openness."

4. Nietzsche, Götzendämmerung, SII, 943.

5. Nietzsche, Also sprach Zarathustra, SII, 335.

6. VA, 196: "Poetizing is in the strict sense of the word a comprehensive taking-measure, through which man first receives the measure of the breadth of his essence. Man essentially is as mortal. . . . Only man dies: indeed he dies continuously as long as he endures on the earth, as long as he dwells. But his dwelling rests in the poetic."

CHAPTER 11

1. Kurt Pinthus, *Menschheitsdämmerung: Ein Dokument des Expressionismus*, first published in 1920, reissued with new material in 1959 (Hamburg: Rowohlt), p. 25. Trakl's poetry, cited in this chapter solely by page number within parentheses, is quoted from the following edition: Georg Trakl, *Die Dichtungen*, 13th printing (Salzburg: Otto Müller, 1938).

2. US, 92: "During the period of Expressionism the realms of poetry and art were constantly present to me. Still more striking, even in my student days before the First World War, were the poems of Hölderlin and Trakl."

3. The photograph (in the possession of the Otto Müller Verlag, Salzburg) is reproduced in Otto Basil, *Trakl* (Reinbek bei Hamburg: Rowohlt, 1965), p. 97.

4. R. M. Rilke, *Briefe aus den Jahren 1914 bis 1921* (Leipzig: Insel, 1938), pp. 36–37. See also the letter to L. v. Ficker immediately preceding and a later one dated 22 February 1917 to Erhard Buschbeck, pp. 126–27.

5. So argues Karsten Harries in "Language and Silence: Heidegger's Dialogue with Georg Trakl," in William V. Spanos, ed., *Martin Heidegger and the Question of Literature: Toward a Postmodern Literary Hermeneutics* (Bloomington: Indiana University Press, 1979), pp. 155–71, following W. H. Rey, "Heidegger-Trakl: Einstimmiges Zwiegespräch," *Deutsche Vierteljahrsschrift für Literaturwissenschaft und Geistesgeschichte*, 30 (1956), 89–136. See also Beda Allemann, *Hölderlin und Heidegger*, p. 201 n. 74, who defends Heidegger against Rey's criticism and exposes Rey's own naive appeal to what is "really there" in Trakl's text.

6. It is perhaps a minor theme. Indeed, the major theme of Heidegger's preoccupation with Trakl—poetic speech as such; speech that allows beings to scintillate in sheer presence; the incantatory *es ist* in Trakl's "Psalm" and "De Profundis" (57–59; 63); the theme of *Ereignis* and the granting of Time and Being—arises only peripherally in his major article on Trakl, only in those three places (US, 38, 65, and 73) where he speaks of "the source of the advancing wave" of Trakl's prosody. On the major theme, see Krell, "The Wave's Source: Rhythm and the Languages of Poetry and Thought," in David Wood, ed., *Heidegger and Language* (Warwick, England: Parousia Press, 1981), pp. 25–50.

7. *Der Schlag* appears at US, 40, 49–50, 66, 78–80; *das Geschlecht* at US, 49–50, 55, 65, 67, 74, 78–80.

8. Cf. Heidegger's analysis of Hölderlin's "Heimkunft" and "Andenken," in EHD, 13–14, and 150. Cf. also ". . . Dichterisch Wohnet der Mensch . . ." in VA, 187–204.

9. Nietzsche, *Jenseits von Gut und Böse*, no. 62 (SII, 623): ". . . in Hinsicht darauf, dass der Mensch das *noch nicht festgestellte Tier ist*." Heidegger cites the phrase in his Trakl article (US, 45) and it is a salient feature of the contemporaneous lecture course *Was heisst Denken?* See pp. 24ff. of the latter.

10. "Womit ist dieses Geschlecht geschlagen, d.h. verflucht? Fluch heisst griechisch *plēgē*, unser Wort "Schlag." Der Fluch des verwesenden Geschlechtes besteht darin, dass dieses alte Geschlecht in die Zwietracht der Geschlechter auseinandergeschlagen ist. Aus

ihr trachtet jedes der Geschlechter in den losgelassenen Aufruhr der je vereinzelten und blossen Wildheit des Wildes. Nicht das Zwiefache als solches, sondern die Zwietracht ist der Fluch. Sie trägt aus dem Aufruhr der blinden Wildheit das Geschlecht in die Entzweiung und verschlägt es so in die losgelassene Vereinzelung. Also entzweit und zerschlagen vermag das "verfallene Geschlecht" von sich aus nicht mehr in den rechten Schlag zu finden. Den rechten Schlag aber hat es nur mit jenem Geschlecht, dessen Zwiefaches aus der Zwietracht weg in die Sanftmut einer einfältigen Zwiefalt vorauswandert, d.h. ein 'Fremdes' ist und dabei dem Fremdling folgt."

11. Ernest Hemingway, "A Natural History of the Dead," in *The First Forty-Nine Stories* (London: Jonathan Cape, 1962), pp. 367–68.

12. Note Heidegger's remark on the relation of poetry and prosaic formulas at *US*, 81.

13. Plato, *Symposium*, 191a–d, translated by Michael Joyce. I am aware of the dangers involved in taking these passages out of their dramatic context. See Samuel Weber, *Freud-Legende* (Olten: Walter, 1979), pp. 171–96; and Krell, "Socrates' Body," as cited in chapter seven, note 6.

14. See, for example, Georges Bataille, *L'érotisme* (Paris: Éditions de Minuit, 1957), which abandons its one fertile idea, *la discontinuité de l'être,* and lapses into an admittedly "theological" explication of eroticism in terms of *l'interdit et la transgression,* decidedly on this side of good and evil. What at first seems the new gesture of Bataille's work turns out to be the leaden gesticulations of the dead god.

15. See *Metaphysische Anfangsgründe,* 26, 171–75, esp. points 1, 2, 6, and 9.

16. The phrase *Dasein lebt, indem es leibt* appears often in Heidegger's early lectures on Nietzsche and even in much later texts. See *NI*, 199 (*Ni 1*, 99); *NI*, 565; *VA*, 214 (*EGT*, 65); and *W*, 326.

17. The most remarkable recent reflection on these matters I take to be Jacques Derrida, "Geschlecht: différence sexuelle, différence ontologique," the first part of which—devoted to Heidegger's 1928 remarks on Dasein and sexuality—is published in *Heidegger,* ed. Michel Haar (Paris: Cahiers de L'Herne, 1983), pp. 419–30. English translation in *Research in Phenomenology,* XIII (1983), pp. 65–83. The second part, presented at Loyola University of Chicago in March 1985 but not yet published, is devoted to Heidegger's Trakl article.

18. Aristotle, *On the Generation of Living Beings,* II, 1 (731b 24–732a 12).

Select Bibliography

The following bibliography lists those books and articles that have been particularly helpful for my reading of Heidegger. It excludes primary sources (that is, works by Heidegger and by other major figures in the history of philosophy, such as Plato, Aristotle, Kant, etc.) and much of the vast secondary literature. In addition to the massive bibliography prepared recently by Hans-Martin Sass, *Martin Heidegger: Bibliography and Glossary* (Bowling Green State University, Ohio: Philosophy Documentation Center, 1982), see the compilation by H. Miles Groth in Thomas Sheehan, ed., *Heidegger, The Man and the Thinker* (Chicago: Precedent, 1981), pp. 275–347; see also J. L. Mehta, *Martin Heidegger: The Way and the Vision* (Honolulu: University Press of Hawaii, 1976), pp. 483–500; and Walter Biemel, *Martin Heidegger: An Illustrated Study*, trans. J. L. Mehta (New York: Harcourt Brace Jovanovich, 1976), pp. 187–206.

Agacinski, Sylviane. "Grammaires du nihilisme." *Nietzsche aujourd'hui?* Two volumes. Paris: Union Générale d'Editions, "10/18," 1973, I, 191–204.

Allemann, Beda. *Hölderlin und Heidegger.* Second, expanded edition. Zürich and Freiburg-im-Breisgau: Atlantis, 1956.

Arendt, Hannah. *The Life of the Mind.* Two volumes. New York: Harcourt Brace Jovanovich, 1977–78.

——. "Martin Heidegger at Eighty." *The New York Review*, October 21, 1971, pp. 50–54.

Barrett, William. *Irrational Man: A Study in Existential Philosophy.* Garden City: Doubleday-Anchor, 1962.

Basil, Otto. *Trakl.* "Rowohlts Monographien Nr. 106." Reinbek bei Hamburg: Rowohlt, 1965.

Ballard, Edward G. *Man and Technology: Toward the Measurement of a Culture.* Pittsburgh: Duquesne University Press, 1977.

——. *Philosophy at the Crossroads.* Baton Rouge: Louisiana State University Press, 1971.

Bataille, Georges. *L'érotisme.* Paris: Editions de Minuit, 1957.

Beaufret, Jean. *Dialogue avec Heidegger.* Volume one: *Philosophie grecque.* Paris: Editions de Minuit, 1973.

Bernasconi, Robert. *The Question of Language in Heidegger's History of Being.* Atlantic Highlands, N.J.: Humanities Press, 1985.

———. "The Transformation of Language at Another Beginning." *Research in Phenomenology,* XIII, 1983, pp. 1–23.

Biemel, Walter. *Heidegger.* "Rowohlts Monographien Nr. 200." Reinbek bei Hamburg: Rowohlt, 1973. English translation by J. L. Mehta. New York: Harcourt Brace Jovanovich, 1976.

Blanchot, Maurice. *L'Entretien infini.* Paris: Gallimard, 1969.

———. *L'Espace littéraire.* Paris: Gallimard, 1955.

Brentano, Franz. *Von der mannigfachen Bedeutung des Seienden nach Aristoteles.* Freiburg-im-Breisgau, 1862. Photographic reprint by G. Olms, Hildesheim, 1960.

Camus, Albert. *L'Homme révolté.* Paris: Gallimard, 1951.

———. *Le mythe de Sisyphe: Essai sur l'absurde.* Paris: Gallimard, 1942.

Caputo, John D. "Language, Logic, and Time." *Research in Phenomenology,* III, 1973, pp. 147–55.

———. "Phenomenology, Mysticism and the 'Grammatica Speculativa': A Study of Heidegger's 'Habilitationsschrift.'" *Journal of the British Society for Phenomenology,* V, 2 (May 1974), pp. 101–17.

Derrida, Jacques. "Différance." *Marges de la philosophie.* Paris: Editions de Minuit, 1972, pp. 1–29.

———. "Envoi." *Actes du XVIIIᵉ Congrès des Sociétés de Philosophie de Langue Française* (Strasbourg, July 1980). Paris: Librairie J. Vrin.

———. *Eperons: les styles de Nietzsche.* Paris: Flammarion, 1978.

———. "Les fins de l'homme." *Marges de la philosophie,* pp. 129–64. English translation in *Philosophy and Phenomenological Research,* XXX, 1, 1969, pp. 31–57.

———. "Geschlecht: Différence sexuelle, différence ontologique." *Martin Heidegger.* Edited by Michel Haar. Paris: Cahiers de L'Herne, 1983. English translation in *Research in Phenomenology,* XIII, 1983, pp. 65–84.

———. *De la grammatologie.* Paris: Editions de Minuit, 1967.

———. "Ousia et Grammé." *Marges de la philosophie,* pp. 31–78. English translation by Edward S. Casey in *Phenomenology in Perspective,* edited by F. J. Smith. The Hague: M. Nijhoff, 1970, pp. 54–93.

———. "La structure, le signe et le jeu." *L'Ecriture et la différence.* Paris: Editions du Seuil, 1967, pp. 409–28.

———. *La vérité en peinture.* Paris: Flammarion, 1978.

Elliston, Frederick, editor. *Heidegger's Existential Analytic.* The Hague: Mouton, 1978.

Emad, Parvis. "The Conception of Logic as the Metaphysics of Truth in Heidegger's Last Marburg-Lectures." *Research in Phenomenology,* IX, 1979, pp. 233–46.

———. "The Place of Hegel in Heidegger's *Being and Time.*" *Research in Phenomenology,* XIII, 1983, pp. 159–74.

Feick, Hildegard. *Index zu Heideggers 'Sein und Zeit.'* Second, revised edition. Tübingen: M. Niemeyer, 1968.

Fink, Eugen. *Metaphysik und Tod.* Stuttgart: W. Kohlhammer, 1969.

———. *Nietzsches Philosophie.* Stuttgart: W. Kohlhammer, 1960.

———. *Spiel als Weltsymbol.* Stuttgart: W. Kohlhammer, 1960.

Frings, Manfred, editor. *Heidegger and the Quest for Truth.* Chicago: Quadrangle Books, 1968.

Gadamer, Hans-Georg. *Kleine Schriften.* Volume one: *Philosophie, Hermeneutik.* Tübingen: J. C. B. Mohr (Paul Siebeck), 1967.

————. "Marburger Erinnerungen." *Alma Mater Philippina*. Marburg am Lahn: Universitätsbund, Winter Semester, 1973–74.

————. "Martin Heidegger und die Marburger Theologie." *Heidegger*. Edited by Otto Pöggeler. Cologne: Kiepenheuer und Witsch, 1969.

————. *Wahrheit und Methode*. Fourth edition. Tübingen: J. C. B. Mohr (Paul Siebeck), 1975.

Georgiades, Thrasybulos. "Sprache als Rhythmus." *Die Sprache*. (In the series "Gestalt und Gedanke," Nr. 5, edited by the Bayrische Akademie der schönen Künsten.) Munich: Oldenbourg, 1959, pp. 109–35.

Granier, Jean. *Le problème de la Vérité dans la philosophie de Nietzsche*. Paris: Editions du Seuil, 1966.

Gray, J. Glenn. *Hegel and Greek Thought*. New York: Harper Torchbooks, 1968.

————. "Heidegger on Remembering and Remembering Heidegger." *Man and World*, X, 1, 1977.

Guzzoni, Ute. *Identität oder nicht: Zur kritischen Theorie der Ontologie*. Freiburg-im-Breisgau: Karl Alber, 1981.

————, editor. *Nachdenken über Heidegger: Eine Bestandsaufnahme*. Hildesheim: Gerstenberg, 1980.

Haar, Michel. "The End of Distress: The End of Technology?" *Research in Phenomenology*, XIII, 1983, pp. 43–63.

————. "Heidegger et le surhomme." *Revue de l'enseignement philosophique*, XXX, 3, February-March, 1980, pp. 1–17.

————, editor. *Martin Heidegger*. Paris: Cahiers de l'Herne, 1983.

————. "La métaphysique dans *Sein und Zeit*." *Exercices de la patience*, no. 3/4, Spring 1982, pp. 97–112.

————. "Structures hégéliennes dans la pensée heidegérienne de l'Histoire." *Revue de la Métaphysique et de Morale*, LXXXV, 1, January-March 1980, pp. 48–59.

Harries, Karsten. "Heidegger as a Political Thinker." *Heidegger and Modern Philosophy*. Edited by Michael Murray. New Haven, Connecticut: Yale University Press, 1978, pp. 304–28.

————. "Language and Silence: Heidegger's Dialogue with Georg Trakl." *Heidegger and the Question of Literature: Toward a Postmodern Literary Hermeneutics*. Edited by William V. Spanos. Bloomington: Indiana University Press, 1979, pp. 155–71.

Heftrich, Eckhard. "Nietzsche im Denken Heideggers." *Durchblicke*. Edited by Vittorio Klostermann. Frankfurt am Main: V. Klostermann, 1970, pp. 331–49.

Janicaud, Dominique. "Presence and Appropriation." *Research in Phenomenology*, VIII, 1978, pp. 67–76.

————. *La puissance du rationnel*. Paris: Gallimard, 1985.

————. "Savoir philosophique et pensée méditante: Penser à partir de Hegel et de Heidegger aujourd'hui." *Revue de l'enseignement philosophique*, XXVI, 3, February-March, 1977.

———— and J.-F. Mattéi. *La métaphysique à la limite*. Paris: Presses Universitaires de France, 1983.

Jaspers, Karl. *Nietzsche: Einführung in das Verständnis seines Philosophierens*. Third edition. Berlin: W. de Gruyter, 1950.

————. *Philosophie*. Three volumes. Berlin: Springer, 1932.

————. *Philosophische Autobiographie*. Expanded edition. Munich: Piper, 1977.

————. *Psychologie der Weltanschauungen*. Third edition. Berlin: Springer, 1925.

Kisiel, Theodore. "En route to *Sein und Zeit*." *Research in Phenomenology*, X, 1980, pp. 307–19.

Lacoue-Labarthe, Philippe. *Le sujet de la philosophie (Typographies 1)*. Paris: Aubier Flammarion, 1979.

Löwith, Karl. *Heidegger: Denker in dürftiger Zeit*. Third edition. Göttingen: Vandenhoeck und Ruprecht, 1965.

———. "Heideggers Vorlesungen über Nietzsche." *Merkur*, XVI, 1962, pp. 72–83.

Marx, Werner. *Gibt es auf Erden ein Mass? Grundbestimmungen einer nichtmetaphysischen Ethik*. Hamburg: F. Meiner, 1983.

———. *Heidegger und die Tradition*. Second edition. Hamburg: F. Meiner, 1980. First edition (Kohlhammer), 1961.

Macomber, W. B. *The Anatomy of Disillusion: Martin Heidegger's Notion of Truth*. Evanston, Illinois: Northwestern University Press, 1967.

Mehta, J. L. *Martin Heidegger: The Way and the Vision*. Honolulu: University Press of Hawaii, 1976.

———. *The Philosophy of Martin Heidegger*. New York: Harper & Row, 1971. (The final three chapters of the first version of *The Way and the Vision*.)

Merleau-Ponty, Maurice. *Phénoménologie de la perception*. Paris: Gallimard, 1945.

———. *Signes*. Paris: Gallimard, 1960.

Murray, Michael, editor. *Heidegger and Modern Philosophy*. New Haven, Connecticut: Yale University Press, 1978.

Pinthus, Kurt. *Menschheitsdämmerung: Ein Dokument des Expressionismus*. Second, expanded edition. Reinbek bei Hamburg: Rowohlt, 1959. First edition, 1920.

Pöggeler, Otto. *Der Denkweg Martin Heideggers*. Second edition. Pfullingen: G. Neske, 1983. First edition, 1963.

———, editor. *Heidegger*. Cologne: Kiepenheuer und Witsch, 1969.

———. *Heidegger und die hermeneutische Philosophie*. Freiburg-im-Breisgau: Karl Alber, 1983.

———. "Heidegger und die hermeneutische Theologie." *Verifikationen: Festschrift für Gerhard Ebeling zum 70. Geburtstag*. Edited by E. Jüngel, J. Wallmann, and W. Werbeck. Tübingen: J. C. B. Mohr (Paul Siebeck), 1982, pp. 475–98.

———. "Heideggers Begnegnung mit Hölderlin." *Man and World*, X, 1, 1977, pp. 13–61.

———. "Neue Wege mit Heidegger?" *Philosophische Rundschau*, XXIX, 1/2, 1982, pp. 39–71.

———. *Philosophie und Politik bei Heidegger*. Freiburg-im-Breisgau: Karl Alber, 1972.

——— and Friedrich Hogemann. "Martin Heidegger: Zeit und Sein." *Grundprobleme der grossen Philosophen*. Edited by Josef Speck. "Philosophie der Gegenwart V." Göttingen: Vandenhoeck und Ruprecht, 1982, pp. 48–86.

Richardson, William J., S.J. *Heidegger: Through Phenomenology to Thought*. The Hague: M. Nijhoff, 1963.

Ricoeur, Paul. *Le conflit des interprétations: Essais d'herméneutique*. Paris: Editions du Seuil, 1969.

———. "The Critique of Subjectivity and Cogito in the Philosophy of Martin Heidegger." *Heidegger and the Quest for Truth*. Edited by Manfred Frings. Chicago: Quadrangle Books, 1968, pp. 62–75.

———. *De l'interprétation: Essai sur Freud*. Paris: Editions du Seuil, 1965.

Rorty, Richard. "Overcoming the Tradition: Heidegger and Dewey." In Michael Murray, listed above; now also in: Rorty, *Consequences of Pragmatism*. Minneapolis: University of Minnesota Press, 1982, pp. 37–59.

———. *Philosophy and the Mirror of Nature*. Princeton, New Jersey: Princeton University Press, 1979.

————. "Heidegger Against the Pragmatists." Unpublished manuscript.

Sallis, John. "End(s)." *Research in Phenomenology*, XIII, 1983, pp. 85–96.

————, editor. *Heidegger and the Path of Thinking*. Pittsburgh: Duquesne University Press, 1970.

————. "Into the Clearing." *Heidegger, The Man and the Thinker*. Edited by Thomas Sheehan. Chicago: Precedent, 1981, pp. 107–15.

————, editor. *Philosophy and Archaic Experience: Essays in Honor of Edward G. Ballard*. Pittsburgh: Duquesne University Press, 1982.

————, editor. *Radical Phenomenology: Essays in Honor of Martin Heidegger*. Atlantic Highlands, New Jersey: Humanities Press, 1978.

————. "Radical Phenomenology and Fundamental Ontology." *Research in Phenomenology*, VI, 1976, pp. 139–50.

————. "Where Does 'Being and Time' Begin?" *Heidegger's Existential Analytic*. Edited by Frederick Elliston. The Hague: Mouton, 1978, pp. 21–43.

———— and Kenneth Maly, editors. *Heraclitean Fragments: A Companion Volume to the Heidegger/Fink Seminar on Heraclitus*. University, Alabama: University of Alabama Press, 1980.

Saner, Hans, editor. *Karl Jaspers in der Diskussion*. Munich: R. Piper, 1973.

Schöfer, Erasmus. *Die Sprache Heideggers*. Pfullingen: G. Neske, 1962.

Sheehan, Thomas. "Caveat Lector: The New Heidegger." *The New York Review of Books*, December 4, 1980, pp. 39–41.

————, editor. *Heidegger, The Man and the Thinker*. Chicago: Precedent, 1981.

————. "Heidegger's 'Introduction to the Phenomenology of Religion,' 1920–21." *The Personalist*, LX, 3, 1979, pp. 312–24.

————. "Heidegger's Philosophy of Mind." *Continental Philosophy* (The Hague: Nijhoff), IV, 1983, pp. 287–318.

————. "On the Way to *Ereignis*: Heidegger's Interpretation of *Physis*." *Continental Philosophy in America*. Edited by Hugh J. Silverman, John Sallis, and Thomas M. Seebohm. Pittsburgh: Duquesne University Press, 1983, pp. 131–64.

Spanos, William V. "The De-struction of Form in Postmodern American Poetry: The Examples of Charles Olson and Robert Creeley." *American Studies/Amerikastudien* (Stuttgart: J. B. Metzler), XXV, 4, pp. 375–404.

————, editor. *Martin Heidegger and the Question of Literature: Toward a Postmodern Literary Hermeneutics*. Bloomington: Indiana University Press, 1979.

Der Spiegel. "Spiegel-Gespräch mit Martin Heidegger." XXX, 23, May 31, 1976, pp. 193–219.

Trias, Eugenio. *Filosofía y carnaval*. Barcelona: Editorial Anagrama, n.d.

Wisser, Richard, editor. *Martin Heidegger im Gespräch*. Freiburg-im-Breisgau: Karl Alber, 1970.

Wood, David. "Metametaphysical Textuality: Heidegger and Derrida." *Heidegger and Language*. Edited by David Wood. Warwick, England: Parousia Press, 1981, pp. 71–100.

Index